THE SPANISH ARCHIVES OF THE

GENERAL LAND OFFICE OF TEXAS

Southern Historical Press, Inc.
Greenville, South Carolina

Please direct all correspondence and orders to:

www.southernhistoricalpress.com
or
SOUTHERN HISTORICAL PRESS, Inc.
PO Box 1267
375 West Broad Street
Greenville, SC   29601
southernhistoricalpress@gmail.com

Originally published: Austin, TX 1955
Copyright 1955 by Virginia H. Taylor
ISBN #0-89308-179-5
All rights Reserved.
Printed in the United States of America

THE SPANISH ARCHIVES OF THE GENERAL

LAND OFFICE OF TEXAS

PREFACE

The Spanish Archives of the General Land Office as a subject of study offer many tempting opportunities for amplification. These I have consistently by-passed in an attempt to present a concise descriptive and chronological narrative which will serve as a composite picture for those who are interested in both the history and the content of these archives.

The work I have done was made possible by Mr. Bascom Giles, the present Land Commissioner. I have received special assistance from Mrs. Eltea Armstrong and Mr. Ray Wisdom of the Land Office staff, Mr. J. D. Freeman of the Stanolind Oil and Gas Company, Mr. Carl F. K. von Blucher of the Humble Oil and Refining Company, Dr. Eugene C. Barker, and

Dr. H. B. Carroll of the University of Texas.

I wish particularly to thank Dr. Carroll for the persistent encouragement and patient instruction which motivated the preparation of this manuscript for lithoprinting. The merits it may have as a private publication should be credited to him, and its defects will be due to my failure to conform to his standards.

Virginia H. Taylor

Austin, Texas

August 25, 1954

CONTENTS

ILLUSTRATIONS

Chapter I

INTRODUCTION

One glance at any map of Texas reveals a Spanish heritage in the multitude of Spanish names applied to cities, towns, rivers, streams, mountains, canyons, and lakes, to diverse landmarks, both notable and minute. From Corpus Christi and Laguna Madre, up the Colorado, Guadalupe, and Nueces, to El Capitán and Amarillo, the liquid language of Castile is undeniably implanted on the plains and forests of Texas. But elsewhere in the Texas scene little that is Spanish meets the eye, and it is generally claimed that Spain left none of her civilization rooted in Texas soil. Nevertheless, there is in Texas another undisputed Spanish heritage, an institution in active existence

1

which sprang full blown into being by virtue of the fact that five thousand Texans had received title of ownership to their lands from the Spanish and Mexican governments.

That institution, the General Land Office of Texas, though it has continued to assume new and greater proportions, yet recalls its origin in its present day functions and currently employs that very concrete legacy of Spanish and Mexican titles as an integral factor and distinctly practical feature. Spanish and Mexican land grants constitute the basis of title to more than twenty-six million acres of land in Texas; and, being written in Spanish, it is necessary that they be translated correctly into English in order that interested individuals, Texas judges, and other government officers, whose duty it is to uphold such titles, may understand them. This curious circumstance is surprising to most persons, even to Texans. Casual visitors find the Spanish Archives immensely inter-esting. Historians and writers have combed the files through the many years of their existence. But the story of those venerable records is more inextricably bound up in the history of Texas than is commonly realized, and in their various phases of legality, land measurement, and historical interest they have im-posed on contemporary lives and customs a deep and visible imprint.

Briefly, the Spanish Archives of the Land Office consist of land grants made in Texas by Spain and Mexico, and records pertaining thereto. The bulk of the Archives proper, now bound in sixty-nine volumes, was assembled in 1837 from the colony land offices of the late State of Coahuila and Texas as the duty of John P. Borden, the first land commissioner of the Republic of Texas. The Land Office, created by the First Congress on December 22, 1836, was opened in

Houston on October 1, 1837.[1] Acting under a law that ordered

> all empresarios, commissioners, political chiefs, alcaldes, and other persons to deliver over to the general land office all titles, books, surveys, papers, documents, or other things in their possession or charge, belonging to the Republic...[2]

Borden collected records made at the new Anglo-American settlements of San Felipe, Liberty, Viesca, Gonzales, and Mina (Bastrop); at the new Irish settlements of Refugio and San Patricio; and at the old Spanish towns of Nacogdoches, San Antonio, and Goliad. The titles of De León's colony at the Mexican settlement of Victoria did not arrive in the Land Office until 1850. Many other records have never been obtained. The number of titles issued by Spain and Mexico has been estimated at 5,000; the present index of

---

[1] H.P.N. Gammel, Laws of Texas, 1822-1838, I, 216; ibid., 1323.

[2] Ibid., 1324.

original grantees lists 4,200 names; and some 330
claims based on original grants not archived in Texas
are otherwise classified.

Fewer than one hundred of the grants preserved
in the Spanish Archives were made by Spain. Most
of them were issued by Mexico between 1824 and 1835
in an area east of San Antonio and north of Corpus
Christi. The Spanish and Mexican grants made between the Nueces River and the Rio Grande were archived in Mexico; for that reason, and because of the
special disposition made of the lands thus covered,
such titles constitute a class unto themselves. The
territory south of the Nueces did not come within the
jurisdiction of Texas until 1848, and since that time
only a few copies, and fewer originals, have made
their way from that area into the Land Office.

Chapter II

ORIGIN OF SPANISH AND MEXICAN LAND
TITLES IN TEXAS

The history of Spanish and Mexican land titles in Texas and their derivation begins with the advent of Spain in the New World and the establishment of the Kingdom of the Indies, claimed by right of conquest and discovery and under the Papal Bull of Alexander VI in 1493, which divided the western world between Spain and Portugal. The vast transoceanic possessions on the continent of America, adjacent islands, Philippine Islands, and others in eastern seas were governed by special laws issued at different times and under different circumstances, which, reunited into one code in 1680, formed the Recopilación de

Leyes de los Reinos de las Indias. This recopilation and the royal ordinances and cedulas issued thereafter were the embodiment of Spanish law prevailing in America until Spain's sovereignty ended.[1]

Under those laws land concessions which emanated directly from the Crown were granted in the King's name by specially delegated officers. Cortés, after the conquest of Mexico in 1521, first exercised that right in New Spain.[2] Then the Supreme Council of the Indies at Madrid and the Royal Audiencia of Mexico City supervised land matters until 1530 when the

---

[1] The fifth edition of the Recopilación de Leyes de los Reinos de las Indias, in Book IV, Title 12, "on the sale, composition, and distribution of lands, lots, and waters" with annotated ordinances and decrees, gives the important regulations relative to the land system. Joseph W. White's Recopilation of the Laws of Spain and the Indies, a translated collection published in 1839, has been recognized as a standard authority by the Supreme Court of Texas. John and Henry Sayles, Early Laws of Texas, 1732-1876, I, 19.

[2] Lucas Alamán, Disertaciones Históricas, I, 171, 172.

King gave his viceroys the prerogative of granting lands.[3] Through the growth of centuries that authority was gradually absorbed by provincial officers who exercised greater power in those places where distance or particular circumstance demanded it.

Such was the case in the remote province of Texas. The great unlimited region beyond the Rio Grande visited by early Spanish explorers had lain forgotten for more than forty years after the departure of Coronado in 1542. With the settlement of the North Mexican states and the gradual extension of their limits

---

[3] The Supreme Council, created in 1524, exercised supreme jurisdiction over the Kingdom of the Indies for three hundred years. Lucas Alamán, Historia de Méjico, I, 34. By royal cedula of December 13, 1527, Charles V instituted the system of audiencias, or tribunals, as a means of governing the possessions in America. Hubert Howe Bancroft, History of Mexico, 1521-1690, II, 277, 278. As a result of the abusive rule of the first audiencia in New Spain, Charles V appointed viceroys to rule in his name. The first viceroy, Antonio de Mendoza, arrived in Mexico in 1535. Ibid., 376-378.

and fortifications, the territory commonly called Texas began to be visited again by devoted missionaries and desultory exploring parties. In 1691 it received official designation as the Province of Texas, New Philippines, and was governed in conjunction with the Province of Coahuila contiguous to the south.[4] In 1727 the King appointed a separate governor, and definite steps were taken for colonization.[5] A viceroy and a specially commissioned judge issued the first land grants to missions and the early settlers of San Antonio and Goliad.[6] Thereafter, and until the system of government was reorganized in the last quarter of the eighteenth century, the governor performed the

[4] Carlos E. Castañeda, Our Catholic Heritage in Texas, 1519-1693, I, 362.

[5] Bancroft, History of the North Mexican States, 1531-1800, I, 604.

[6] The Spanish Archives of the General Land Office, vol. 50, p. 13; vol. 42, p. 98. Cited hereafter as Spanish Archives, G.L.O.

duty of distributing lands under the supervisory control of the viceroy and the privative judge of lands and waters.[7]

In Texas and other northern provinces, where the Spanish population was in continuous struggle with savage Indian tribes and where the inhabitants formed military colonies, an immediately absolute and entirely military authority was needed. Hence, in 1776, the creation of the Commandancia General, an administrative and military division comprising the interior provinces as so regarded from Mexico City; they were under the authority of their governors and a commandant general, who was entirely independent

---

[7] Ibid., Decree of Don Jacinto de Barrios, governor and captain general of Texas, 1759, vol. 50, p. 149; Title to Andrés Hernández and Luis Menchaca, 1758, vol. 42, p. 98; Grant of Eleven Leagues to Mission of San José, 1766, vol. 50, p. 50; Protection Granted to Bernabé Carabajal by Privative Judge in Mexico City, 1765, vol. 50, p. 153; Decree of Privative Judge, Mexico, 1770, vol. 50, p. 25.

of the viceroy and responsible directly to the King.

The Interior Provinces were Nueva Vizcaya (Durango

and Chihuahua), Texas, Coahuila, New Mexico, So-

nora, Sinaloa, and the Californias, and the capital city

was located at Chihuahua.[8] After undergoing numer-

ous revisions, the organization of the Commandancia

General in 1793 was substantially the same as that of

1776. It included all the original provinces except

the Californias and was subject only in a limited de-

gree to the viceroy.[9] In 1813 a final change was made.

The Interior Provinces were divided into two separate

commands, those of the east and those of the west.

The Provincias Internas del Oriente were Nuevo León,

---

[8] Bancroft, History of the North Mexican States,
1531-1800, I, 636-638. Herbert E. Bolton, Guide to
Materials for the History of the United States in the
Principal Archives of Mexico, 75; Herbert E. Bolton,
Athanase de Mézières and the Louisiana-Texas Fron-
tier, 1768-1780, II, 147, 148.

[9] Bancroft, History of the North Mexican States,
1531-1800, I, 641.

Nuevo Santander (Tamaulipas), Coahuila, and Texas.

The commandant general was Joaquín de Arredondo,

and his headquarters were at Monterrey.[10]

Though Texas also was attached nominally to the

fiscal Intendencia of San Luis Potosí, she retained

her military status, and for the last half-century of

Spanish rule was subject, with few exceptions, to the

authority of the Commandancia General.[11] The mili-

tary took precedence over the civil at all times, and

---

[10] Vito Alessio Robles, Coahuila y Texas, I, 41, 42, 67.

[11] In 1786, to strengthen the power of the Supreme Government, all of New Spain was divided into twelve intendencias, each taking the name of its capital, under the administration of an intendant governor and sub-delegates. This was the political system in existence until the Mexican revolution was consummated. Bancroft, History of the North Mexican States, 1531-1800, I, 642. Antonio Cordero, governor of the state of Coahuila and ad interim governor of Texas in 1807, made three grants, one being located in Coahuila, in which he stated that by royal cedula of February 14, 1805, it was necessary that the grantee, in person or by attorney, receive confirmation from the Intendencia

Quedo enterado de quanto Vm. refiere
en informe n.º 229, de 7 del mes ultimo
à cerca de los reconocimientos que hà
practicado sobre los Rios de S.ᵗ Antonio
y Guadalupe, en union del R.P. Fr. Manuel Silva y otros sugetos para buscar
Parage à proposito en que establezca la
nueva Mission del Refugio: y quando
Vm. me dé cuenta de las resultas del
que iva à egecutar del Rio de las
Nueces, haré à Vm. las prevenciones
que me ocurran.

Dios gūe. à Vm. muchos años.
Chihuagua 4 de Diciembre de 1794.

Pedro de Nava

M.
S. Governador de Texas.

nador, y Alcalde de los Naturales por no saver Es=
cribir pusieron una señal de cruz quedando ad=
vertidos que es la Justificacion de la Verdad, hizi=
eronlo los testigos de mi asistencia con quienes
actuo, como dicho es Doy Feé.

℞ ☩ Man.⁷ ℞₡no ——— Fr.⁰ Jose Manuel Pedrajo

Jose Errera   ☩ ☩ Pedro Thurac

Tes.⁰   Tes.⁰
Andres Bon.⁰ Gonzs.⁵   fran.⁰ Xavier Perez

En dicha Mision y en veinte y tres dias del refe[ri]
do mes de Julio de este Corriente año de Mil Seteci
entos noventa, y quatro. Yo el anotado Comisario
que actuo con testigos de asistencia. Dixe: que se pasen po
señonar de las tierras y frutos que Ay en ellas à
Yndios; respecto à estar medidas desde el dia diez y se[is]
à el veinte y dos del mismo y à este efecto estando en
la labor con dichos Yndios, y el Justicia Español
con el Agrimensor, y con presencia del P.⁰ Minis
tro Fr.⁰ Jose Manuel Pedrajo se entregaron à los
mencionados Yndios veinte y ocho suertes de t[res]
cientas varas de Largo y dos cientas de ancho
cada una, y à los tres Gentiles dos suertes para que
hagan sus Huertas y se impongan en los lab[o]r[es]

a "political and military governor" issued land titles under the close and cognizant supervision of the commandant general.[12]

In 1820 a provincial deputation was formed to govern the interior provinces, and it went into operation a few months before Spain's withdrawal from the continent.[13] Settlers were instructed to receive their titles from the ayuntamiento of the municipality in which they lived.[14] One grant thus acquired is of record,

of San Luis Potosí. Those grants were not completed with respect to their final confirmation. Spanish Archives, G.L.O., vol. 42, p. 119; vol. 58, p. 173; vol. 31, p. 255. No other reference is found to this order in subsequent titles.

[12] Carlos E. Castañeda, A Report on the Spanish Archives of San Antonio, Ugarte to Cordero, 113; Salcedo to Governor of Texas, 119. Spanish Archives, G.L.O., Titles issued by Spanish Authorities, vol. 37; Pedro de Nava to Carlos Martínez, vol. 30, p. 149; Title to Ramón de Legarreta, vol. 37, p. 398.

[13] Castañeda, A Report on the Spanish Archives of San Antonio, 122.

[14] Ibid., 123.

and it later received confirmation from Mexico.[15]

---

[15] This grant of four leagues to Nicolás Carabajal was issued in the name of the King and the Constitution on March 9, 1821, by the Alcalde of La Bahía del Espíritu Santo (Goliad). The Mexican authorities confirmed one league. Spanish Archives, G.L.O., vol. 43, p. 165.

Chapter III

LAND GRANTS MADE BY SPAIN IN TEXAS

To establish her national claim to ownership, Spain maintained her three outposts at San Antonio, Nacogdoches, and Goliad from 1718 to 1821 with little attempt toward permanent colonization. Of her century of active rule in Texas no more than seventy land titles remain of record in the archives of the Land Office. Doubtless, many have been lost or destroyed. Fiftytwo of those concessions were made at Nacogdoches where the settlers had received their lands by "verbal permission" from Captain Gil Ybarvo[1] when, after

---

[1] A request to the governor for approval of a grant, written and signed by Ybarvo in 1782, is found attached to a later title issued to Pedro Procela by the Spanish government. Spanish Archives, G.L.O., vol. 38, p. 501.

the abandonment of the East Texas forts and missions in 1773, he returned to establish the town in spite of government orders.[2] In 1792 Don Juan Cortés, lieutenant governor and commandant of the post, made public proclamation of a decree by which he was designated to grant lands to "those not so supplied." Cortés and successive commandants issued titles until 1810 when the governor, Don Manuel de Salcedo, came from the capital at Béjar and was engaged for several months attending to land matters. He confirmed previous grants and approved titles to new settlers and to those who had acquired land "extrajudicially" by inheritance and transfer.

The peso was the unit of exchange, but live stock, "material for skirts," jewelry, and vermillion figured prominently in local trades. Grants varied in size

---

[2] Herbert E. Bolton, Texas in the Middle Eighteenth Century, 439.

Don Antº Gil y Barvo capitan de Milicia y teni
ente de Govrº del Pueblo de Nª Sª del Pilar de Nacogdo
ches y su Jurisdicion &

Atendiendo al pedido por el Vecino y poblador
de dhº Pueblo Miguel de Cordova demandandose este
un sitio de tierra para formar un Rancho y la
bor de siembra de Semillas con una legua en con
torno para pastuar sus ganados y Caballerias
en el parage Nombrado el atascoso Rumbo al orien
te y atendiendo a las buenas Circunstancias que le
adornan y por otra parte ser acredor a ello y que
dhº sitio se alla en distancia de no perjudicar a otro
vecino e benido en Concedersele en Nombre de Su
M.q.D.G para el y sus eredero. Suplicando
a la Superioridad se dine aprobarlo y atender
dhº demandante Segun lo meresse. a quien le otorg
la presente firmada de mi mano en el Pueblo de
los Nacodoches a los quatro dias del mes de abril
del año de mil Setecientos ochenta y dos

Antº Gil Barvo

from a "plot of ground" for sowing <u>frijoles</u> and corn
to large four-league tracts which were surveyed by
beginning at the settler's dwelling and measuring one
"league to each wind," or in all four directions. Oc-
casionally the timber prevented the use of the <u>cordel</u>,
and the tract was surveyed <u>a pasos de caballo</u>, or by
the steps of a horse; the distance was calculated afterward by the length and number of the steps. Lands
were often declared unsuitable for farming and stock
raising because of the prevalence of ticks and horse-
flies and the scarcity of water, and a tract of more
than 17,000 acres was sometimes appraised at seven
<u>pesos.</u>

Though lands were of trifling value, the procurement of a title was tedious in its requirements. It
was necessary that a colonist address a formal petition for his land to the governor, or his delegate, who
signed an approval ordering a specially designated

local officer to make a reconnaissance, survey, and appraisal of the tract and give official possession to the applicant. A written acknowledgment of the order was recorded by the notary in attendance who proceeded with the notification of the commissioned officer and the petitioner, making a certification of the act which was signed by all three parties. The special officer, accompanied by witnesses, appraisers, and adjacent landowners, summoned to prevent boundary conflicts, went to the tract and made the vista de ojos, or visual inspection, survey, and demarcation. At that point the official act of possession took place, and the grantee, as a token of his true ownership, performed ceremonial demonstrations such as walking to and fro over the tract, throwing rocks, pulling grass, cutting bushes, and digging holes in the ground. All those proceedings were incorporated into a report signed by the officer, the witnesses, and the interested

party who, in most cases, carefully rendered his signature with the sign of the cross. The complete record of events, written contemporaneously with their
occurrence and in continuation of the original petition, constituted a title in its simplest form.

If contingent circumstances necessitated the in-
clusion of more than one order from the governor,
testimonials of witnesses as proof of occupation and
ownership, adjustments with adjacent landowners, appointments of substitute officers, or certified copies
of previous titles or transfers, a longer and more
complex document resulted, and months or even years
were expended in its completion.

In the absence of a notary a title could be legalized by a local officer acting with attendant witnesses.
An official notary accompanied Governor Salcedo to
Nacogdoches, but at that far-away post the stamped
paper required for legal instruments was not provided

for use. The omission always was carefully noted
and explained in every document.[3]

The titles issued at Nacogdoches were archived in
the presidio under the charge of the commandant of
the post. They were consulted from time to time at
the request of landholders desiring certified copies
of previous titles, deeds, or transfers. Several copies
taken as early as 1800 appear in later records. The
land covered by those early grants was an extensive
outlying area around the town of Nacogdoches, including the present limits of Nacogdoches County and
parts of adjacent counties. Many of the old ranches
and farms established there were abandoned during
the turmoil of the revolutionary years between 1812

---

[3] The stamps were of four different values varying from three dollars to one-sixteenth of a dollar.
Every instrument, deed, judicial record, will, or contract was required to be written on paper of the corresponding stamp. Recopilación de las Indias, Book
VIII, Title 23, Law 18.

and 1821 and never were reclaimed. Only twenty-five
of the existing titles of record appear on present official maps.[4]

From San Antonio and Goliad, where land grants
were issued by Spain more than two centuries ago
and throughout a period of ninety years, the records
of the Land Office are few and fragmentary. They
consist of one volume of grants, inventories, and orders relative to the establishment and maintenance
of certain missions and towns, an assortment of miscellaneous records and incomplete grants, and six
land concessions that are considered as actual titles.
Of these six, only three have been recognized as valid.

---

[4] A few of these titles overlapped into Louisiana.
They appear as "unlocated grants" in the index of
original grantees in the Spanish Archives of the Land
Office. Grants issued by Spain in Louisiana in the
period between 1763 and 1803 are found in the National
Archives in Washington. The final disposition of the
lands thus covered was made by the United States government.

It may be presumed that the immense size of the
ranches in that region and the limited areas of safety
from the constant and terrific menace of the Apache
and Comanche Indians precluded the issuance of an
extremely large number of grants. Again, a great
many Spanish settlers were living on lands without
authority, and they later secured titles from the Mexican government, as did many whose titles had been
lost.[5] Yet it is known that numerous ranches and
farms existed in the areas immediate to those two
oldest settlements in Texas, and that many titles,

---

[5] Castañeda, *A Report on the Spanish Archives of
San Antonio*, 119. Incomplete grants issued between
1792 and 1810 reveal that the petitioners were living
on lands for which they had never received titles.
Spanish Archives, G.L.O., vol. 40, part 1. Manuel
Barrera, a prominent citizen who had served a long
period as alcalde in San Antonio before 1810, received
a Mexican title in 1833 for land which his father had
occupied for years under Spain. By virtue of occupancy, eleven leagues were granted by Mexico to the
heirs of Simón de Arocha, a descendant of the Canary
Islanders. *Ibid.*, vol. 49, p. 9; vol. 31, p. 47.

though the number is indeterminable, were actually issued by the Spanish government.[6] The mystery is that such records should be so conspicuously absent from provincial archives. It usually was required that titles be registered or protocoled in the place where they were issued,[7] and the archives of San Antonio and Goliad should have contained the land records covering those rural areas settled under the Spanish regime.[8] Time cannot be regarded as a necessarily destructive element because countless records of grants for lots and buildings within the limits

---

[6] Fray Juan Agustín Morfi, History of Texas, 1673-1770, translated with biographical introduction and annotations by Carlos E. Castañeda, part I, 79, 102; ibid., part II, 418; Bolton, Texas in the Middle Eighteenth Century, 382, 386; Spanish Archives, G.L.O., vol. 50, p. 153; vol. 50, p. 24; vol. 50, p. 197.

[7] Spanish Archives, G.L.O., vol. 50, p.153; vol. 50, p. 24; vol. 50, p. 197.

[8] Castaneda, A Report on the Spanish Archives of San Antonio. There are as many as fifteen completed

of the old city of San Antonio, dating from 1736 through 1820, have been preserved in the same archives from which the few titles in the Land Office were obtained.[9]

From evidence available in the titles later issued by Mexico to the Spanish settlers at San Antonio it is reasonably certain that the government archives were greatly damaged and mishandled when Arredondo and his troops occupied the city in 1813. Ignacio de Arocha, in his petition to the Mexican government for lands granted in 1782 to his grandfather, Simón de Arocha, stated that "Arredondo and the enemies of the repub-lican system" deliberately despoiled the original Aro-cha title. Angel Navarro, alcalde of San Antonio in 1832, further explained that the archives had passed

---

land grants listed in this report which appear to be titles to lands abandoned by the grantees, some of whom received later titles from Mexico.

[9] *Ibid.*, Castañeda's report lists and classifies the records of those archives. The report was prepared in 1923.

through many hands during the revolutionary turmoil of 1813 and that when Arredondo took possession of them the greater part was lost and the remainder carried away to Laredo. Navarro also added that the few Spanish titles then existing under his charge had been found accidentally, mutilated and torn, in the dwelling of Baron de Bastrop, who had possession of them by unknown authorization.[10]

Whatever disposition was made of the records in question, all positive vestiges of individual occupancy did not disappear with the titles, and lands in the San Antonio-Goliad area are yet held by virtue of original ownership under "presumed grants" from

---

[10] Spanish Archives, G.L.O., Title to Heirs of Simón de Arocha, vol. 31, p. 47. Governor Antonio Martínez wrote in an official communication to Commandant General Arredondo in 1817 that the archives were in a state of confusion and disorder due to their mistreatment during the revolutionary years. Letters of Antonio Martínez to the Commandant General, No. 101, September 6, 1817, Nacogdoches Archives.

Spain.[11] The several grants which have thus sur-
vived and the three valid ones of record in the Land
Office are located along the San Antonio River, beginning south of the city of San Antonio, where the
mission lands terminated, and extending southeast-
ward on both sides of the river to the limits of Bexar
County and into parts of Wilson and Karnes counties.
They comprise approximately 200,000 acres of land.[12]

Among the small remnant of Spanish records of that
area are the two oldest titles in the Land Office. One
is a copy of a grant made in 1713 by the viceroy to the
three missions of Concepción, San Juan Capistrano,
and San Francisco de la Espada at San Antonio. The
copy was taken on October 2, 1772, from its original,
which was then in the archives of the Royal Presidio

---

[11] Paul v. Pérez, Texas Reporter, Book 7, p. 338.

[12] General Land Office, Bexar County Map, 1932;
Wilson County Map, 1921; Karnes County Map, 1921.
These are original grantee maps.

of Béjar.[13] The other, the oldest grant in original form, is dated April 12, 1758, and was made to Luis Menchaca and Andrés Hernándes. It is an agreeable settlement of the conflict and litigation which had a-risen over a fifteen-league tract claimed by both parties under previous titles from Spain.[14]

The third valid title is the concession for fifteen leagues made on June 7, 1788, by Luis Cazorla, captain of the presidio of Bahía del Espíritu Santo, to Carlos Martínez as an award for sixteen years of valiant and honorable service in the King's campaigns against the "Apachería." Governor Rafael Pacheco for unstated reasons revoked the grant. An appeal was made to Juan Ugalde, commandant general of the Interior Provinces, who wrote in "Respondido No. 354" that La Bahía was a military settlement, the

---

[13] Spanish Archives, G.L.O., vol. 50, p. 13.

[14] Ibid., vol. 42, p. 98.

Martínez grant had been legitimately acquired, and the action of the governor was unjust. The decision was transmitted to Governor Pacheco with the added warning "to take care to preserve justice and protect the poor when the landed and powerful try to oppress them."[15] After surviving controversy under Spanish authorities, and having been twice upheld by Texas courts, the Carlos Martínez grant is not entirely free from conflict.[16]

The Medina River, as it flowed eastward to its confluence with the San Antonio, was officially considered

---

[15] Juan Ugalde was one of the imposing military figures that flashed across the pages of Texas' earliest history; the name of the present town of Uvalde commemorates his successful Indian campaigns in the upper Nueces valley. Bolton, Texas in the Middle Eighteenth Century, 127; Alessio Robles, Coahuila y Texas en la Epoca Colonial, 570.

[16] Spanish Archives, G.L.O., Title to Carlos Martínez, vol. 30, p. 149. J. M. Martínez et al. v. John Littleton et al., No. 333, Decree of District Court of Karnes County; Case No. 711, Divine v. Comett et al.,

as the dividing line between the provinces of Coahuila

and Texas, and the Nueces as that between Texas and

Nuevo Santander.[17] The strategically important east-

ern boundary of Texas was in dispute until 1819 when

it became the Sabine by treaty with the United States.

The northern boundary was considered generally as

the Red River. New Mexico was on the west, and the

Big Bend country and El Paso supposedly belonged

to the district of Chihuahua.[18] Within these limits

District Court of Bexar County; General Land Office, Map of Karnes County, 1921.

[17] Spanish Archives, G.L.O., vol. 43, p. 119, Power and Hewetson's Contract with the State of Coahuila and Texas, Appendix to Empresario Contracts, vol. 56, p. 21.

[18] The question of whether the presidio at San Saba belonged to the jurisdiction of Texas or New Mexico was debated during the eighteenth century. Alessio Robles says that in 1805 Texas increased her juris- diction westward when the boundaries were extended toward the proximity of the Pecos River. Alessio Robles, Coahuila y Texas en la Epoca Colonial, 8. Arredondo's map of 1815 shows the boundary line of

and centered at the three settlements of Nacogdoches,

San Antonio, and Goliad were the 3,334 Spanish sub-

jects who, on August 18, 1824, became citizens of the

Mexican Republic.[19]

Texas and New Mexico sharply indented to a point approximating the location of the presidio of San Saba. The constituent congress in 1824 fixed the northern boundary of the State of Chihuahua as "a straight line run from east to west from the point or town called Paso del Norte." By this authority Chihuahua claimed jurisdiction over the territory situated south of the parallel leaving the source of the Gila River and terminating at the Pecos River.

[19] Alessio Robles, Coahuila y Texas, I, 30.

Chapter IV

THE COLONIZATION OF TEXAS BY MEXICO

In the transition from empire to republic no changes were immediately visible in Texas. The recently installed provincial deputation, overshadowed by the authority of the commandant general, continued with the administration of the government. The despotic Arredondo, loyal first to Spain, then to General Iturbide, finally was forced to flee to Havana by the increased strength of republican troops in Nuevo León and Coahuila. Gaspar López, who succeeded Arredondo on August 14, 1821, usurped the civil power of the deputation and the junta provisional until the installation of the sovereign constituent congress in 1823. Antonio Martínez, the last Spanish governor,

-

took the oath of independence at the opportune moment
and remained in office until April 1, 1822.[1]

That same provincial deputation, meeting in Monterrey under the aegis of Spanish liberalism, granted permission to Moses Austin to settle three hundred foreign families in the province of Texas and thereby set the pattern of future colonization. In 1797, Moses Austin, a native of Connecticut, obtained a land concession from the Spanish government in the territory of Missouri. With his family established near the village of Saint Genevieve, he devoted sixteen years to the successful operation of the lead mines on his plantation. By means of the mines and other business ventures he developed a sizable estate, but the failure

---

[1] Alessio Robles, Coahuila y Texas, I, 70-75. José Felix Trespalacios, one of Iturbide's colonels, replaced Governor Martínez. Ibid., I, 117. On the fall of Iturbide, Brigadier Felipe de la Garza succeeded Gaspar López as commandant general, and Lieutenant Colonel Luciano García succeeded Trespalacios as governor. Ibid., 150.

of the Bank of St. Louis, in which he had large invest-
ments, brought losses that he barely was able to sustain. It was then that he conceived the idea of a new
enterprise in fairer fields - a colonial settlement in
Texas on the Colorado River, "latitude 27 N on the
Spanish Main, a spot beautiful to behold," where he
would regain his health and prosperity.

Early in December of 1820 Austin traveled to San
Antonio and laid his plans before Governor Martínez,
who forwarded a formal petition to the provincial authorities at Monterrey. Austin received notice of the
confirmation of his grant in March, 1821, soon after
his return to Missouri.[2] He immediately wrote his
son, Stephen Fuller Austin, at New Orleans, urging
his participation in the enterprise. On June 17, Stephen

---

[2] Moses Austin had been informed of the confirmation of his grant by letter from the Spanish officials
at Natchitoches. Barker (ed.), The Austin Papers, I,
397-401.

F. Austin set out for Natchitoches to join his father
and the two Spanish officials who were waiting to conduct him to the site of the new colony. Informed of
his father's death on reaching Natchitoches,[3] Stephen
F. Austin proceeded with the Spanish emissaries and
sixteen Americans to San Antonio where he was ac-
knowledged as the representative of his father and
fully empowered to carry out the original project.

With his party of Americans and a guide, Austin
explored the country between the Colorado and Brazos
rivers as far as the sea coast. Convinced that this
territory would be a desirable location for a flourishing colony, he returned to the United States to make
further arrangements; he fitted out a schooner, the
Lively, with eighteen men, provisions, arms, ammu-
nition, and farming tools, and it left New Orleans on

---

[3] Moses Austin died on June 16, 1821. The news of
his death was received by S. F. Austin on July 1. Ibid.,
395, 396.

November 20, 1821. A day later, Austin proceeded overland with ten colonists to meet her at the mouth of the Colorado. He arrived there some time in January; he waited three weeks, and finally giving up all hope of meeting the schooner, returned to San Antonio on March 15, 1822.

Governor Martínez gave Austin a cordial reception and thereupon informed him of the recent change in the political affairs of the country. Martínez advised that circumstances made it necessary to secure approval of the colonization contract either from the new commandant general at Monterrey or from the national congress at Mexico City. Austin set out for the capital on March 20, 1822, and arrived there on the 29th of the following April. Fifteen months later, he returned to the colonists he had left in the Texas wilderness.[4]

---

[4] Ibid., I, 1-5.

Meanwhile, in Mexico City, General Iturbide, who had proclaimed himself emperor after consummating the revolution, promulgated the National Colonization Law of January 4, 1823.[5] By imperial decree of February 18, he ratified the concession for which Austin had made long and diligent solicitation.[6] On March 19, after the appearance of the "liberating army" in Mexico City, Emperor Iturbide abdicated; the national congress reassembled and promptly confirmed Austin's same concession.[7] Under authority extended by

---

[5] Alamán, Historia de Méjico, V, 599-601; 875. A copy of the National Colonization Law of 1823, printed in Mexico, appears in vol. 53, pp. 192, 193, of the Spanish Archives, G.L.O.

[6] Eugene C. Barker, The Life of Stephen F. Austin, 48-75.

[7] Alessio Robles, Coahuila y Texas, I, 170; Alamán, Historia de Méjico, V, 740. Congress convened on March 29. Ibid., V, 744. No other contracts were made under the Colonization Law of 1823 as it was suspended at the same time Austin's concession was confirmed.

the sovereign constituent congress and the supreme executive power by decrees of April 11 and 14, Austin's enterprise finally was launched.

The provincial deputation at Monterrey, re-instated by the new government,[8] provided the particular regulations governing the establishment of the first colony, and Governor Luciano García appointed the Baron de Bastrop as its commissioner. The grant called for the settlement of three hundred families, and it comprised the territory between the San Jacinto and Lavaca rivers, extending northward to the old San Antonio road, and leaving free the ten-league coast reserve. Acting with the provincial deputation of Texas, Empresario Austin[9] and Commissioner Bastrop issued their first

---

[8] Spanish Archives, G.L.O., vol. 51, p. 1.

[9] The National Colonization Law of 1823 defined an empresario as one who contracted with the government to introduce at least two hundred families to settle the vacant tracts deemed suitable to their corresponding industries and resources. The empresario

title on July 7, 1824, to Sylvenus Castleman for two and one-half leagues and two labors (11,073 acres) of land on the lower Colorado River.[10]

Specific orders required that original titles be retained in the archives of the colony and that a duplicate copy, or <u>testimonio</u>, be given to each owner. For further security Austin was instructed to keep a special record book into which every title was copied with a sketch of each survey and the signatures of the empresario, commissioner, alcalde, and two attendant witnesses. The recorded titles were prefaced by the special laws, decrees, and instructions issued for the establishment of the colony and its capital, the town of San Felipe de Austin. This register or record book of original titles, now in the Land Office, is a

would receive fifteen leagues and two labors as premium lands for each two hundred colonists he introduced.

[10] Spanish Archives, G.L.O., vol. 1, p. 22.

masterpiece of workmanship.

Other records of the first colonization enterprise include two volumes of original titles, Austin's Field Note Book, Austin's Census of 1826, correspondence relative to colony affairs, Austin's Application Book and Register of Families, the Minutes of the Ayuntamiento of San Felipe de Austin, and copies of the laws, decrees, orders, and appointments made for the organization and government of the colony. Beyond the intrinsic worth of 297 legal land titles and the containment of valuable historical and genealogical information, these records unfailingly reflect the genius by which Austin effected the settlement of Texas under the colonization laws of Mexico.

Within six months after the issuance of the first title, Austin secured a second colonization contract for 500 families, but from a new authority, the free and sovereign state of Coahuila and Texas. By the

adoption of the Constitution of 1824 Mexico became
a republic of federated states. A national colonization law, outlining general principles, was passed by
the sovereign constituent congress on August 18 of the
same year.[11] By that law the Mexican nation offered
to foreigners, who might come to establish themselves
within its territory, security of their persons and
property provided that they subjected themselves to
the laws of the country. The object of the law was the
colonization of the unappropriated lands of the nation.
The state congresses were instructed to form their
respective laws and regulations within the briefest
time possible.

The congress of Coahuila and Texas, having convened at Saltillo on August 15, 1824, immediately dis-
solved the provincial deputation of Texas and created

------

[11] Alessio Robles, Coahuila y Texas, I, 169, 170.
Copies of the Constitution of 1824 and the National

Plot West side Brazos

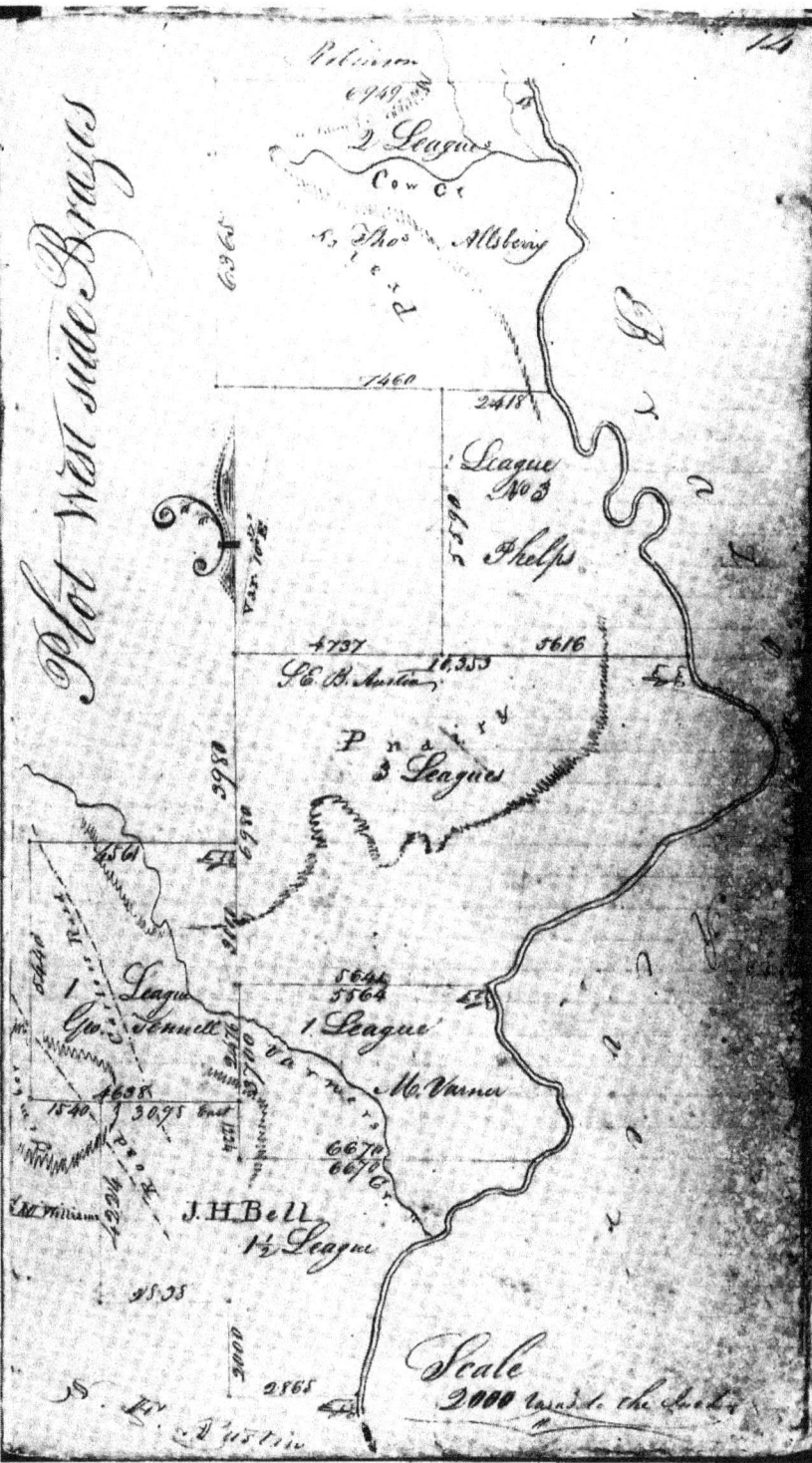

Robinson
6949
2 Leagues
Cow Cr
Thos Allsberry

1460
2418

League
No 3

Phelps

4737   5616
S. E. B. Austin   16,353

P r a i r y
3 Leagues

4561

1 League
Geo. Jennell

5644
5564

1 League

McVarna

4638
1540   3075 East

6670
6670

J. H. Bell
1½ League

2865

Scale
2000 varas to the Inch

the office of chief of the department of Texas.[12] The

local deputation had been installed on October 31,

1823,[13] and during its brief existence had issued many

land titles and approved Martin de León's proposal

to colonize forty-one Mexican families in Texas.[14]

State authorities later confirmed De León's contract

but nullified most of the titles for non-payment of

stipulated fees and lack of conformity with existing

regulations. José Antonio Saucedo, the first political

chief of the new government, was occupied primarily

Colonization Law of 1824 appear respectively in vol.
57, pp. 25-41, and vol. 53, pp. 195, 196, Spanish Archives, G.L.O.

[12] Laws and Decrees of the State of Coahuila and
Texas, 8, 11.

[13] The provincial deputation of Texas was instituted
by decree of the federal congress on August 18, 1823.
Nettie Lee Benson, The Provincial Deputation in Mexico, Precursor of the Mexican Federal State, dissertation, 127.

[14] Spanish Archives, G.L.O., vol. 56, pp. 1-3.

with land problems projected by inrushing colonists.[15]

Among his immediate duties were the delivery of a formal inventory of the provincial archives to the governor and secretaries of state and the confirmation of a number of controversial land titles.

After six months of careful deliberation, a comprehensive colonization law containing forty-eight articles was drafted and passed by the congress on March 24, 1825.[16] The terms were generous and carried few restrictions. Provisions were made for the distribution of lands by sale or award to Mexicans and for the introduction of both foreign and Mexican colonists by empresarios or contractors. Subsequent legislation by the state congress provided new regulations

[15] Ibid., vol. 51, pp. 34-37. José Antonio Saucedo was also the political chief of the province of Texas under the former government and had directed the provincial deputation.

[16] Laws and Decrees of the State of Coahuila and Texas, Decree No. 16, pp. 15-23.

as new problems arose. To facilitate and effect the equitable distribution and location of lands, special instructions were issued to commissioners on September 4, 1827.[17] These instructions and the colonization law of March 24, 1825, governed the issuance of the majority of titles in Texas during the colonial period.

Under the empresario system almost the entire state was contracted for settlement. By formal invitation the east-west tide moved into Texas.[18] Ten thousand people were reported to be already at the eastern frontier.[19] Forty-one different contracts with

---

[17] Ibid., 70-73. Additional Article, ibid., 73, 74.

[18] Alessio Robles, Coahuila y Texas, I, 177, 178. Alessio Robles says that the westward movement began at the precise moment when the English established themselves on the Atlantic coast.

[19] Bastrop to the legislature of Coahuila and Texas, March 6, 1825, in Barker (ed.), The Austin Papers, II, 948.

individuals and companies were authorized by the government, but only two empresarios, Austin and De
León, were successful in settling their quota of families. Fourteen contracts were partially fulfilled, four
were cancelled or forfeited, and under the remainder
not a single title was issued.[20]

Austin's second contract, made on June 4, 1825,
authorized the settlement of 500 additional families
within the specified boundaries of his first colony.[21]
Gaspar Flores and Miguel Arciniega as commissioners issued 460 titles.

Austin's "Little Colony" was designed to open communications into the interior and establish the new
town of Bastrop. The contract for 100 families was

---

[20] Spanish Archives, G.L.O., Original and Other
Documents in Spanish, vol. 52; Appendices to Empre-
sario Contracts, vols. 53, 54, 55, 56, and the General
Index.

[21] Ibid., vol. 3, pp. 1-12.

made on November 20, 1827.[22] The grant comprised two-thirds of the present county of Travis and one-half of that of Bastrop, including the site of the city of Austin. Commissioner Arciniega issued fifty-nine titles.

Austin's "Coast Colony," by contract of July 9, 1828, was established with the view of extending settlement to the coast and developing harbors and ports of entry.[23] The territory comprised the littoral leagues between the Lavaca and San Jacinto rivers. The contract called for the settlement of 300 families. Austin was appointed commissioner, and 175 titles were issued.

A fifth contract to settle 800 foreign and Mexican families in the "Upper Colony" was granted to Austin and Samuel M. Williams on February 25, 1831. By

---

[22] Ibid., vol. 9, pp. 1-4.

[23] Ibid., vol. 7, pp. 1-35.

this contract the boundaries of Austin's first colony were extended northward into central Texas, covering the territory between the Colorado River and the dividing ridge of the waters of the Brazos and Trinity.[24] Most of this area had been originally comprised in the grant held by Robert Leftwich and the Nashville Company. On April 29, 1834, the supreme government returned the colony to the Nashville Company and recognized Sterling C. Robertson as empresario. On May 18, 1835, the colony was restored to Austin and Williams.[25] Commissioner Robert Peebles issued 152 titles.

Sterling C. Robertson, by contract of April 29, 1834, was authorized to settle 800 families in the former Austin and Williams Colony.[26] While Robertson was

---

[24] Ibid., vol. 54, pp. 171, 172.

[25] Ibid., vol. 43, p. 304.

[26] Ibid., vol. 54, pp. 277, 278.

in control, Commissioner William H. Steele issued

279 titles at the town of Viesca.[27] Robertson's colony

register, which contains an incomplete record of sur-

veys and applicants, is in the Spanish Archives.

Benjamin R. Milam's colony, by contract of Janu-

ary 12, 1826, for 300 families, lay between the Guada-

lupe and Colorado rivers and above the upper San

Antonio road.[28] Commissioner Talbot Chambers, at

---

[27] A Texas court later rejected Robertson's claim
for 221 families introduced after the closing of the land
offices but allowed him credit for 307 families. One
hundred and eight of the 279 titles issued were to single men. The court ruled that three single men were
equivalent to one head of a family, and the total number of families was reduced to 207. Therefore, Robertson was credited with 100 families which he claimed
to have settled but to whom he had issued no titles.
Virginia Henderson, "Minor Empresario Contracts,"
The Southwestern Historical Quarterly, XXXI, (April,
1928), 315-324. Twelve leagues of the twenty-four
that Robertson had received as premium lands were
later cancelled. Herndon v. Robertson, 15 Texas 593;
Houston v. Robertson, 2 Texas 35; Houston v. Robertson, 3 Texas 374.

[28] Spanish Archives, G.L.O., vol. 55, pp. 6, 7.

the town of Mina (Bastrop), issued fifty-three titles

to settlers in the year of 1835. Milam's register,

containing the oaths of allegiance of sixty-five colo-

nists with their signatures, ages, occupations, nation-

alities, and family statuses, is on file in the Spanish

Archives. Milam's contract expired in 1832, and the

territory it covered was granted to Juan Vicente Cam-

pos, the agent of a Mexican company which made no

effort to colonize it.[29]

The adjoining grants of Burnet, Zavala, and Vehlein

were located in a compact area in East Texas. George

Anthony Nixon was the commissioner for the three

colonies. On December 22, 1826, David G. Burnet ob-

tained his contract for the settlement of 300 families

northwest of Nacogdoches,[30] between the Navasoto

and Sabine rivers, leaving clear the twenty-league

[29] Ibid., vol. 52, pp. 381-384.

[30] Ibid., vol. 55, pp. 43-45.

strip bordering on the United States boundary line. Commissioner Nixon issued 251 titles at Nacogdoches.

Joseph Vehlein's first contract for 300 families was made on December 21, 1826.[31] The colony was located between the San Jacinto and Sabine rivers, leaving free the twenty border leagues and extending southward from the town of Nacogdoches to the littoral belt. His second contract for 100 families, dated November 17, 1828, extended the boundaries of the first contract through the coast reserve to the Gulf of Mexico.[32] Three hundred and fifty-eight titles were issued by Commissioner Nixon at Nacogdoches.

Lorenzo de Zavala received his contract for 500 families on March 12, 1829. It included the border leagues between Vehlein's grants and the Sabine River. The gulf was the southern boundary and the road

[31] Ibid., vol. 55, pp. 29-31.

[32] Ibid., vol. 55, pp. 58, 59.

from Nacogdoches to Natchitoches the northern.[33] At Nacogdoches and San Augustine Commissioner Nixon issued 464 titles.

Martin de León's contract, which was made with the provincial deputation of Texas on April 13, 1824, authorized him to settle forty-one Mexican families on the Guadalupe and establish the town of Victoria.[34] No specific boundaries were delineated until he received permission to introduce an additional 150 families.[35] The second agreement was cancelled later by state authorities because its designated limits conflicted with the territory assigned to Green De Witt and to Power and Hewetson.[36] The federal government

---

[33] Ibid., vol. 55, pp. 67-69.

[34] Ibid., vol. 56, pp. 1-3.

[35] Ibid., vol. 52, pp. 95, 96. The date of this second contract was April 30, 1829.

[36] Ibid., vol. 52, pp. 97-99.

intervened in behalf of De León, and his commissioner was instructed to continue the issuance of titles in conformity with the second contract.[37] Thereafter, most of De León's colonists were settled in an area between Coleto Creek and the Lavaca River and extending to the sea coast. Commissioner Fernando de León issued 162 titles at the town of Guadalupe Victoria.

James Power and James Hewetson contracted on June 11, 1828, to introduce 200 Irish and Mexican families into the ten-league coast reserve between the Guadalupe and Lavaca rivers.[38] By special petition the grant was later extended to the Nueces River, and citizens of Germany, England, and North America were admitted. The seat of government was Refugio, and Commissioner José Jesús de Vidaurri issued 174

---

[37] Ibid., vol. 56, pp. 109-115.

[38] Ibid., vol. 56, pp. 144, 145.

titles.[39]

· The contract of John G. Purnell and Benjamin Drake Lovell[40] was conceded to John McMullen and James McGloin. Those two associates received permission on August 17, 1828, to settle 200 families in an area south of the Medina and San Antonio rivers, extending to the Nueces, with the old road from Bexar to the presidio of Rio Grande as the northwest boundary, and leaving clear the coast reserve on the southeast.[41] At San Patricio, José Antonio Saucedo and José María Balmaceda issued eighty-five titles.

Green DeWitt's contract for 400 families was made on April 15, 1825. The territory covered was located within the following boundaries: beginning on the right

---

[39] Ibid., vol. 56, pp. 146, 147. The extension was granted on April 2, 1829. Translations of Empresario Contracts, 149, 150.

[40] Ibid., vol. 55, pp. 169, 170.

[41] Ibid., vol. 55, pp. 165-168.

SELLO TERCERO: DOS REALES

HABILITADO POR EL ESTADO DE COAHUILA Y TEXAS PARA EL BIENIO DE 1828 Y 29

Por Comicionado en esta Colonia
de Green de Witt.

Juan Martin de Veramendi, natural de la Ciudad
de Bexar y residente en ella, à V. tercera vez me pre-
sento y digo: Que haciendome V. acordado en diez del
presente mes el título de posecion correspondiente à los
dos Sitios de tierra unidos q.e pedi en el oro de Agua
del Comal, y en onse de el mismo mes, el del otro sitio
de Agua q.e llaman de Guadalupe, en cuenta de los
Sitios q.e me correspondere por havermelos concedido com
poblador el Gobierno Supremo del Estado, segun consta
de los documentos originales à que se refiere el Certificado q.e V. mismo me libro y adelantam.te, acompaño la
q.e se agrega à este Expediente; he de merecer de su
Bondad, se sirva ponerme en posesion de los dos sitios
restantes q.e pretendo en la inmediacion del rio de San Marcos
fuera de esta Colonia, con los cuales se completan los cinco
q.e se me hallan garantisados por el Gefe del Ayuntamiento; y encuanto q.e sea à la posesion, me hará V.
la Justicia y favor de darme una Copia de esta en forma
q.e pueda certificar y pedir en donde y cuando me
convenga, los otros sitios q.e me quedan faltando, Lo
que no procede de Malicia &.c.   Villa de Gonzales

18 de Noviembre de 1831.

Juan Martin de Veramendi

presentado y admitido: Agreguese á con-
tinuacion el Certificado que acompaña esta
parte á su instancia y en vista de ser cierto
que el Gobierno Supremo del Estado le
concedio como poblador los once sitios de tierra que indica y hayandome con facultad
bastante del Sôr Gefe de Policia del de-
partamto Ciudadano Ramon Musquiz, para
meter en posesion al interesado de cinco sitios de tierra, de los cuales tiene ya recividos
dos en el ojo de agua del Comal y otro en el
de Guadalupe, siendo como son baldios y no
perteneciendo á Empresa alguna los dos que so-
licita por la presente instancia en las Cave-
zeras del Rio de San Marcos; librese el
Utso de propiedad, para que por medio de él
los posea y disfrute con entero arreglo á las
Leyes; Y desele el Certificado que pide pa
que pueda hacer constar en donde y cuando
le convenga, quedarle faltando todavia
seis pa completar los once que le perte-
necen: Yo Cosé Antonio Navarro, Co
misionado Como queda dicho: Por este autori-
lo proveo, mando y firmo en esta villa de Gon-
zalez á los diez y nueve dias del mes de
Noviembre de mil ocho cientos treinta y uno;
lo que certifico y firmo con dos testigos de mi
asistencia.   José Antonio Navarro
            de asª   de asmª
Josê Ramon Bedford   Thomas R. Miller

bank of the Lavaca River, ten leagues from the coast; thence up the river to the San Antonio-Nacogdoches road, west along said road to a point parallel with the river and downward to the ten border leagues.[42] At Gonzales, Commissioner José Antonio Navarro issued 189 titles.

Arthur G. Wavell, by contract of March 9, 1826, for between four and five hundred families, introduced a number of settlers into his colony on the Red River.[43] Benjamin R. Milam was appointed commissioner, but the contract expired before any titles were issued.

James Grant and John Charles Beales contracted on October 9, 1832, to settle 800 families between the Nueces and Rio Grande.[44] The contract states that the grant was bounded on the south by the Laredo-San

---

[42] Ibid., vol. 54, pp. 176, 177.

[43] Ibid., vol. 55, pp. 14, 15.

[44] Ibid., vol. 55, pp. 219-228.

Antonio road and extended westward to the 24th meridian. Fortunato Soto issued nine land titles to native Mexicans who had an interest in the colony. The first foreign colonists introduced by Beales established the town of Dolores on Las Moras Creek, near the present site of Eagle Pass. They were reported to have been massacred by the Indians. The second shipload of emigrants joined other colonists in South Texas. Though Beales made pretentious preparations for further settlement, the members of his last expedition dispersed immediately on the outbreak of the Texas revolution.[45]

Haden Edward's contract of April 15, 1825,[46] for the settlement of 800 families in East Texas was annulled

---

[45] Doctor John Charles Beales et als., Memorial to the United States Congress, Second Session, December, 1870, part 1, pp. 10-20 (Deposition of T. H. O'Sullivan Addicks).

[46] Spanish Archives, G.L.O., vol. 52, pp. 61-64.

because of mismanagement.[47]

John Cameron failed in two colonization enterprises. His first contract was made on May 21, 1827, for 100 families to be located in central West Texas.[48] The second on September 19, 1828, provided for the settle- ment of 200 families south of the Red River.[49] This territory formerly had been conceded to Reuben Ross, who was killed shortly after his contract was granted. José María Portillo was appointed commissioner on July 28, 1825, but no titles were issued.

Robert Leftwich relinquished his contract of April 15, 1825, for 800 families to the Nashville Company.[50] This contract expired before any colonists had been settled, and the territory was assigned to Austin and

[47] Ibid., vol. 52, pp. 189-213.

[48] Ibid., vol. 55, pp. 113, 114.

[49] Ibid., vol. 55, pp. 119-121.

[50] Ibid., vol. 52, pp. 33-60.

Williams.

No titles were issued under the following contracts: Frost Thorn, April 15, 1825, 400 families; John Lucius Woodbury and José Vehlein, November 14, 1826, 200 families; Richard Exeter and Stephen Julian Wilson, February 23, 1828, 100 families; Colonel Juan Domínguez, February 6, 1829, 200 families; Juan Antonio Padilla and Thomas J. Chambers, February 12, 1830, 800 families; General Vicente Filísola, October 15, 1831, 600 families; Fortunato Soto and Henry Egerton, January 1, 1834, 800 families; Manuel R. Arispe,[51] November 12, 1828, 200 families; Juan Vicente Campos, agent for a Mexican company composed of Mariano Domínguez, Fortunato Soto, Juan Mila de la Rosa, and John Charles Beales, May 1, 1832, 800 families; the

---

[51] The contracts of Manuel Arispe and of Fortunato Soto and Henry Egerton are listed in Louis J. Wortham's History of Texas, I, 186, 187. The remainder of the contracts listed are of record in the Spanish Archives of the Land Office.

Shawnee Indians, April 16, 1825; the Cherokee Indians, September 1, 1831; and Stephen Julian Wilson, May 27, 1826, 200 families.

Williams, Johnson, and Peebles, on May 13, 1835, were granted 400 leagues of land to be disposed of by sale. The grant was made in compensation for the maintenance of a state militia to be composed of 1,000 armed men.[52] The authority of the governor to make such a contract was derived from Decree No. 278 of the state congress of April 19, 1834. Radford Berry, alcalde of Nacogdoches, issued forty-one individual titles to lands in eastern and northern Texas which were later voided by the Texas constitution of 1836.[53]

James Grant was sold 100 leagues by virtue of De-cree No. 297, issued by the congress of Coahuila and

---

[52] Spanish Archives, G.L.O., vol. 52, pp. 385-388. Samuel M. Williams, Francis W. Johnson, and Robert Peebles.

[53] Ibid., vol. 34, titles, index, and preface.

Texas on April 7, 1835. The land was resold by Empresario Grant, and Commissioner John Cameron issued ten titles for ten leagues each in counties that border on the Red River.[54] The titles became invalid because they were issued after the closing of the land offices by the Consultation of Texas.

One hundred and twenty-four leagues purchased by Durst and Williams from the state government by Decree No. 293 of March 14, 1835, were resold to fifteen purchasers. The land was located principally in the Red River counties. Carlos S. Taylor issued the titles before the closing of the land offices, but the general congress of Mexico declared the claims invalid because the grant violated the national colonization law.[55]

---

[54] Ibid., vol. 35, titles, index, and preface, pp. 1-188.

[55] Ibid., vol. 35, titles, index, and preface, pp. 189-300.

Ten titles covering ninety-five leagues in northeast Texas were issued by James Bowie under the contract of John T. Mason.[56] Mason's contract, made by authority of Decree No. 278 of April 19, 1834, was voided by the first Texas constitution.

Special commissioners issued titles to colonists, both foreign and Mexican, who settled outside the limits of contracted areas. Those who received grants by direct application to the governor were permitted to make their locations in any of the vacant or unrestricted districts or within any established enterprise by consent of its empresario. Such grantees applied to the corresponding commissioner for possession. In the defect of a commissioner, the alcalde of the respective municipality or another local officer was officially commissioned to put the grantee

---

[56] Mason's contract was made on June 19, 1835; the titles are filed in volume 30 with other grants in east Texas.

in formal possession of the designated lands. Only
the supreme government could grant land in restricted
areas.

Under the colonization law of March 24, 1825, Mexicans were privileged to acquire lands from the government by purchase. As many as eleven leagues
could be bought in any location suitable to their interests.[57] Vicente Aldrete, José Manuel del Moral,

---

[57] Articles 22 and 24 of the state colonization law
of March 24, 1825, set the price of purchased land at
100 pesos per league for grazing land and 150 pesos
per league for grazing land and 150 pesos for unirrigable farming land (less than two and one-half and
three and one-half cents respectively per acre), and
arranged for payment to be completed six years after
settlement in three installments, on the 4th, 5th, and
6th years. New settlers who received land by concession were required to pay only about seven-tenths
of a cent per acre for grazing land and less than one
and one-half cents for unirrigable farming land. In
1830 the Mexican monetary unit was about the same
value as the North American. Alessio Robles, Coahuila y Texas, I, 204.
    In spite of generous terms, few Mexicans could af-
ford the large eleven-league tracts, and most of such
purchases were transferred immediately to American

and José María Balmaceda, special commissioners to

give possession to Mexican purchasers, issued fifty-

six titles in East and Central Texas. Commissioned

alcaldes issued 120 titles, mostly to Mexicans, at San

Felipe de Austin, Nacogdoches, and Liberty.[58]

The "new colonization law" of April 28, 1832,[59]

offered additional inducements to Mexicans, and the

"republican citizens" at San Antonio and Goliad re-

ceived lands gratis for services rendered in the revo-

lution against Spain. From 1831 to 1834, the alcaldes

of Goliad and San Antonio were invested, by special

---

buyers. These floating eleven-league grants formed
the basis of most of the early land speculation in Texas.

[58] They were Luke Lessassier, Radford Berry, Ira
H. Lewis, J. B. Woods, Horatio Chreisman, Adolfo
Sterne, Manuel de los Santos Coy, José María Mora,
Vital Flores, Encarnación Chirino, and José Ygnacio
Ybarvo.

[59] Laws and Decrees of the State of Coahuila and
Texas, Decree No. 190, pp. 189-194.

decree, with the authority to make land concessions in their jurisdictions without the approval of governor or commissioner. When the decree was rescinded on March 7, 1834, commissioners were appointed for the Bexar and Goliad districts.[60] Various alcaldes and commissioners issued sixty-one titles in those areas.[61]

Commissioner Miguel Arciniega gave possession to twenty-one special grantees, both Mexicans and foreigners, in Austin's colonies.

After the resolutions of the general government in April and August of 1828, which authorized the granting of land to certain colonists who had settled in the

---

[60] Spanish Archives, G.L.O., vol. 51, pp. 90, 95, 96, 97, 119, 120.

[61] They were Manuel Ximenes, José Miguel Aldrete, Francisco Xavier Bustillo, José Antonio Navarro, José María Salinas, James G. Patrick, Juan Nepomuceno Seguín, José Antonio Vásquez, Angel Navarro, and Andrew Ponton.

border and coast reserves,[62] José Francisco Madero made seventy-eight concessions to citizens residing on the Sabine, Trinity, and San Jacinto rivers.[63] By virtue of the same resolutions and the colonization law of 1834,[64] Carlos S. Taylor and George H. Smyth were commissioned to sell land on the eastern frontier. They issued 336 titles in northeast and southeast Texas.

---

[62] Spanish Archives, G.L.O., vol. 52, pp. 247-254; 327-334.

[63] Juan Antonio Padilla, appointed on December 4, 1828, to the new office of commissioner general, had the authority to grant lands throughout the state and was specially commissioned to give titles to those settlers who had received approval from the supreme government to settle in the restricted leagues on the border and coast. Padilla's office terminated abruptly when he was imprisoned on a murder charge early in 1830. The office of commissioner general was abolished, and special commissioners were provided for the various enterprises. Spanish Archives, G.L.O., vol. 58, file 214; vol. 51, pp. 80, 85.

[64] The colonization law of March 26, 1834, repealed the law of 1832 and provided for the sale of the public lands of the state to both foreigners and Mexicans.

By the law of April 6, 1830,[65] the federal government summarily closed its doors to all emigration from the United States. General Manuel Mier y Terán, however, gave a special interpretation to article 11 of the same law and permitted Americans to enter in Austin's and Green DeWitt's colonies.[66] Three years later, when article 11 was repealed,[67] and certain contracts were extended, colonization was resumed in accordance with the law of March 24, 1825.

The state colonization laws of Mexico simplified the procurement of land titles. Generally, they were

---

The law of March 24, 1825, remained in force for unfulfilled contracts. Laws of the State of Coahuila and Texas, Decree No. 272, pp. 247-252.

[65] Spanish Archives, G.L.O., vol. 51, pp. 160, 161.

[66] Barker, The Life of Stephen F. Austin, 296-328; Ohland Morton, Terán and Texas, 95-136.

[67] Article 11 was officially abrogated on December 7, 1833, but its actual repeal did not take effect until six months later. Alessio Robles, Coahuila y Texas, I, 476.

Agrimensura N° 7 en clase N° 8 de una labor p.ª siembras de temporal medida al Ciud.º Manuel Ximenes, y Situado en el lado oriental del arroyo del Sebolo y acia del Camino q.º pasa p.ª Gonzales, por el lado de abajo, y distante como vente y nueve millas de Bejar, Empesando por una estaca puesta para la esquina de arriba de la medida N° 8. Donde está un encino prieto de 12 pulgadas de diam.º y rumbo N. 11. E. á distancia de 28½ varas y un musquite de 11 pulgadas de diam.º y rumbo S. 30. E. á distancia de 3 varas.

y con la linea de dicha medida N° 8

Rumbo	Distancia	
N 61 E.	1000	varas
N 29 O	1000	"
S 61. O.	945	"
S 40 E.	290	"
S 5. O.	50	"
Sur	150	"
S 26 E.	70	"
S 35 E.	310	"
S 11 E.	80	"
S 80 E.	90	"
S 26 E.	30	"

Se puso una estaca p.ª la esquina N. E. de esté medida, Donde está un musquite de 11 pulgadas de diam.º y rumbo N. 13. E. á distancia de 14 S. y otro de 8 pulgadas de diam.º y rumbo N. 42 O. á distancia de 14 varas.

y siguiendo en linea recta

Se puso una estaca p.ª la esquina N. O. de este medida, Donde está un encino prieto de 14 pulgadas de diam.º y rumbo N 36 E á distancia de 13½ varas

y siguiendo en linea recta.

Al barranco de dicha arroyo, Donde se puso una estaca p.ª la esquina de arriba de este medida, Donde está un musquite de 11 pulgadas de diam.º y rumbo N. 7 O. á distancia de 5 varas.

y hora abajo de dicho arroyo por todas sus vueltas,

hasta cerrar donde comensé la primera medida en esté medida todos son planes y buenos tierras

Nota = Todas las lineas son hechos con variación de 10 grados y 30 minutos y la variación es al E.
8 de Marzo de 1834. Byrd Lockhart

Survey No. 7 en clase No. 8 of one labor of land made for Don Manuel Ximenes, It is situated on the Easterly side of the Sibolo Creek near the Gonzales road and on the lower side of said road about twenty nine miles from Bexar, begining at a stake set for the upper corner of survey No. 8., from which there is a live oak 10 inches in dia bears N. 11. E. 20½ varas. and a musket 14 inches in dia bears S. 31. W. 3 varas.

Thence with said Survey No. 8.

N. 61. E.	1000 varas	Set a stake for the N. E. corner of this survey from which there is a musket 14 inches in dia bears N. 13. E. 14 varas. and an other 8 inches in dia bears. N. 42. W. 14 varas.
		Thence on a true line
N. 29. W.	1000 "	Set a stake for the N. W. corner of this survey from which there is a live oak 12 inches in dia bears N. 31. E. 13½ varas.
		Thence on a true line
S. 61. W.	945. "	To the bank of said Sibolo creek where set a stake for the upper corner of this survey from which there is a musket 11 inches in dia bears. N. 7. E. 5 v̄ Thence down said Sibolo creek with its meanders.
S. 40. E.	290 "	
S. 5. W.	50 "	
South	100 "	
S. 26. E.	75 "	
S. 35. E.	310 "	
S. 11. E.	80 "	
S. 8. E.	90 "	
S. 26. E.	35 "	To the place of begining.

All of the above lines were extended at a variation of Ten degrees and 30 minutes and the variation is East 5th March 1834.

Byrd Lockhart

required to pass through the hands of only three officers for completion. The ordinary component parts were reduced to the petition of the applicant, decree of governor or commissioner, report of empresario, order of survey, field notes, and decree of possession. In form and expression, the expediente, or file of documents making up the title, became standardized in conformity with the conditions governing the respective enterprises. By 1828, printed forms were often used in Austin's colonies. Local circumstances and personalities, however, always lent themselves to variation, and any title, having passed through vicarious hands, was necessarily a document of heterogeneous style and composition.

The field notes or land descriptions were in every case highly variable. Surveying had become an important factor of colonial development, and as many as seventy-two surveyors were appointed to measure and delineate the tracts designated in the various land

concessions.[68] The land descriptions or field notes

made by those surveyors were incorporated into each

title. The law required that all titles be written in

Spanish. Most surveyors were Americans, and they

wrote their notes in English. It then became nec-

essary to employ a translator in each office to con-

vert English field notes into Spanish; and thereby was

created a unique body of literature, technical to a de-

gree and highly colloquial in its scientific expres-

sions, topographical descriptions, and the multiplicity

of names of Texas trees.

Each surveyor returned his notes to the respec-

tive government office where they were examined and

translated into the title in supposedly identical form.

The original English field notes now supply important

---

[68] Spanish Archives, G.L.O., Index to Surveyors of
the Texas Colonies.

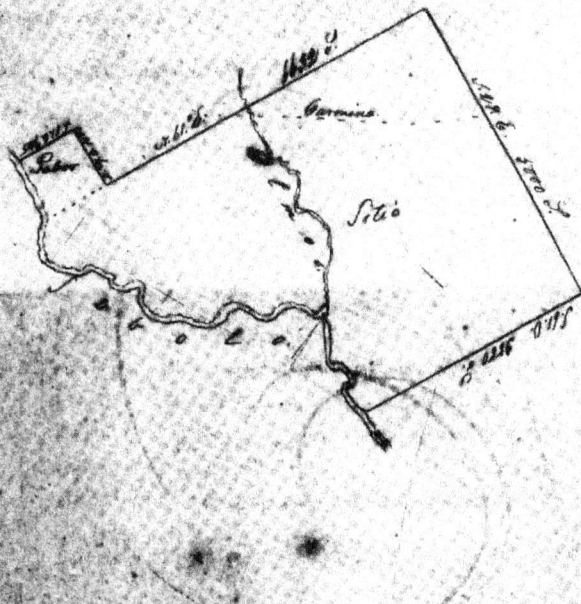

Medida N.° 7 en clase N.° 8 de
una labor, y N.° 8 en el mismo clase
de un sitio medida p.ª el Guard.°

Manuel Navarro

locative data and serve to interpret the titled notes, but the courts have held that the title controls in boundary controversies. And, strangely, the Spanish notes now must be translated into English for present day use.

State laws, in accord with the federal law of October 6, 1823, regulated the use of stamped paper.[69] It was required that original titles be written on paper of the third stamp and testimonios, or duplicates of the original, on that of the second. Paper of the first and fourth stamps was designated for wills, deeds, transfers, certified copies, and other legal instruments. Each stamp had its corresponding fee, and the number of the stamp and the amount of the fee were printed on each page with appropriate biennial dates. If paper of the required stamp was not available

[69] Laws and Decrees of the State of Coahuila and Texas, Commissioners' Instructions of September 4, articles 8, 9, and 71.

for titles or other instruments, captions in manuscript were legalized by the signature of a local officer.

The Spanish Archives contain some 3,800 land titles
issued by the State of Coahuila and Texas. Supple-
mentary records of the same period comprise titles
to town lots in Victoria, Liberty, and San Patricio;
empresario contracts; appendices to empresario contracts with pertinent files of original correspondence,
official communications, orders, and reports; government decrees; appointments of officers; English
field notes and sketch books; unfinished titles; colony
registers and colonists' character certificates.

Chapter V

THE TEXAS VARA

The survey of a land tract and the record thereof
was as important as the title itself, for by no other
means could the title-holder's grant be located or
identified. The demarcation of lands, one of the oldest customs in existence, reached Texas through the
long circuit of Roman, Spanish, and Mexican law. The
Roman foot was introduced into Spain where it under-
went changes in various parts of the country. Three
Spanish feet became recognized under the generic
term "vara," the English cognate of which is bar.
The vara of Burgos, later known as the Castilian vara,
was the Spanish standard for many years. The Castilian vara containing three Castilian feet was between

834 and 835 millimeters in length, or slightly less than 32.9 inches.[1]

The Castilian vara was adopted by Spanish colonists in America. It later became known as the Mexican vara and presumably was still equivalent to three Castilian feet. It is not known exactly when the length of the Mexican vara was changed, but the national colonization law of 1823 officially defined the vara as

---

[1] Pequeño Larousse Ilustrado, Paris, 1945, defines the Castilian foot as 28 centimeters and the Castilian vara as 835 millimeters. Walter E. Jones, in a study of the vara entitled "Some Information for Surveyors," in the Miscellaneous Files of the Spanish Archives, G.L.O., quotes the following as given to him by the United States Department of Commerce, Bureau of Standards: F. Altes, in Traite comparatif des Monnais, Poids, et Mesures entre la France, L'Espagne et L'Angleterre, states that three Castilian feet constituted one vara and that the Castilian foot was 27.83 centimeters. Melitón Martín, in Nuevo sistema legal de pesas y medidas puesta al alcance de todos, Madrid, 1876, gives the Castilian foot as 27.86 centimeters.

Joaquín Escriche, in Diccionario de Legislación, Madrid, 1842, pp. 425, 478, 479, quotes Law I, Title 9, Book 9 of the Recopilación Novísima which, in explanation of the ancient and modern vara, states that

containing three geometrical feet.[2] The vara at that
time appears to have been between 827 and 839 millimeters, or slightly above 32.9 inches.[3]

There was much confusion among early surveyors
as to the exact length of the vara. No vara chain was

---

the vara used in New Spain contained four palmos. A
palmo is defined by most dictionaries as one-fourth
vara, or a hand's spread from the thumb to the little
finger. Appleton's New Dictionary, New York, 1940,
gives eight inches as the length of the palmo.

[2] Melitón Martín, quoted by Walter E. Jones, gives
the geometrical foot of Spain as 27.7777 centimeters,
a value which he calculated on the assumption that it
was exactly defined as the 1/400,000 part of a degree
of the earth's quadrant expressed as 10,000,000 meters, and he concludes that the geometrical foot was
shorter than the foot of Burgos. Jones states that the
geometrical foot similarly defined as the 1/400,000
part of a degree of the earth's quadrant was used in
ancient Egypt where it had a length of about 27.8 centimeters. Gaspar y Roig, Diccionario Enciclopédico
de la Lengua Española, Madrid, 1867, defines the geo-
metric foot as the ancient Roman foot which had the
proportion of 1,000 to 923 to the Castilian foot.

[3] The following information is taken from Walter
E. Jones, "Some Information for Texas Surveyors":
The length of 837 millimeters is contained in an agree-
ment dated September 15, 1837, between the minister

then known. Mexican surveyors used a cordel, composed of fifty Mexican varas and made of pita en-
cerada,[4] which had to be remeasured several times
a day. The surveyors who came from Louisiana and
Missouri brought with them the French arpent chain
which was used in those states. The ones who came
from other states brought the Gunter chain, or the
100-foot chain. All tried to convert their chains into

---

plenipotentiary of the Mexican republic and his agents
in London with holders of Mexican bonds (quoted in
Report of U.S. General Land Office, 1854, p. 27). Values as high as 839 millimeters ascribed to Humboldt
(1810) and including the value of 838.01 millimeters
of a Mexican decree are cited in US v. Perot, 98 US
428.

The Department of Weights and Measures in Mexico
gave the official length of the vara as 32.9927 inches
(English) and the foot as 10.9976 inches on April 18,
1910, in a letter to H.M. Henderson, surveyor, Port
Lavaca, Texas.

In the Spanish Archives Handbook, J. V. Haggard
gives 32.9931 inches as the standardized length of the
Mexican vara.

[4] A cord or rope made from the waxed fiber of the
pita plant.

a ten-vara Mexican chain, largely by guessing how long the Mexican vara was.

Consequently, chains were of varying lengths. As used by Seth Ingram in Austin's colonies, the ten-vara chain measured twenty-seven feet, ten inches, with fifty links of 5.68 inches.[5] The vara was 33.4 inches.[6] James Kerr, in De León's colony, used a vara of two feet, nine and one-third inches, or 33 1/3 inches, making a chain of twenty-seven feet, nine and one-third inches, with links of 6 2/3 inches.[7] In East Texas, Empresario Haden Edwards instructed James Gaines, surveyor, to adjust his chain to eleven varas and defined the linear league as 5,000 varas; but later

---

[5] <u>Lamar Papers</u>, V, 128.

[6] On July 1, 1824, the Mexican vara was expressly stated by Stephen F. Austin and Commissioner Baron de Bastrop to be 2.6 inches less than the English yard, or 33.4 inches. Spanish Archives, G.L.O., Record of Original Titles, 18.

[7] <u>Lamar Papers</u>, V, 128.

Commissioner George Anthony Nixon issued official instructions calling for a chain of ten varas with links of 6 2/3 varas.[8]

Finally, by agreement among themselves, colonial surveyors converted the awkward and elusive Mexican vara into the convenient 33 1/3 inch vara.[9] As a decimal inch measure (three varas equal one hundred inches), it is an ideal unit and is easily calculated into English feet, yards, and acres. When the General Land Office was organized, John P. Borden, the first commissioner and previously one of Stephen F. Austin's surveyors, was doubtless responsible for recognizing 33 1/3 inches as the established length of

[8] Spanish Archives, G.L.O., vol. 55, pp. 146, 147; Commissioner George Anthony Nixon's Instructions to Surveyors, Miscellaneous Files.

[9] Ibid., Miscellaneous Files. H. M. Henderson in an article on the vara quotes the deposition of Francis W. Johnson, surveyor of Austin's colonies, in Ayres v. Harris, 77 Texas 108.

the vara.[10] All lands surveyed in Texas since it became a republic have been or supposedly have been
surveyed with a 33 1/3 inch vara. By silent acceptance
and without statutory recognition,[11] it has been used
to survey and grant hundreds of millions of acres of
land. Texas is the only place that knows or uses it.
It stands alone in the standard measures of the world
and is a monument to the old Austin colony surveyors
who originated it; and it is perpetuated in the field
notes of every survey of land granted by the republic
and state of Texas. "After Texas independence all

---

[10] Ibid., Deputy Surveyor's Field Note Book and Instructions from General Land Office, San Patricio
instructed the county surveyor of San Patricio County
to use the 33 1/3 inch vara as the unit of measure.

[11] Commissioner Francis W. White's Instructions
to Surveyors, May 31, 1858, stated that all field notes
must give distances in varas and defined the vara as
33 1/3 inches. Report of Commissioner, 1845-1891,
pp. 260-263. Not until February 11, 1919, was the vara
defined by an act of the legislature. General Laws
of the State of Texas, 36th Legislature, 1919, p. 32.

grants of land were in acres, and any length chain or unit of measure could be used without affecting the number of acres in the survey. But the field notes sent to the General Land Office had to give the length of lines in varas of 33 1/3 inches for no other measure has ever been accepted in surveying public lands.''[12]

Many other measurements were in common use under the Spanish and Mexican regimes. The legua, or league, was the linear unit for long distances. It was the equivalent of 5,000 varas, or approximately 2 5/8 statute miles.

A square league, or 25,000,000 square varas was called a sitio, or 4,428.4 acres. This unit was also called a sitio de ganado mayor, or a ranch for large stock (cattle and horses). A sitio de ganado menor, a ranch for small stock (sheep and goats), was an area

[12] Spanish Archives, G.L.O., Miscellaneous Files, article by H. M. Henderson, surveyor.

of 11,111,111 square varas. Areas sometimes were expressed in square varas, but these resulted in astronomical proportions, even in describing ordinary tracts, and other units grew into use.

A labor was 1,000,000 square varas, or 177.1 acres. It was said to be the quantity of land that could be worked effectively by one family. Correctly, it was a farm.

An hacienda was an estate of five or more square leagues.

A caballería was a very ancient land term in Spain. Originally, it meant that part of the spoils of war in real estate which was allotted to a cavalryman in the victorious armies of the king. In the frontier states of America it came to mean a parcel of ground granted to a colonist who would keep one armed and mounted man in readiness at all times and subject to the call of the state. It was often used to measure land grants in Texas and was equivalent to 105.7 acres.

Porción, meaning part or portion, was the amount of land assigned to Spanish colonists in the towns established on the lower Rio Grande. The size of the porción varied according to the classification of the colonist. The minimum amount granted to one individual was two leagues for small stock, and the maximum was two leagues for large stock and twelve caballerías.[13]

A number of primitive terms were employed for describing linear measurements and areas of land. Huebra was the amount of a day's plowing by a yoke of oxen. A fanega was the amount of land required for sowing a fanega, or about one and one-half bushels of grain. A suerte was a plot of ground originally

---

[13] This was a double portion awarded for special service. It was twice the amount granted to an original settler (two leagues for small stock and twelve caballerías).

drawn by lot when lands were parcelled among share-holders. A <u>solar</u>, as used in Spanish and Mexican land titles in Texas, was a town lot. <u>Pasos</u> <u>salomones</u> were long double steps measuring 1 2/3 yards.

Since a court decision may depend on the translation of one Spanish word, particularly in the case of field notes, a precise interpretation of terms having various connotations or special meanings is required. Extensive research is often necessary to establish correct definitions, and Spanish translators have continuously compiled a reference list of such definitions, the majority of which do not appear in ordinary dictionaries.

Chapter VI

SPANISH AND MEXICAN GRANTS BETWEEN THE

NUECES RIVER AND THE RIO GRANDE

The territory between the Nueces River and the Rio Grande was colonized under circumstances peculiarly different from those governing the settlement of other regions of Texas. Under Spanish rule that area was the northernmost extent of Tamaulipas, the last stronghold of the Indians of Mexico. As Spanish conquest expanded the Indians took refuge in the wild sierras, and no Spaniard was able to subdue them successfully until 1746 when José de Escandón was commissioned[1] to undertake a vigorous campaign designed

---

[1] The Royal Treasury appropriated an initial sum of 115,000 pesos with a yearly stipend of 29,000 pesos,

for their complete subjugation. Escandón's ability and understanding won the confidence of the Indians, and he succeeded in making peaceful and permanent settlements as he advanced through the new province of Nuevo Santander. Pushing forward to the Rio Grande, Escandón established towns along the river from Matamoros to Laredo. The Rio Grande region was soon flourishing with cattle ranches, and peaceful prosperity reached a degree which was never attained in other parts of Texas during its early history.

---

and the war council appointed the man who had performed the similarly impossible feat of subjecting and pacifying the Sierra Gorda. Escandón had carried on his first campaign with little expense to the Crown, employing his own personal fortune to maintain his troops. His exemplary conduct had won for him the friendship of the Indians as well as the respect of the government and the colonists. He had been made Count of Sierra Gorda in consideration of his services, and in the conquest of Tamaulipas he achieved still greater laurels. Bancroft, History of Mexico, 1600-1803, III, 339-341. For the work of Escandón, see Lawrence Francis Hill, José de Escandón and the Founding of Nuevo Santander.

In 1767, a royal commission visited the towns of Mier,
Reynosa, Guerrero, Camargo, and Laredo, and gave
some 400 inhabitants formal possession of their lands.
Porciones, or portions of equitable variation were
allotted to original, old, and new settlers.[2] The porciones were surveyed in long narrow strips on both
sides of the Rio Grande with at least 1,000 varas front-
age on the river and extending back for quantity. The
grant to each town and its individual settlers, entitled
La Visita General, was drawn up in legal form for a
permanent record. None of the originals of those acts
of distribution is to be found in Texas, but certified
copies and translations of all five Visitas are on file
in the Spanish Archives of the Land Office. They are

---

[2] Two leagues for small stock and twelve caballerías to the sons of original settlers and those with
six years residence and service, and two leagues for
small stock to new settlers. Copy and Translation
of the Visita General, Charter Granting Reynosa Porciones, 164, Spanish Archives, G.L.O.

the basis of title to some 170 porciones lying north

of the Rio Grande and within the present boundaries

of Texas.[3]

The Crown also made large individual grants to col-

onists for purposes of settlement, and titles were is-

sued to lands as far north as the Nueces River. Nuevo

Santander, like Texas, became an interior province

in 1776 and was attached to the intendencia of San Luis

Potosí in 1786. Under the new organization it was

required that land concessions be approved in San

---

[3] By act of April 24, 1871, the legislature made provisions for obtaining transcriptions and translations
of the acts, charters, and grants founding the towns
of Mier, Reynosa, Camargo, Laredo, and Guerrero.
J. L. Haynes was appointed as agent, and he secured
from the archives of those towns copies of all acts,
charters, and grants with an annexed table of measurements taken from the "Ordenanzas de Tierras y
Aguas" of the Spanish and Mexican governments. All
these documents, duly certified by Mexican authorities, were copied and translated by J. L. Haynes and
deposited for record in the Land Office within one
year after passage of the act. Gammel, Laws of Texas, 1866-1871, VI, 958.

Luis Potosí and Mexico City and that full payment
in cash be made to the royal treasury after the lands
had been offered by public auction to the highest bid-
der. Though variations in procedure appear with relation to time and circumstance, the ordinary title
generally consisted of the application or denouncement, certification, appointment of surveyors, examination, survey, and appraisal of the designated tract,
approval, auction, citation of adjacent landowners,
and act of possession, all duly and consecutively recorded. After the completion of the required proceedings, accomplished with many attendant difficulties
and some irregularities, a testimonio or duplicate
copy of the file of documents constituting the title was
given to the owner, and a certified copy was deposited
in the archives of the town where the final step was
concluded. The original file was returned to San Luis
Potosí.

Land Office records list some forty individual concessions, excluding <u>porciones</u>, made by Spain between
1757 and 1819 in the area south of the Nueces. None
of those grants in original form has ever reached the
Land Office, and only a few copies have been obtained
from the records of Texas counties where owners
recorded their titles after that territory was acquired
from Mexico. <u>Testimonios</u> of that period, as well as
originals, are rarely found in Texas.[4] Only two such
<u>testimonios</u> appear of record in the Spanish Archives
of the Land Office.

One of the <u>testimonios</u> on file is the title to José
Manuel Pereda for four leagues of land issued in San
Luis Potosí on August 10, 1810. It is written on fifteen

---

[4] The <u>testimonio</u>, or owner's duplicate of the original, is in one sense considered an original document.
The original titles of that area were archived in Mexico, and few owners' copies have withstood the rav-
ages of time. Some certified copies have been obtained from Mexican archives and unofficially deposited in the General Land Office.

pages, front and reverse, of heavy linen paper bearing the seals of Charles IV and Ferdinand VII. When it was deposited in the Land Office in 1902, it had been folded to pocket size in three horizontal sections, and three blood stains, diminishing proportionately on the successive pages, had penetrated forty-five thicknesses of paper.[5] The land covered by the Pereda title is situated in the present county of Zapata. The following description and appraisal of the tract was made by government authorities in 1807:

> ...the plants are chaparral, huisache, mesquite, and retama, and such vegetation is so plentiful that it makes the land inhabitable and beneficial to him ₵the grantee₃. The animals are tigers, leopards, wolves, coyotes, rabbits, hares, deer, antelope, and snakes, and these last-named are abundant. The birds are buzzards, hawks, owls, and partridges. There is no timber which can be used to any advantage; there is only pasturage for stock, and I do not consider the tract suitable for any kind of settlement whatsoever.... Skilled appraisers value the leagues at ten pesos each as water is absolutely lacking....

---

[5] Spanish Archives, G.L.O., vol. 67, p. 11.

ma el peyote, en cuyo ambito se midie
ron ciento quarenta cordeladas que hacen siete
mil varas castellanas, y mande se reviere, y
puso lindero fixo donde reunió esta me
dida por el rumbo las demarcaciones corres
pondientes, con lo que se concluyó el tercero lado
de su paralelo; para cuya constancia lo firma
ron el Agrimensor, y los dos Contadores con migo
y los dos testigos de mi asistencia, con quienes ac
tuo como dicho es, y de todo doy fee = Jose Grediano
Vaez Benavides = Francisco Cardenas = Don Dionisio
Uribe = Jose Pio de la Garza = an el = Don Ramon de
la Garza = an el = Juan Angel de Cuellar =
dia mes y año de dicho Capitan y Con
tuando en el campo en el sitio parage
nombrado Santa Catarina donde se concluyó la
tercera medida que se contiene en mi anterior
auto del dia de hoy, sin omitir la medida del
cordel cada cien cordeladas a las cincuenta va
ras dichas mande al Agrimensor y demas per
sonas dichas exercer cada una su oficio, y
la medida al quarto lado de su parale
lo del Nordeste al Sudueste hasta el citado para

Many of those Spanish grants have claimed attention beyond their dramatic survival and endurance through almost two centuries of conflict and controversy. The largest concession made by Spain in Texas was the San Juan de Carricitos grant to José Narciso Cabazos in 1792. It contains more than 600,000 acres of land in what is now Cameron, Willacy, and Kenedy counties. The Padre Island grant, made to Nicolás Ballí and his nephew, Juan José Ballí in 1800, was upheld by the Texas Supreme Court after a long contest over the validity of title and the amount of land covered thereby. Title to the entire island was confirmed to the original grantee on December 20, 1944.[6] The grant of San Salvador del Tule attained legal and historical fame in 1866 when the Reconstruction Constitutional Convention passed an ordinance releasing ''to the owners of the soil all mines and

---

[6] State of Texas v. Ballí, 190 SW 2d 71.

mineral substances that may be on the same," and

thus ended the operation of Spanish and Mexican min-

eral law in Texas.[7] The question had arisen over the

title to "El Sal del Rey," the salt lake of which the

state of Texas had taken possession and which was

located within the boundaries of the grant made to

Juan José Ballí in 1798. Other notable grants were

the "Rincón del Oso," made to Enrique Villarreal

in 1810 and including the present site of the city of Cor-

pus Christi; "El Potrero del Espíritu Santo," fifty-

nine and one-half leagues granted to José Salvador de

la Garza in 1781 and occupied by the original grantee

and his descendants until the approach of the United

States army in 1846; and "La Barreta," the Spanish

grant to José Francisco Ballí,[8] the title to which has

---

[7] Wallace Hawkins, El Sal del Rey, 56, 57.

[8] An order from the Supreme Court of Mexico was
required to obtain this copy. It was presented as evidence in Civil Action No. 614, the Sun Oil Company

long been sought and was found only recently in the archives of San Luis Potosí.

The province of Nuevo Santander became the state of Tamaulipas under the Mexican Constitution of 1824. A state colonization law, which differed slightly from that of Coahuila and Texas, was enacted in 1829.[9] Recognizing established Spanish grants in conformity with the national colonization law of 1823, state authorities proceeded to concede unoccupied lands to new claimants and to confirm grants to those who had failed to perfect their titles under the Spanish

---

v. the Humble Oil Company et al. in the U.S. District Ct., Southern District of Texas, April 29, 1950. In this case, the Sun Oil Company, plaintiff, was claiming under the State; the court ruled that the defendants had no title to the lands in controversy and that the State made out a prima facie case for the recovery of said lands, which in this instance were tidewater lands in Laguna Madre.

[9] December 15, 1829. A copy of this law is published in Laws and Decrees of the State of Coahuila and Texas, and translated by J.P. Kimball, Telegraph Power Press, Houston, 1839.

government. Land concessions from the state of Tamaulipas required the approval of the governor and payment to the treasury at Ciudad Victoria, the capital of the state, where the original files were protocoled. Copies "for due evidence at all times" were retained in the archives of the court of the constitutional alcalde, who gave formal possession to the grantee.

The first congress of the republic of Texas, on December 19, 1836, declared that its southern boundary extended to the Rio Grande, but the occupation and possession of the territory south of the Nueces was realized only by the Mexican war and the treaty of Guadalupe Hidalgo. The state of Tamaulipas continued to issue titles in that area until 1848. Those Mexican titles to Texas lands have remained in the archives of Reynosa, Matamoros, Laredo, Guerrero, Mier, Camargo, and Ciudad Victoria. Official records list some 120 valid Mexican grants south of the

Agostad.º de los Sauces.

Sur

Oriente.　　　　　　　　Poniente.

Norte

Notas

La superficie que encierran el cuadrado á. b. c. d. es de 400. mil.
leguas cuadradas i cuatro sitios de Agostaderos de ganado mayor según la
unidad fijada por V. Ley del Senado y... las medidas legaria... ...referida...
...los cuatro linderos angulares con que la Demarcacion está...
... Demarcado por V. el P.... Long.ª y se llaman del m.do siguiente la
linea del rincon... el paso... linea de San Ant.º ...
...arroyo de S.to Fernando y Charco de los Sauces en el arroyo del Chil...
...dijo... esta medida fue hecha con la mayor exactitud geometrica po-
sible, corregida la Inclinacion del Aguijon y cuidando de remedia el Con...
del casa media legua. El agostadero queda perfectam.te cuadrado por
...dado igual n.º de cordeladas por cada uno de los cuatro lados así como
...en el Mapa... queda lindante por el Poniente con el agostadero medido al... Marcelino Lopez y por los demas rumbos con terre-
nos baldios. Lo que por constancia y en cumplim.to de mi Deber...

haciendo devolución de los autos fecho en Camargo a 2.
de Agosto de 1831 — Ant.o Canales —

y conforme con su original. C. Vict.a Nov.e
5 de 1831. 3.o de la instalacion del Cong.o del Estado

Ant.o Canales

Se agrega al título como se previene y f.o f la del
Gobernador, y para constancia se anota

Sumano
Sria.

Nueces, but no more than thirty-five certified copies

and owners' testimonios have been deposited in the

Land Office.

Chapter VII

SPANISH AND MEXICAN LAND GRANTS

IN CHIHUAHUA

In the district of Chihuahua, Spain granted lands to
the towns of Isleta and Socorro and to the presidio of
San Elizario.[1] There are no originals or copies of
those grants in the Land Office, but the state legislature of Texas confirmed the claims[2] at an early date
by virtue of occupancy and subsequent confirmations
by Mexico which appear in the records of El Paso

---

[1] General Land Office Files, Bexar 1-1342; Bexar
1-1499; Bexar 1-1447; Bexar 1-1007.

[2] Gammel, Laws of Texas, 1854-1861, IV, 42, 53,
1027, 1094; ibid., III, 1847-1854, 1362. The legislature
also confirmed to the town of Isleta two additional
leagues which originally belonged to the inhabitants
of Senecú, a branch mission of Isleta.

County.

No authentic record was ever found of the "La Prieta" grant for 325 leagues in El Paso County though an abstract in circulation in 1908 represented that the concession was made by the King of Spain on March 13, 1751, and was three times confirmed by the state of Chihuahua. Commissioner J. T. Robison went to Mexico in 1909 and examined the records at Juárez, Chihuahua, Durango, Mexico City, Torreón, Guadalajara, and Zacatecas, but he found nothing that even related to the grant.[3] Numerous claims based on the alleged grant for many years were never prosecuted.[4]

---

[3] Report of Commissioner, 1908-1910, pp. 11, 12.

[4] In 1910 Commissioner J.T. Robison reported that he had made repeated appeals to the attorney general to take some action which would clarify the situation in El Paso County where those claiming under the "La Prieta" grant were clouding the titles of school land, University land, and private land. Report of Commissioner, 1908-1910, p. 11. In 1912 Robison again reported that the attorney general had filed suit in

Chihuahua became a state in the Mexican republic
in 1824, and its northern boundary was defined as a
line running east to west from the source of the Gila
River to the Pecos River.[5] By authority of the ayuntamiento of Paso del Norte, two Mexican grants, "El
Canutillo" and "Rancho de Ponce," were made to
individuals. The "Rancho de Ascarete" appears to
have been claimed by virtue of occupancy under the
Mexican government.[6] By special legislative acts
the state of Texas relinquished those lands to the

the district court of Travis County against C.T. Greg-
ory, W.H. Yoakum, and J.O. Wiley who claimed interest in the "La Prieta" grant; Report of Commissioner, 1910-1912, p. 5. The suit, State v. James O.
Wiley et al., was dismissed on November 25, 1913.

[5] Alessio Robles, Coahuila y Texas en la Epoca
Colonial, 11.

[6] A copy of the title to Juan María Ponce de León
is found in Texas Supreme Court Records, C.R. Johns
et al. v. Samuel Schutz, 47 T 578. General Land Office Files, Bexar 1-1390; Bexar 1-2212; Bexar 1-1382.

original claimants.[7]

A land grant of 225 square leagues, or approximately 1,000,000 acres, situated in the present counties of Jeff Davis, Presidio, and Brewster, was alleged
to have been made to José Ygnacio Ronquilla in 1832
by the authorities of the state of Chihuahua. The story
of the grant is contained in the records of the case
of Ernest Dale Owen, trustee, <u>versus</u> the Presidio
Mining Company, No. 12, in the United States Circuit
Court for the Western District at El Paso. The court
held that the alcalde of Presidio del Norte was not
constitutionally authorized to make the concession,
that it was never confirmed by the congress of Chihuahua, and the same was, therefore, invalid. A copy
of the title taken from Bexar County records, where
it was recorded on July 10, 1851, is in Letter File No.
210,482 of the Land Office.

---

[7] Gammel, <u>Laws of Texas</u>, <u>1854-1861</u>, IV, 1027.

Chapter VIII

THE REPUBLIC AND STATE OF TEXAS

After the outbreak of open hostilities between Texas and Mexico, the Consultation, meeting at San Felipe de Austin to consider the general welfare of the country, suspended all operations concerned with the granting of land and ordered that all government archives be deposited in safe places under the authority of the provisional government.[1]

When subsequent events led to a final break with Mexico and the winning of Texas independence, the constitution of the new republic designated November 13, 1835, as the official date of the closing of the various

---

[1] Gammel, Laws of Texas, I, 541, Journals of the Consultation, Article XIV.

land offices and declared null and void all titles, surveys, and locations of land made thereafter.[2] The new
government immediately adopted the Mexican civil
law and validated all land titles made in conformity
with the colonization laws governing their issuance,
i. e., the land laws of Spain and Mexico.[3] Further,
since all titles, perfected or unperfected, remained
dependent upon those laws, they were excepted from
the act of 1840 which substituted the common law of
England;[4] and they have since continued to form the
rule of decision in determining property rights which
accrued when the same laws were in force.

Having made their lands secure, the charter citizens of the republic made generous provisions for
the new constituency. From the public domain land

---

[2] Ibid., I, 1081.

[3] Ibid., I, 1077, 1282.

[4] Ibid., II, 177.

grants would be made to colonists who had failed to

obtain their titles from Mexico, to new settlers, and

to all soldiers who had rendered service in the Texas

army.[5] The General Land Office was created, and

its chief officer, the land commissioner, was enjoined

"to superintend, execute, and perform all acts and

things touching or respecting the public lands of the

republic of Texas."[6] Thus John P. Borden set out

for Houston in July, 1837, to assume an arduous task

in a vast and troubled territory with absolutely no

means at his disposal.

Borden wrote the Senate that when he reached Hous-

ton there was no office in which to house the records

already sent in by Green DeWitt. The legislature had

not provided funds for the transportation of the govern-

ment archives, and no one seemed inclined to perform

---

[5] Ibid., I, 1079, 1282.

[6] Ibid., I, 1276.

that important and necessary duty merely for the sake
of honor. Borden assumed the first expenses himself. When the treasury finally sent $189.50, it was
not enough to pay the three men who had been assist-
ing him. The means of conveyance was a wagon and a
team, and Borden admonished the men he engaged to
exert great care in handling the records, "to see that
they did not get wet," and "proceed with a suitable
escort."

With the exception of Austin, DeWitt, and Carlos S.
Taylor, the authorities seemed reluctant to give up
their archives. At Nacogdoches, former Commissioner G.A. Nixon had the records at his house and
insisted he was too ill even to turn them over to Borden's representative. The archives at San Antonio
could not be located. After investigation[7] they were

---

[7] Only under threat of invoking the penalty of the
law were the records finally obtained from Nacogdoches and San Antonio.

discovered to be in the hands of individuals who did not choose to release them. It was reported that William O'Docharty, the surveyor of McMullen and Mcgloin's colony, had carried the San Patricio records to Mexico, and De León's archives at Victoria were believed to be destroyed James Kerr considered the field notes of his surveys in De León's colony as his own personal property and refused to send them in. Other records in the hands of special commissioners and officers were lost, destroyed, or deliberately withheld.

Without the archives, Borden could not correctly ascertain the lands that were vacant and those that were covered with valid titles. With the records that he was able to assemble gradually by diplomacy and coercion, his assignment assumed inconceivable proportions. Through the services of one Spanish translator, three clerks, and a small staff of surveyors, all provided by statute, Borden undertook to translate, record, and locate each Spanish and Mexican grant; simultaneously, and with the same force of surveyors and clerks, he began to survey and register the grants so rapidly issuing to the clamoring hordes of the new republic.

In his report to the legislature on April 10, 1838, Borden enumerated the obstacles with which he was confronted; the archives in general, having been hastily collected through various channels, were in a confused state; the records received from Nacogdoches were a "mere mass of Spanish documents," the contents of which could not be determined except by close and attentive examination; government officers could not collect outstanding dues because they could not read Spanish nor did they know the proper monetary exchange; the claims presented were so complex in their nature that the land laws themselves were an uncertain guide; special legislation would be neces-

sary before just decisions could be made; the excess

in the old grants would necessitate resurveys; county

boundaries were indefinite; surveyors lacked proper

reference maps; endless litigation would be inevitable

because surveys were being heaped one upon another

in spite of strict orders; new certificates were being

issued to many who had already received their grants

from Mexico; some citizens were receiving two cer-

tificates from different boards of land commission-

ers; and designing speculators were obtaining land

by fraudulent methods.[8]

---

[8] Spanish Archives, G.L.O., Letters, 1837-1841, pp.
65-68. A First Class Certificate entitled "all persons except Africans and their descendants, and Indians, living in Texas on the day of the Declaration
of Independence" to one league and one labor of land
(4,605.5 acres) if they were the heads of families and
to one-third of a league if single. A Second Class
Certificate entitled heads of families who arrived in
Texas after the Declaration of Independence and prior
to October 1, 1837, to receive 1,280 acres and single
men 320 acres. The above-described claims were

One by one Borden admitted and rejected surveys, reiterating that his office had to be governed by the archives as they were and not as they should be, repeatedly instructing surveyors to respect the boundaries of the old grants, and always insisting that rather than himself the judiciary should be the proper tribunal of doubtful claims.

Six months later on November 7, 1838, Borden reported that the archives were still incomplete. The records of De León's colony had not yet been deposited in the Land Office. It was, therefore, impossible to form any correct idea of the situation of titled lands in that colony except from a map returned by

---

known as headrights. Other grants made to individuals by the republic and state were homestead donations (preemptions) and donations to veterans. The last homestead donation was made in 1898. The recognition of this class of claims came to an end because there was no more land on which homesteads could be located. Bascom Giles, History and Disposition of Texas Public Domain, 9-11.

Major Edward Linn and compiled from field notes in
the possession of James Kerr. Only a few grants along
the San Antonio River and not within the limits of any
colony were on file. Those titles, issued by the alcaldes of San Antonio and Goliad with no plats and field
notes, probably never had been surveyed. Neither the
titles nor the field notes of McMullen and McGloin's
colony were of record. The lines of the old surveys
in the prairie country of that colony could not easily
be found, and it was impossible to know with certainty
which lands were vacant. All of Austin's titles were
of record with field notes filed together and a connected map of all surveys. The archives of Austin
and Williams's colony, including titles and field notes,
had been deposited. The records of Sterling C. Robertson were on file with the exception of two or three
titles and a few sets of field notes not yet delivered.
The archives of De Witt's colony were of record and

in good order; nearly all the surveys were represented on maps made by Byrd Lockhart. Power and
Hewetson's titles with only a few sets of original field
notes had reached the Land Office in November, 1837,
but it was doubtful whether they could ever be located
because of the vague and indefinite land descriptions.
The titles of Milam's colony were of record with maps
of nearly all surveys. The titles issued by Carlos S.
Taylor and George W. Smyth on the eastern frontier
were on file and partially located. The records sent
in by Durst and Williams, James Grant, and Williams,
Johnson, and Peebles had been examined and classified.[9]

Further, the republic had issued 10,890 certificates
amounting to 26,242,199 acres of land, of which only
793 corresponding surveys had been registered in the

---

[9] Synopsis of Spanish Archives in report of November 7, 1838. Spanish Archives, G.L.O., Letters, 1837-
1841, pp. 176-178.

Land Office. Borden explained that he could not continue to make new locations until additional authoritative instructions were received and county boundaries
were established, nor could his small staff of clerks
with limited salaries determine the existing locations
unless remedial measures were taken. He appealed
for a clarification of the land system by the legislature in session with the warning that he and his
officers were "toiling in a labyrinth" and by per-
severing in the same course, "they would only become
more entangled."[10]

Again on March 28, 1839,[11] Borden directed a similar appeal to President Mirabeau Lamar and repeated
his request for a clerk to assist the translator,[12] who

---

[10] Ibid., pp. 172-175.

[11] Ibid., pp. 200-202.

[12] At that time, next to the commissioner, the Spanish translator was the highest paid officer in the Land
office. The first translator was Thomas G. Western.

was constantly busy with the voluminous material at hand and did not have time to record and file titles. The attached synopsis of the Spanish Archives stated that the amount of land covered by titles of record was 4,286 leagues, or 18,979,400 acres, to which might be added an estimated 600 leagues, or 2,657,040 acres, making an approximate total of 21,636,440 acres of titled lands.

Meanwhile, fraudulent and irregular practices compelled the government to discontinue the issuance of patents. On April 20, 1839, Borden addressed a notice to the public explaining that such a measure was necessary to protect both the interests of the individual and the republic. Few counties had yet furnished the Land Office with connected maps of their respective territory as required by law; owing to the irregularity that had prevailed in locating and surveying lands, it was utterly impracticable to issue further patents without the aid of such maps. Special agents would be dispatched to examine the records and transactions of the boards of land commissioners. When reports were obtained and connected maps of the various counties were received, patents would issue again, giving the evidence and fidelity proper to a government title.[13]

After six months, on October 23, 1839, Borden reported the results of the investigations and the status of the land situation in the republic.[14] That fraud had been practiced in procuring certificates was evident from the total number issued and from the quantity in the hands of one individual.[15] By virtue of 2,402

---

[13] Spanish Archives, G.L.O., Letters, 1837-1841, pp. 208, 209.

[14] Ibid., 258-264.

[15] Borden said in his report that an individual holding less than ten certificates was considered a small operator.

headrights and 507 bounty warrants and donations, 6,456,607 acres of land had been surveyed and registered.[16] As yet only seven connected county maps had been received. That was largely due to lack of knowledge of the extent of old surveys, the uncertainty of county limits, and particularly the prospect of payment for surveying at the rate of $3.00 per mile in promissory notes.

Borden followed his report with a special request for an appropriation for a clerk in the translator's office, adding that the assistant clerks in other departments were working after prescribed hours copying Spanish titles or field notes of new surveys.[17] Then on November 21, 1839, in reply to an inquiry from

---

[16] But 14,300 certificates, amounting to 33,046,679 and 1/8 acres, had been issued.

[17] Spanish Archives, G.L.O., Letters, 1837-1841, p. 270. Report to Committee on Finance, November 19, 1839.

the House of Representatives as to the probable time
it would take to translate all Spanish documents, he
answered that it would be impossible to form any
correct idea because of their great number and the
difficulty of execution.[18] In a report to the Committee
on Finance on December 9, 1839, he also pointed out
that by direction of the president he was employing
a clerk as assistant to the translator although such
an office was not authorized by law.[19]

For another year Borden continued to struggle with
problems that multiplied rather than diminished. The
Congress ignored not only his repeated suggestions

[18] Ibid., 270, 271.

[19] Ibid., 278. In 1839, there was a force of seven
in the Land Office which was composed of the commissioner, translator, chief clerk, and four clerks.
They were drawing $12,000 in salaries, and the con-
tingent expenses were $500: commissioner, $3,000;
translator, $2,000; chief clerk, $1,600; two assistant
clerks, $1,200 each. Ibid., 265, Report to Chief Clerk,
State Department.

for the establishment of a separate bureau under the supervision of a surveyor general but also his urgent requests for the services of a draftsman. When no permanent provision was made for the office of a translator after the repeal of the land laws of December, 1837, the translation of titles was greatly curtailed. It ceased abruptly when the small sum appropriated for translations by commission became exhausted. Borden considered the legislative land acts of 1840 and 1841 insufficient and in many respects unwise. He had received little relief in the way of explicit instructions and authoritative interpretations of ambiguous or inconsistent laws and was constantly besieged with the responsibility of issuing patents indiscriminately upon appropriated lands. His repeated instruction to all county surveyors, on advice of the attorney general, was not to allow locations to be made on lands once disposed of by former governments and for which titles had issued, whether forfeited or not. Borden's

replies to the chairman of the Committee on Public

Lands, very ably covering the situation of titled lands,

particularly in those counties where conflicts or ab-

sence of records demanded legislative action, were

his last reports.[20] He resigned on December 12, 1840,

soon after the beginning of his second term.[21]

Thomas William Ward, the second land commis-

sioner, wrote the president that John P. Borden had

done magnificent work on a task only just begun.[22]

---

[20] Spanish Archives, G.L.O., Letters, 1840-1845,
100-105; 108-111.

[21] Ibid., 113. On December 22, 1840, H. W. Raglin,
chief clerk and acting commissioner, made a special
report on large grants located within the restricted
leagues of the coast and border reserves. The constitution had declared invalid all eleven-league grants
in those areas. Ibid., 116-119.

[22] Ward wrote also that the country owed a debt of
gratitude to Stephen F. Austin for the accuracy with
which he had represented the titled surveys in his
colonies. Ibid., 208.

In continuation of that immediate task, Ward was har-
assed by the same obstacles and restrictions that had
thwarted Borden in his earnest desire to administer
Texas lands to the best interests of the citizenry.
Inadequate funds, defective laws, and lack of authoritative instructions made it impossible to halt the growing confusion. Ward's first report to the legislature
was a vigorous denouncement of the existing land system.[23] Bluntly setting forth its inherent evils, he
asked for complete reform. It was too late, he said,
to sectionize the lands of the republic according to
the expressed intent of the constitution. It would be
necessary to perfect the established order. The quantity and location of titled lands could never be ascertained unless the legislature took some action to force
the registry and establishment of claims for which
there was no record in the Land Office. Holders of

---

[23] Ibid., 207-219.

unrecorded titles should be compelled to deposit their claims within a certain period of time under penalty of forfeiture of rights.[24] The accurate and permanent establishment of all such titles could not be left to accidental circumstances, nor could the land thus covered be withheld from location indefinitely. What was to be done about the many eleven-league claims of doubtful validity. Also what was the status of titles complete except for field notes in the possession of the surveyor. The appropriation for translations made by the last congress had been expended. If the

----

[24] The law stating that "Any person who owns or claims land of any description by deed, lien, or other color of title, shall, within twelve months from the 1st day of April next, have the same proven in open court and recorded in the office of the county clerk of the county in which said land is situated, etc.," was merely directory, and it was optional with the individuals to comply with or disobey it. And consider the costly litigation when thirty-six claims in Milam County were patented and only a few days afterward they were ascertained to be covered by an eleven-league grant from the Mexican government.

government considered it necessary to preserve the substance of those titles of record, a sufficient appropriation should be made for their translation before the deterioration of age destroyed them.

In the face of an already chaotic situation, President Sam Houston ordered the seat of government removed from Austin. Then occurred the famous Archive War, and after being closed for six months,[25] the Land Office opened in Washington-on-the-Brazos without benefit of the national archives which the citizens of Austin had seized and refused to surrender. The absence of records perforce interrupted the progressive and continuous operation of the land business which was vital to the interests of all Texans. Therefore, after temporizing for eight months, Ward reopened the office in Austin in January, 1844, and the

[25] The Land Office was closed from September 2, 1842, to May 1, 1843.

archives were again placed in his custody. By order
of the legislature they were examined by an appointed
committee and the commissioner and with slight exceptions found to be intact.[26]

When business was resumed in March, Ward re-
newed his struggle to remove the obstacles that were
blocking any orderly management of Texas lands. He
began with a spirited protest to the president against
the insufficient appropriation made for the land office
staff.[27] His annual report[28] of 1844 recited old and
new grievances in convincing terms: There had been

---

[26] Spanish Archives, G.L.O., Letters, 1840-1845,
pp. 328-332.

[27] Ibid., 346, 347. By statute, the staff had been
increased to eleven officers. Ten clerks, including
the chief clerk, the Spanish translator, one draftsman, and an assistant draftsman had been provided
by the legislature, but the last appropriation was for
only seven clerks and one draftsman.

[28] President Houston reappointed Ward as commissioner for three years on July 4, 1843.

no consideration for measures formerly recommended; the land commissioner was called upon to exercise judicial power when his acts should be strictly ministerial; the diversified and discordant system precluded the possibility of harmony and justice to all without the interposition of the judiciary; land laws, crude and uncertain, were a mass of incongruities that delayed rather than expedited the final settlement of routine problems; the laws relative to county boundaries were vague and indeterminate; counties, organized for the purpose of representation, had been adopted also as land sections; therefore, it was imperative to establish definite boundaries and let them remain unchanged; county surveyors, elected by the people, were incompetent and not subject to control; the price for surveying, now only $2.00 per mile, did not permit efficiency (in the United States the minimum was $4.00 and the maximum $8.00); the Land

Office should be allowed to make official county maps

because surveyors' maps were glaringly incorrect,

and all the time of clerks was consumed by the con-

stant investigation of errors; it was impossible to

put Power and Hewetson's surveys on maps because

no metes and bounds were given in the original titles;

some measure was necessary to secure those lands

to colonists and guard them against rapacious specu-

lators; unless it was required that all old titles be

recorded in county or Land Office, it would be im-

possible to place them on maps, and the land would

again be subject to location; the Land Office needed

a new roof and many other repairs; the records were

getting damp and wet, and business had to be sus-

pended during heavy rains; the last Congress had not

made any provision at all for a Spanish translator; ex-

penses had increased, and appropriations fell doubly

short because money was worth only fifty cents on

the dollar.[29]

On February 3, 1845, a special session of Congress adjourned without taking any action to alleviate the land situation. Then in the summer of that year the proposed annexation of Texas to the United States was sharply projected into the foreground. President Anson Jones summoned a convention to consider the terms of annexation offered by the joint resolution of the United States Congress. A special session of the Texas Congress voted unanimously in favor of annexation, and the convention adopted an ordinance accepting the terms of the joint resolution, the main proviso of which modestly stated that Texas would retain dominion of her public lands. Ward's brief report to the convention read as follows: Texas contained 254,284,160 acres; of this amount 50,000,000

---

[29] Spanish Archives, G.L.O., Letters, 1840-1845, pp. 454-470.

acres were covered by claims issued by the republic, 26,000,000 acres of which were comprised in legal claims and 24,000,000 in fraudulent claims; Spanish and Mexican authorities had issued titled grants covering 22,980,000 acres; the public domain unsurveyed and subject to location comprised 181,991,403 acres.[30]

On December 29, 1845, the United States Congress accepted the constitution of the new state of Texas, and the sovereignty of the republic passed to the United States. The state constitution adopted all the laws of the republic not contrary to the constitution of the United States, the joint resolution, or the provisions of the same constitution. On May 12, 1846,[31] the first Texas legislature passed an act to establish a general

---

[30] Spanish Archives, G.L.O., Miscellaneous Letters Sent, 1845-1850, pp. 77, 78.

[31] Section 3 provided for a staff composed of the chief clerk, Spanish translator, two draftsmen, and eight assistant clerks. Gammel, Laws of Texas, 1838-1846, II, 1538.

land office for the state of Texas. Thomas William Ward, elected as land commissioner by the legislature, soon announced that the demand for patents had trebled immediately after annexation and an appropriation of $61,000,000 would be necessary to carry on the increased business.[32]

When the House of Representatives requested a special report on the condition of the Spanish Archives after annexation to the United States, Ward presented the following exhibits: 1) Thirty-five titles deposited by individuals since January 1, 1846. 2) Eighty-five titles of McMullen and McGloin's colony received from Mexico. 3) Ten volumes of Spanish documents received from the archives of Bexar through the office of the Secretary of State, October 13, 1846; they were laws, decrees, and orders of the governments of Spain,

---

[32] Spanish Archives, G.L.O., Miscellaneous Letters Sent, 1845-1850, pp. 106, 107.

Mexico, and Coahuila and Texas with relation to grants

of land, colonization, missions, etc.[33]

On February 8, 1850, an act of the legislature au-

thorized the transfer of the long missing records of

De León's colony from the office of the Secretary of

State to the General Land Office.[34] That addition

marked the completion of the Spanish Archives insofar

as time and circumstance had permitted government

authorities to assemble original records from known

and available sources. Other records, not originals

but having the force of titles, had been deposited in

the Spanish Archives. They were *testimonios* and

deeds, issued prior to March 2, 1836, on paper of the

second or third seal, which were accepted as evidence

---

[33] Spanish Archives, G.L.O., Report of Commissioner, 1845-1891, p. 138. The report was made on
January 27, 1848.

[34] Gammel, Laws of Texas, 1847-1854, III, 580. No
evidence as to how or when they reached the office of
the Secretary of State has been found.

of ownership when there was no original title of record.[35] Such titles continued to be deposited at intervals by individuals until 1876 when the new state constitution declared invalid all claims received or recorded after that date.[36]

By ruling of the Texas Supreme Court, the above-mentioned deeds and testimonios were not considered as original documents or archives;[37] and owners, by provision of the legislative acts of February 11, 1850, and January 11, 1862, were permitted to withdraw those evidences of title on "leaving a receipt therefor, naming the grantee of the land and the quantity thereof, together with its location...and the date

---

[35] A testimonio, under the Mexican colonization law, was the copy taken immediately from the original and delivered to the owner "for his security." It is sometimes called the second original.

[36] Gammel, Laws of Texas, 1873-1879, VIII, 822.

[37] Vernon's Civil Statutes of the State of Texas, Revision of 1925, articles 250, 251, 252, pp. 565-570.

of such paper."[38] Of 185 titles deposited by indi-

viduals in the Spanish Archives, sixty-five have been

withdrawn.[39]

---

[38] Gammel, Laws of Texas, 1847-1854, III, 638;
ibid., 1861-1866, V, 479.

[39] The Spanish Archives were further depleted on
December 24, 1851, when the legislature authorized
the placing of Volume 45 in the County Clerk's office
in Refugio. This volume contains 169 titles to town
lots in Refugio. Gammel, Laws of Texas, 1847-1854,
III, 900.

Chapter IX

THE SPECIAL DISPOSITION OF TITLED LANDS

BETWEEN THE NUECES AND RIO GRANDE

On the same day that De León's records were com-
mitted to the Spanish Archives, the legislature in-
itiated a new development in the history of Spanish
and Mexican titles to Texas lands by passage of an
act which provided for the "investigation of land titles in certain counties therein mentioned."[1] Most
of the counties mentioned in the act were those comprised within the recently extended limits of the San
Patricio district, or the territory between the Nueces
River and the Rio Grande. Certificate holders had
made little infiltration into that area until the de facto

[1] Gammel, Laws of Texas, 1847-1854, III, 582-587.

125

jurisdiction of Texas was established there by the presence of General Zachary Taylor's army. Then the Spanish and Mexican grants were attacked so frequently that the legislature was called upon for relief. A special investigation became necessary to ascertain the validity of claims made more complex because all original titles were archived in Mexico. The only records of title available in Texas were transfers already recorded in county offices and testimonios yet in possession of the original grantees or their descendants. William H. Bourland and James B. Miller, appointed as commissioners to make the investigation, were instructed to enter upon their duties at the county seat of each county where notice should be posted requiring all persons to present their claims with a full description of the land, all evidences of title, and sworn affidavits of ownership. The commissioners were invested with the authority to summon witnesses and take testimony in support of or against the validity of claims. After due examination, there should be submitted to the legislature an abstract of every claim with the accompanying evidence and a statement recommending or rejecting confirmation on the basis of the "principles of justice and the laws, ordinances, rules, and customs of the government... under which the claim originated."

The legislature in session on September 4, 1850, promptly confirmed Bourland and Miller's first recommendations for Webb County.[2] Fourteen months later, the commissioners completed their investigations and submitted the final results with the general report which follows:

"Austin, Nov. 11th, 1851.

His Excellency
    the Governor

---

[2] Gammel, Laws of Texas, 1847-1854, III, 798.

The undersigned Commissioners appointed in conformity with an Act "to provide for the investigation of land titles in certain counties therein mentioned," approved February 8th, 1850, beg leave to present the following report: That in consequence of delays necessarily incurred in preparing for the discharge of their duties assigned them, they were unable to reach the County of Kinney by the first Monday of May succeeding the passage of the Act, and desiring not to disarrange the times prescribed for holding their sessions in the other and more important counties of their district, they commenced their official operations at Laredo in the County of Webb, and after giving the notices required by the law, they proceeded to investigate such titles and claims as were presented to them and to take testimony in respect to their validity, a report of which investigation and the results of it they have heretofore had the honor to present for the action of the Honorable Legislature.

The undersigned deem this a proper occasion to state, that when they first entered upon the discharge of their official duties they had to encounter much opposition and embarrassment, growing out of an impression which seemed to prevail in the valley of the Rio Grande, that the act under which the board was held, was devised to destroy rather than to protect their rights (if honestly acquired) to their lands.

Knowing, as the undersigned did, that this act had its origin in a sincere desire on the part of the Legislature to protect a class of citizens but recently brought into, and identified with the State, and who were but little accustomed to our laws, usages & customs, from the harassing vexations of tedious and expensive law suits in respect to their land titles, they were not prepared for that opposition, and probably would have been unable to overcome it, but for the influence and exerting of the Honorable H. B. Bee. Many of the citizens of Laredo were induced to lay their claims before the board and to produce the evidence upon which they relied to sustain them, and the fairness with which the investigations were conducted, and the subsequent confirmation by the Legislature, of those titles recommended for confirmation, had the effect of removing the whole of this unfounded prejudice, and to cause them to look upon the act as a generous boon extended to them, rather than as a trap laid to ensnare them and deprive them of their rights. The Commissioners, therefore, since that period, have had no difficulties thrown in their way by the people, but have been approached with confidence and a full belief and reliance that justice would be done them.

After getting through with their duties in the County of Webb, as far as they could be performed during the time they remained there, the undersigned proceeded to the other Counties in their district and investigated all the claims and titles presented to them in those counties. The whole of them will be found represented in the accompanying abstract marked A.

The applications from each County are numbered seperately on the abstract, and the petitions and testimony relating to each, marked respectively with the corresponding numbers of the abstract, will be found in the package of land titles for the County to which it pertains, marked also with the corresponding number on the abstract.

In respect to the County of Kinney, the undersigned
ask an indulgence of a few days longer to make their
report. The reason of their requiring this indulgence
is, that for the causes before stated, they were unable to visit that County previous to the present year,
and the people not expecting that a session of the board
would be holden there, were unprepared to present
their claims; consequently, they came in at a late
date, and the evidence in support of them is not yet
fully arranged. There are but few claims, however,
from that County, and they only for pasture lands.
So soon as the abstract and evidence can be prepared,
they will be submitted.

The reason why the undersigned were not prepared
to make their report on or before the first Monday
of the present month (November) had its origin in the
unfortunate wreck of the Steamer Anson, while on her
passage from the Brazos ₑBrazos Santiago Pass₃ in
(November 1850) and by which all the papers and original titles connected with the claims presented in Cameron County were lost. This accident forced upon the
Commissioners the necessity of going over the whole
of that work again and to which was superadded the
difficulty of procuring duplicates and other evidences
of the lost titles and documents connected with them.

The undersigned, in their investigations of the whole
of the claims and titles presented to them, were governed strictly by the provisions of the act under which
they received their appointment, and expecially by the
instructions contained in the 5th, 6, 7, & 8th Sections
of that act. The decisions of the Board were pred-
icated upon the evidence of the title and the testimony
offered in reference to the claim and when from that

evidence it satisfactorily and conclusively appeared
that the claim was a good, genuine, and bona fide one
against Mexico on the 2nd day of March, 1836, it has
been recommended for confirmation; but when the
evidence was not sufficient to establish that fact the
claim was invariably rejected. The undersigned beg
leave to call the attention of the Legislature specially
to the Copies herewith presented of the original grants
made to the citizens of Guerrero, Mier, Camargo,
and Reynosa. These are grants of a peculiar character and known as "porcion" grants. The lands were
originally surveyed into tracts of uniform size by the
government and disposed of to citizens, and a document was given to them as the evidence of their right,
which they have preserved with great care, supposing
it to be a perfect title to their lands. These documents
would not probably be construed by the Courts of this
country as full and complete titles; but that they are
genuine there is no doubt, and there is no class of
claims in that region that is better entitled to protection and confirmation. The owners of them have
resided upon the lands and cultivated them for a long
series of years, as will be seen from the evidence,
and their rights to them have always been unques-
tioned under the Government of Mexico.

The undersigned cannot close this report without
expressing their sincere wish that the Honorable Legislature will proceed to act upon the claims now presented with the dispatch and in the same spirit that was
manifested in reference to the claims heretofore presented from the County of Webb. They have recommended no claim for confirmation which they do not
honestly believe ought to be confirmed. If they have
erred at all, they believe they have done so in holding

the claimants to a too strict and rigid complyance
with the requirements of the law. They are satisfied
they have not erred in releasing them.

The people of those Counties now look with confidence to the action of the Legislature upon this subject, a confidence which has been planted in their
minds by its former action upon a similar class of
claims, and we sincerely trust that they are not des-
tined to meet with disappointment.

                              Respectfully Yours,

                              J. B. Miller
Commissioners
                              Wm. H. Bourland."

On February 10, 1852, in "an Act to relinquish the
right of the State to certain lands therein named,"
the legislature confirmed 192 grants recommended
by Bourland and Miller in Kinney, Webb, Starr, Nueces, and Cameron counties.[3] The act listed the name
of each grantee with the acreage and the Spanish name
by which the grant was commonly known. The Bourland and Miller abstract and copies of their general

---

[3] Gammel, Laws of Texas, 1847-1854, III, 941.

report and the report of the committee to whom the bill was referred are in the Spanish Archives.[4] What disposition was made of the actual files prepared as evidence by Bourland and Miller cannot be ascertained. No more than four or five have been found in the records of the Land Office.

Two years later, by act of February 11, 1854, a second board of commissioners was created to investigate land titles in Webb, Starr, Hidalgo, Cameron, Nueces, Kinney, Presidio, and El Paso counties.[5] No confirmations appear to have been made by the commission, and only one reference to the act is found in subsequent laws.[6]

---

[4] Bourland and Miller's general report in manuscript and the printed report of the Select Committee are original records of the State Archives.

[5] Gammel, Laws of Texas, 1847-1854, III, 1538.

[6] Ibid., 1861-1866, V, 135. The legislature authorized the treasury to pay $240.00 to the heirs of Blas

Then on February 11, 1860, the legislature authorized original grantees, their heirs, or legal assigns,
who claimed land between the Nueces River and the
Rio Grande by titles from former governments issued
prior to March 2, 1836, to present their claims for
confirmation in the corresponding district court within three years after passage of the act.[7] By amend-
ment in 1862, the time limit was extended to February
11, 1865.[8]

Again on August 15, 1870, provision was made for
confirmation of the same class of claims by the legislative act which directed that such claims be presented

————

Uribe as reimbursement for taxes erroneously collected by the commission of 1854.

[7] Ibid., 1854-1861, IV, 1471

[8] Ibid., 1861-1866, V, 479. On April 14, 1881, the
legislature allowed the same provisions for cases begun within the limits specified by the acts of 1860 and
1862 but not completed because of complications aris-
ing from the Civil War. Ibid., 1877-1889, p. 197.

to the district court of Travis County for adjudication within the term of two years after that date.[9]

The act of September 3, 1901, "to provide for ascertaining and adjudicating certain claims against or in favor of the State for land, titles to which are claimed to have emanated from the Spanish or Mexican governments" was devised for testing the validity of those claims situated between the Nueces River and the Rio Grande and having their origin "at such time as to be, and being within the protection guaranteed by the Treaty of Guadalupe Hidalgo entered into between the United States and Mexico" on July 4, 1848; for determining the exact location and boundaries of such lands when the evidence on file in the General Land Office did not sufficiently identify the land claimed; and also for enabling the State to recover lands held or claimed under titles emanating from the Spanish or Mexican

[9] Ibid., 1866-1871, VI, 375.

governments when no valid evidence was to be found

in the files or records of the land office; suits were

to be brought, prosecuted, and tried in the district

court of Travis County within two years from and after

passage of the act.[10]

Some fifty Spanish and Mexican titles were con-

firmed under the acts of 1860, 1870, and 1901.[11] Special

confirmations were also made to certain individuals

---

[10] General Laws of the State of Texas, First Called
Session of the 27th Legislature, 1901, pp. 4-7. By virtue of the guarantees made by the Treaty of Guadalupe Hidalgo, the Mexican government presented some
200 individual land claims amounting to $10,000,000
to the General Claims Commission, United States and
Mexico. The claims were disallowed, and the evidences of title were deposited in the National Archives
a number of years ago. This information was obtained from M. P. Shaner of the Legal Division of the
State Department by Senator Lyndon Johnson at the
request of Bascom Giles, the present land commissioner.

[11] In 1900 Commissioner Charles Rogan presented
to the legislature a list of forty-three alleged Spanish
and Mexican grants for which there was no evidence
of title in the Land Office. Two years later titles

by the legislature at intervals when no validating act

was in effect. The recognized grants between the

Nueces and Rio Grande are classified as first class

headrights, and most of them have been resurveyed

and patented to the original grantee or his heirs. The

first class files contain a few original testimonios

and copies of titles procured from Mexico and from

county records. By act of March 16, 1881, it was re-

quired that a copy of every validated title, of which

there was no evidence on file, be placed in the Land

Office, either in the form of the owner's testimonio

or of a certified copy taken from county records.[12]

---

were found to seven of the grants mentioned. Rogan
stated that he believed that many of the grantees would
be able to establish their titles, while on the other
hand, it was possible that the state would recover at
least 500,000 acres where the claimants had no title
or where excess existed. Report of Commissioner,
1898-1900, p. 31; ibid., 1900-1902, pp. 38-42.

[12] Gammel, Laws of Texas, 1879-1889, IX, 129. Commissioners Spence, Kuechler, and Groos made strong

Apparently, the requirements of the act were never

fully complied with as the records reveal very few

titles deposited after that date.

The 3,780,000 acres of land confirmed to grantees

between the Nueces River and the Rio Grande brought

the total amount of titled lands in Texas to 26,280,000

---

appeals for the passage of this law. They protested
repeatedly against the withdrawal of testimonios of
valid titles, which were important not only as evidence
of title but also as a source of essential locative data.
Report of Commissioner, 1845-1891, pp. 371, 409, 424,
437. Heading W. C. Walsh's report on September 1,
1880, was the following request for a change or modi-
fication of the law regulating Spanish and Mexican
land titles: "The Constitution, Article XIV, Sec. 2,
provides three modes by which such titles may be
recognized as valid: (1) by being mapped and archived
in this office; (2) by being recorded in the county; and
(3) by possession of the grantee or those holding under
him. Of the three modes the last two, as the law now
stands, are beyond the knowledge of this office; and
in default of the first there is nothing to indicate to
the Commissioner what grants are entitled to respect.
This difficulty is greatly increased by the require-
ment of Art. 3916, Revised Statutes (adopted from the
Act of Feby. 10, 1852) which directs the Commissioner
to strike from the maps all surveys for which no valid titles are on file in his office. Were the letter of

acres.[13] It was the work of John P. Borden, Thomas

William Ward, and successive commissioners to as-

semble, preserve, and locate all the Spanish and Mexi-

can grants comprised in that area and scattered over

one-third of the surface of the state.[14] In sections

where early surveying was done with care and precise

records were kept, the majority of claims appear to

be definitely established; in others, where the grant-

ing of lands was accomplished in such a manner as

---

this Statute observed and the land declared vacant by
the Commissioner, a conflict with Sects. 2 and 8, Art.
XIV of the Constitution would result. The law should
provide some mode by which this office can be advised of what surveys are entitled to respect by reason
of compliance with the second and third conditions
prescribed by the Constitution.'' Ibid., 500.

[13] Ibid., 373.

[14] It was not until after 1866 that official maps were
compiled in the Land Office. Before that time maps
made by county surveyors and filed in the Land Office
constituted the official maps. Report of Commissioner, 1932-1934, p. 4. The first protective measure for
the preservation of the Spanish Archives was made

to defy all probability of eventual settlement, the situ-

ation is strongly reminiscent of Borden's and Ward's

early predictions. But regardless of any nebulous or

categorical status, the Spanish Archives have been and

remain the major source of conclusive evidence in

the location and establishment of thousands of claims

in the gigantic jigsaw puzzle of Texas lands. The old

records are consulted from day to day as property .

rights are being called into question at the present

time. The old surveys are examined daily to de-

---

in 1873 when the legislature provided for the making
of copies which could be used in court proceedings
with the same force and effect of originals. Gammel,
Laws of Texas, 1873-1879, VIII, 180. Since that time
certified copies of titles have been made on order by
the Spanish translator. The policy of retaining carbon
copies of translations is employed to save the originals from the wear and tear of daily use. But "unless
some provision is made for the retirement of these
records the constant use of these century old documents will result in their partial destruction which
would prove an irreparable damage to landowners of
the State." Bascom Giles, Report of Commissioner,
1938-1940, p. 15.

termine vacancies, excesses, and existing boundaries. Along with modern developments in law, eco-
nomics, and industry, the old grants assume new sig-
nificances and importance. Their utilitarian force
enhances their aura of sentiment and antiquity as they
yet serve the purpose for which they were issued,
"that he ⸢the grantee⸣ may possess and enjoy the tract
that has been conceded to him - he, his children, heirs
and successors, or whoever from him or from them
shall have cause or right."

BIBLIOGRAPHY

Secondary Works

Alamán, Lucas

Disertaciones sobre la Historia de la República Megicana, J. M. Lara, Mégico, 1844.

Historia de Méjico, J. M. Lara, Méjico, 1849.

Alessio Robles, Vito

Coahuila y Texas, Mexico, 1945.

Coahuila y Texas en la Epoca Colonial, Editorial Cultura, Mexico, 1938.

Bancroft, Hubert Howe

The Works of Hubert Howe Bancroft, San Francisco, 1899: The History of Mexico; The History of the North Mexican States.

Barker, Eugene C.

The Austin Papers, Washington, 1924.

The Life of Stephen F. Austin, Founder of Texas, 1793-1836, Cokesbury Press, Nashville, 1925.

142

Benson, Nettie Lee

The Provincial Deputation in Mexico, Precursor of the Mexican Federal State, Dissertation, Austin, May, 1949.

Bolton, Herbert E.

Athanase de Mézières and the Louisiana-Texas Frontier, 1768-1780, Cleveland, 1914.

Guide to Materials for the History of the United States in the Principal Archives of Mexico, Carnegie Institute, Washington, 1913.

Texas in the Middle Eighteenth Century, University of California Press, 1915.

Castañeda, Carlos E.

A Report on the Spanish Archives in San Antonio, Texas, Yanaguana Society, San Antonio, 1937.

Fray Agustin Morfi, History of Texas, 1673-1779, The Quivira Society, Albuquerque, 1935.

Our Catholic Heritage in Texas, Von Boeckmann-Jones Company, Austin, 1942.

Gammel, H. P. N.

The Laws of Texas, The Gammel Book Company, The Gammel Book Company, Austin, 1898.

Giles, Bascom

History and Disposition of Texas Public Domain, Austin, 1945.

Hawkins, Wallace

El Sal del Rey, The Texas State Historical Association, Austin, 1947.

Henderson, Virginia

"Minor Empresario Contracts," Southwestern Historical Quarterly, XXXI, April, 1928.

Kimball, J. P.

Laws and Decrees of the State of Coahuila and Texas, Telegraph Power Press, Houston, 1839.

Morton, Ohland

Terán and Texas, A Chapter in Texas-Mexican Relations, The Texas State Historical Society, Austin, 1948.

Sayles, John and Henry

Early Laws of Texas, The Gilbert Book Company, St. Louis, 1891.

Vernon Law Book Company

Civil Statutes of the State of Texas, Revision of 1925, Kansas City, Missouri, 1927.

Documentary Sources

General Laws of the State of Texas, Thirty-sixth Legislature, 1919.

Recopilación de Leyes de los Reinos de las Indias, Madrid, 1841.

Manuscript Sources

General Land Office Files

Lamar Papers, State Archives

Nacogdoches Archives, State Archives

Spanish Archives, General Land Office

INDEX

Madero, José Francisco, 63
Martínez, Antonio, 31, 33, 35
Martínez, Carlos, 27
Mason, John T., 59
Matamoros, 81, 90
McGloin, James, 52. See McMullen and McGloin
McMullen, John, 52. See McMullen and McGloin
McMullen and McGloin, 104, 121
Medina River, 28
Menchaca, Luis, 27
Mexican grants, number of, 5; procurement of, 64; state of Tamaulipas, 90; state of Chihuahua, 94
Mexican Republic, 30
Mexico City, 10, 35, 36, 84, 93
Mier, town of, 82, 90, 131
Mier y Terán, Manuel, 64
Milam, Benjamin R., 47, 53; records of, 105
Miller, James B., 126, 132
Mina, town of, 4, 48
Monterrey, 12, 32, 33, 35, 37

Nacogdoches, 4, 15, 20, 30, 48, 49, 50, 61, 99, 101
Nacogdoches County, 20
Nashville Company, 46, 55
Natchitoches, 34, 50
Navarro, Angel, 24, 25
Navarro, José Antonio, 53
National Colonization Law, of 1823, 36, 70, 89; of 1824, 40
New Mexico, 29
New Orleans, 34
Nixon, George Anthony, 48, 49, 50, 74, 99
Nueces River, 29
Nuevo Santander, 12, 81, 83, 89

Owen, Ernest Dale, 95
O'Docharty, William, 100

Pacheco, Rafael, 27, 28
Padilla, Juan Antonio, 56, 63n
Padre Island grant, 87
Pasos salomones, 79
Patents, discontinuance of, 107
Pecos River, 94
Peebles, 46. See Williams, Johnson, and Peebles

Pereda, José Manuel, 85
Porción, 78, 131
Porciones, survey of, 82
Portillo, José María, 55
Power, James, 51. See Power and Hewetson
Power and Hewetson, 50, 105
Presidio Mining Company, 95
Presumed grants, 25
Province of Texas, official designation of, 9; appointment of separate governor for, 9
Provincial Deputation of Texas, formation of, 41; dissolution of, 46; De León's contract with, 50
Provincial Deputation of the Interior Provinces, 13, 31, 32, 37
Provincias Internas del Oriente, 11
Purnell, John G., 52

Rancho de Ascarete, 94
Rancho de Ponce, 94
Reconstruction Constitutional Convention, 87
Recopilación de Leyes de los Reinos de las Indias, 6
Red River, 29
Refugio, town of, 4, 51
Resolutions of April and August of 1828, 62
Reynosa, town of, 82, 90, 131
Rincón del Oso, 88
Robertson, Sterling C., 46; records of, 104
Robison, J. T., 93
Ronquilla, José Ygnacio, 95
Ross, Reuben, 55
Royal Audiencia, 7

Sabine River, 29
Saint Genevieve, 32
Salcedo, Manuel de, 16, 19
Saltillo, 40
San Antonio, 4, 5, 9, 15, 20, 21, 24, 30, 34, 35, 61
San Augustine, 50
San Elizario, presidio of, 92
San Felipe, 4, 38, 61, 97
San Francisco de la Espada, Mission of 26
San Juan Capistrano Mission, 26
San Juan de Carricitos grant, 87

APPENDIX

Name and Date of Title	Amount	Colony or Commis- sioner	Present Location
Abbott, Lancelot, Oct. 29, 1835	1/4 lea. *	Austin 5	Waller
Acosta, Jose Mariano, Apr. 24, 1834	1 lea.	Aldrete	Bowie (?)
Acosta, Jose Mariano, Sept. 14, 1835	1 lea.	Smyth	1/3 Smith 2/3 Hender- son
Acosta, Juan, May 10, 1810	7 1/2 lab. * *	Procela	Nacogdoches
Acosta, Juan Jose, Sept. 30, 1833	11 lea.	Lessassier	1 Burleson 2 Falls 8 Milam
Acosta, Juan Nepomuceno, Nov. 21, 1833	11 lea.	Aldrete	5 Limestone 3 Freestone 3 Anderson
Acosta, Isidro, Dec. 20, 1831	1 lea.	Santos Coy	Nacogdoches
Adams, Francis, Oct. 22, 1830	1/4 lea.	Austin 3	Jackson
Adams, James, Dec. 22, 1835	1 lea. 1 lab.	Taylor	Cherokee (?)
Adams, John, Oct. 14, 1835	1 lea.	Burnet	Anderson
Adams, John W., March 25, 1835	1 lea.	Vehlein	San Jacinto
Adams, Thomas, July 30, 1835	1 lea. 1 lab.	McMullen and McGloin	Live Oak
Aguilera, Casildo, Apr. 30, 1835	1 lea.	Burnet	Nacogdoches
Aguilera, Jose Ygnacio, Nov. 26, 1833	11 lea.	Aldrete	1/2 Anderson 1/2 Free- stone
Aguirre, Antonio, Apr. 18, 1834	11 lea.	Soto	Zavala
Aguirre, Narciso, Apr. 18, 1834	11 lea.	Soto	6/7 Zavala 1/7 Dimmit
Aguirre, Pedro Jose, Apr. 18, 1834	11 lea.	Soto	Zavala
Aguirre, Rafael de, Oct. 4, 1833	11 lea.	Lessassier	McLennan
Aguirre, Rafael de, Oct. 22, 1833	11 lea.	Lessassier	10 William- son 1 Falls
Albarado, Faustino, Apr. 10, 1835	1 lea.	F. de Leon	Calhoun
Albright, John A., Nov. 5, 1835	1 lea.	Taylor	Jefferson (?)
Aldrete, Jose Maria, Sept. 22, 1834	1/4 lea.	Power and Hewetson	Refugio
Aldrete, Jose Miguel, Sept. 22, 1834	4 lea.	Power and Hewetson	Refugio

* League
* * Labor

151

Name and Date of Title	Amount	Colony or Commissioner	Present Location
Aldrete, Jose Miguel, Sept. 22, 1834	1 lea.	Power and Hewetson	Refugio
Aldrete, Jose Miguel, See Jesusa de Leon			
Aldrich, Collin, Feb. 14, 1835	1 lea.	Vehlein	Houston
Aldrich, Peter, Oct. 22, 1830	1/4 lea.	Austin 3	Jackson
Alexander, Amos, Oct. 31, 1832	1 lea.	Austin 4	Travis
Alexander, Archibald, Oct. 5, 1835	1/4 lea.	Austin 5	Montgomery
Alexander, Caleb P., May 5, 1831	1 lea.	DeWitt	Caldwell
Alexander, Daniel, Feb. 5, 1835	1/4 lea.	Robertson	Milam
Alexander, Hannah, Nov. 21, 1835	1 lea.	Zavala	Hardin (?)
Allcorn, Elijah, July 10, 1824	1 1/2 lea. 1 lab.	Austin 1	1 lea. Ft. Bend, 1/2 lea. Washington, 1 lab. Walle
Allcorn, Elliott, Mch. 31, 1831	1 lea.	Austin 2	Washington
Allcorn, John H., Mch. 20, 1831	1/4 lea.	Austin 2	Washington
Allen, Augustus C., Jan. 27, 1836	10 lea.	Grant, Durst and Williams	(?)
Allen, Ethan, May 11, 1835	1 lea.	Vehlein	Walker
Allen, George, June 2, 1831	1 lea.	DeWitt	Guadalupe
Allen, George, July 29, 1835	1 lea.	Robertson	Falls
Allen, George, August 27, 1835	1 lea.	Vehlein	1/2 Tyler 1/2 Falls
Allen, James, Apr. 25, 1831	1/4 lea.	Madero	Chambers
Allen, John, July 23, 1835	1 lea.	Zavala	Orange
Allen, John K., Jan. 27, 1836	10 lea.	Grant, Durst and Williams	(?)
Allen, John M., Nov. 27, 1831	1/4 lea.	Austin 3	Brazoria
Allen, Martin, July 19, 1834	1 lea. 1 lab.	Austin 1	lea. Wharto lab. Austi
Allen, Miles N., May 21, 1827	1/4 lea.	Austin 2	Austin
Allen, Miles N., Nov. 29, 1832	3/4 lea.	Austin 2	Austin
Allen, Nathaniel, Apr. 6, 1835	1 lea.	Zavala	Tyler
Allen, N. G., April 20, 1835	1 lea.	Burnet	Leon
Allen, Philip J., May 23, 1835	1 lea.	Milam	Hays
Allen, Samuel T., July 29, 1835	1 lea.	Robertson	Williamson
Allen, Samuel T., Dec. 21, 1832	1/4 lea.	Austin 4	Brazos
Allen, William S., June 2, 1835	1 lea.	Vehlein	Montgomer
Alley, John, May 14, 1827	1 lea.	Austin 1	23 lab. Jackson 2 lab. Lavac
Alley, Rawson, Aug. 3, 1824	1 1/2 lea.	Austin 1	Colorado
Alley, Thomas, Apr. 4, 1831	1/4 lea.	Austin 2	Fayette
Alley, Thomas and Wm., July 29, 1824	1 lea.	Austin 1	Brazoria
Alley, John, for Heirs of William, May 16, 1827	1 lea.	Austin 1	Fayette
Allison, Elihu C., Oct. 16, 1835	1 lea.	Burnet	Cherokee
Allison, Patrick, Apr. 20, 1831	1/4 lea.	Austin 2	Fayette
Allison, William F., Oct. 19, 1835	1 lea.	Burnet	Rusk
Allphin, Ranson, May 22, 1835	1 lea.	Vehlein	Madison

Name and Date of Title	Amount	Colony or Commissioner	Present Location
Allphin, Shelton, June 27, 1835	1 lea.	Burnet	3/4 Madison 1/4 Leon
Alsberry, Thomas, July 8, 1824	2 lea. 1 1/2 lab.	Austin 1	1 1/2 lea. Brazoria 1/2 lea. Ft. Bend 1 1/2 lab. Waller
Alsberry, Chas. G., Aug. 3, 1824 Harvey Horatius	1 1/2 lea.	Austin 1	Brazoria
Amador, Nasario, Mch. 6, 1835		De Leon	Victoria
Amador, Refugio, Mch 25, 1833	1 lea.	De Leon	4/5 Dewitt 1/5 Victoria
Amador, Refugio, Apr. 8, 1835		De Leon	Victoria
Amador, Thomas, Mch. 5, 1835		De Leon	Victoria
Amory, Nathaniel, Oct. 5, 1835	1/4 lea.	Vehlein	San Jacinto
Anderson, David, Feb. 12, 1835	18 lab.	Robertson	Bell
Anderson, David, Nov. 30, 1835	1/3 lea.	Taylor	Houston (?)
Anderson, Elijah, Apr. 30, 1835	1 lea.	Vehlein	Walker
Anderson, Ephraim, Apr. 23, 1831	1 lea.	Austin 2	Fayette
Anderson, Harriett, Aug. 26, 1835	1 lab.	Robertson	Falls
Anderson, Simon Asa, Aug. 10, 1824	1 lea.	Austin 1	Fayette
Anderson, Thomas, Mch. 14, 1835	1 lea.	Milam	Travis
Anderson, Uriah, Oct. 24, 1835	1/4 lea.	Vehlein	Liberty
Anderson, William, Dec. 27, 1834	1/4 lea.	Power and Hewetson	Bee
Anderson, William B., Sept. 26, 1835	1 lea.	Zavala	Angelina
Anding, George, July 18, 1835	1 lea.	Burnet	Anderson
Andrada, Antonio, Sept. 18, 1835	1 lea.	Taylor	Trinity
Andrews, Edmond, Nov. 30, 1830	1 lea.	Austin 3	Brazoria
Andrews, John, July 7, 1824	1 lea. 1 lab.	Austin 1	1/2 Colorado 1/2 Fayette Labor Waller
Andrews, John, Jr., May 31, 1828	1 lea.	Austin 2	Jackson
Andrews, Richard, Mch. 30, 1831	1/4 lea.	Austin 2	Washington
Andrews, Richard, Nov. 23, 1832	3/4 lea.	Austin 2	Bastrop
Andrews, William, July 15, 1824	1 lea. 1 lab.	Austin 1	Ft. Bend
Angier, Samuel, Thos. Bradley, Geo. B. Hall, Aug. 16, 1824	1 lea.	Austin 1	Brazoria
Angier, Samuel, Aug. 24, 1824	1 lab.	Austin 1	Brazoria
Angier, Samuel, Dec. 10, 1830	2/3 lea.	Austin 3	Brazoria
Anglin, Elisha, Feb. 28, 1835	1 lea.	Robertson	Limestone
Anthony, D. W., Nov. 20, 1832	1/4 lea.	Austin 2	Ft. Bend
Anthony, Francis J., Jan 29, 1836	10 lea.	Grant, Durst and Williams	(?)
Araujo, Gavino, Mch. 17, 1834	11 lea.	Aldrete	4 22/25 Tyler 3/25 Polk 1 Red River 2 Louisiana 1 Lamar 2 Bowie
Archer, Branch T., Nov. 18, 1832	1 lea.	Austin 3	Brazoria

153

Name and Date of Title	Amount	Colony or Commissioner	Present Location
Arciniega, Miguel, Sept. 22, 1835	11 lea.	Berry	4 Hunt 2 Gr son (?) 5 Harrison
Arco (de), Santos, Oct. 21, 1835	11 lea.	Del Moral	1 Harrison Balance ('
Armour, Robert, Oct. 5, 1835	1 lea.	Austin 5	Grimes
Armstrong, Henry F., Mch. 3, 1831	1/4 lea.	Austin 2	Washington
Armstrong, Jacob, Aug. 12, 1835	1/4 lea.	Vehlein	Chambers
Arnold, Daniel, May 9, 1831	1 lea.	Austin 2	3728.4 acre Grimes about 700 acres Bra
Arnold, William, Apr. 15, 1833	1 lea.	Austin 3	Calhoun
Arocha, Jose Ygnacio, Sept. 23, 1835	1 lea.	Berry	Lamar
Arocha, Jose Ygnacio, Apr. 4, 1835 (J. and A. Seguin)	2 lab.	Berry	Red River
Arocha, Jose Nepomuceno, Apr. 29, 1834	4 lea.	Aldrete	Bell
Arocha, Jose Ramon, Oct. 22, 1835	1 lea. 1 lab.	Berry	Fannin
Arocha, Heirs of Juan and Simon, Feb. 18, 1834	8 lea.	Bustillo	Wilson
Arrington, William W., June 16, 1832	1/4 lea.	DeWitt	Guadalupe
— Arriola, Antonio, June 6 (?), 1810 (?)	18 lab. (?) 270,000 sq. vs. (?)	De la Bega	Nacogdoche
Arriola, Dolores, Oct. 16, 1835	1 lea.	Austin 5	Madison
Arriola, Eduardo, Oct. 17, 1835	1 lea.	Austin 5	Madison
Arriola, Eduardo, Nov. 6, 1835	1 lea. 1 lab.	Taylor	Hardin
Arriola, Francisco, Nov. 5, 1835	1 lea. 1 lab.	Taylor	lea. Hardin lab. (?)
Arriola, Leandro, Nov. 5, 1829	2 lea.	Del Valle	Bexar (?)
Arriola, Maria Josefa, May 11, 1810 ?	2 1/2 lea.	Flores	Nacogdoche
Arthur, John, June 18, 1835	1/4 lea.	Burnet	Anderson
Ashby, John M., July 16, 1831	1 lea.	DeWitt	Lavaca
Ashley, Aaron, Oct. 4, 1835	1 lea.	Zavala	Angelina
Atkins, Wm., Apr. 18, 1831	1 lea.	Austin 2	Montgomer
Aughinbough, Jesse, July 9, 1835 Augustine	1 lea.	Vehlein	Houston
Augustine, Henry W., Oct. 13, 1835	1 lea.	Vehlein	Polk
Austin, Emily M., See J. F. Perry			
Austin, Henry, Oct. 13, 1830	1 lea.	Austin 3	Brazoria
Austin, Henry, June 20, 1831	3 lea.	Austin 3	Brazoria
Austin, Henry, Oct. 6, 1835	1 lea.	Austin 3	Brazoria
Austin, Henry, May 30, 1831	5 lea.	Austin 3	3/4 Colora 1/4 Fayet
Austin, Henry, May 30, 1831	1 lea.	Austin 3	Washington
Austin, James B., Aug. 24, 1824	1 lab.	Austin 1	Brazoria
Austin, James E. B., Aug. 19, 1824	3 lea. 1 lab.	Austin 1	3 lea. Braz 1 lab. Wa
Austin, John, July 21, 1824	2 lea.	Austin 1	Harris
Austin, John, Aug. 24, 1824	1 lab.	Austin 1	Brazoria
Austin, John, May 16, 1831	1 lea.	Austin 2	Brazos
Austin, Mary Holly, June 13, 1831 Widow	1 lea.	Austin 3	Galveston

154

Name and Date of Title	Amount	Colony or Commissioner	Present Location
Austin, Stephen F., May 31, 1828	5 lea.	Premium	Brazoria
Austin, Stephen F., May 31, 1828	7 1/3 lea.	..	Brazoria
Austin, Stephen F., May 31, 1828	1/3 lea.	..	Brazoria
Austin, Stephen F., May 31, 1828	1/2 lea.	..	Brazoria
Austin, Stephen F., May 31, 1828	1/4 lea.	..	Brazoria
Austin, Stephen F., May 31, 1828	1 3/4 lea.	..	Brazoria
Austin, Stephen F., May 31, 1828	2 1/8 lea.	..	Brazoria
Austin, Stephen F., May 31, 1828	3 1/6 lea.	..	Wharton
Austin, Stephen F., May 31, 1828	2 lea. 3 lab.	..	2 lea. Wharton 3 lab. Brazoria
Austin, Stephen F., Jan. 15, 1830	4 lea.	..	Austin
Austin, Stephen F., Jan. 15, 1830	1 lea.	..	Austin
Austin, Stephen F., Jan. 15, 1830	2 lab. and 350,000 sq. vs.	..	Waller
Austin, Stephen F., Jan. 15, 1830	2 lab. and 650,000 sq. vs.	..	Austin
Austin, Stephen F., Dec. 20, 1831	4 lea.	..	2/3 Lee 1/3 Burleson
Austin, Stephen F., Dec. 20, 1831	1 lea.	..	Washington
Austin, Stephen F., Dec. 20, 1831	1 lea. 8 1/2 lab.	..	Washington
Austin, Stephen F., Dec. 20, 1831	1 lea.	..	Bastrop
Austin, Stephen F., Dec. 20, 1831	1/2 lea.	..	Bastrop
Austin, Stephen F., Dec. 20, 1831	1 lea.	..	Austin
Austin, Stephen F., Dec. 20, 1831	4 lab.	..	Washington
Austin, Stephen F., Dec. 20, 1831	1 lea.	..	Wharton
Austin, Stephen F., Dec. 20, 1831	9 lab. and 187,500 sq. vs.	..	Wharton
Austin, Stephen F., Dec. 20, 1831	812,500 sq. vs.	..	Waller
Austin, Stephen F., Dec. 20, 1831	4 or 5 lab.	..	Waller
Austin, Stephen F., Dec. 18, 1830	2 lea.	..	Jackson
Austin, Stephen F., Dec. 18, 1830	1 lea.	..	Matagorda
Austin, Stephen F., Dec. 18, 1830	1 lea.	..	Brazoria
Austin, Stephen F., Dec. 18, 1830	1 lea.	..	Brazoria
Austin, Stephen F., Dec. 18, 1830	2 lab.	..	Matagorda
Austin, Stephen F., Dec. 18, 1830	3 lab.	..	Brazoria
Austin, Stephen F., Feb. 25, 1832	1 lea.	..	Brazoria
Austin, Stephen F., Feb. 25, 1832	1 lea.	..	Brazoria
Austin, Stephen F., Feb. 25, 1832	1 lea.	..	Brazoria
Austin, Stephen F., Feb. 25, 1832	1 lea.	..	Galveston
Austin, Stephen F., Feb. 25, 1832	1 lea.	..	Galveston
Austin, Stephen F., Feb. 25, 1832	3 lab.	..	Galveston
Austin, Stephen F., Feb. 25, 1832	1 lab.	..	Brazoria
Austin, Stephen F., Feb. 25, 1832	1 lab.	..	Brazoria
Austin, William T., Apr. 25, 1831	1 lea.	Austin 2	Ft. Bend
Avent, Durham, Oct. 26, 1835	1 lea.	Smyth	Freestone
Avery, Willis, Nov. 13, 1832	1 lea.	Austin 4	Williamson
Awalt, Henry, Oct. 11, 1835	1 lea.	Burnet	Freestone
Ayers, David, Nov. 15, 1832	1 lea.	Austin 4	Washington
Ayers, Lewis, June 25, 1835	1 lea. 1 lab.	McMullen and McGloin	Live Oak

Name and Date of Title	Amount	Colony or Commissioner	Present Location
Babbit, Benjamin, Nov. 22, 1832	1/4 lea.	Austin 4	Grimes
Babbit, Benjamin, Oct. 3, 1835	3/4 lea.	Austin 5	Austin
Badillo, Gordiano, July 6, 1835	1 lea.	Burnet	Houston
Badillo, Gordiano, May 15, 1834	1 lea.	Aldrete	(?)
Badillo, Gordiano, May 18, 1834	1 lea.	Aldrete	Louisiana
Badillo, Gordiano, Nov. 20, 1834	9 lea.	V. Flores	Louisiana
Badillo, Gordiano, Nov. 28, 1832	8 lea.	J. M. Mora	Houston
			Madison
			Trinity
			Walker
Bailey, Alexander, Mch. 31, 1831	1/4 lea.	Austin 2	Washington
Bailey, Henry, Nov. 14, 1834	1 lea.	Burnet	Nacogdoch
Baily, James B., July 7, 1824	1 lea.	Austin 1	Brazoria
Baine, Moses, Apr. 26, 1831	1 lea.	Austin 2	Brazos
Baird, Charles, Oct. 17, 1832	1 lea.	Zavala	2/3 Angeli
			1/3 Jasp
Baird, William, Oct. 3, 1835	1 lea.	Austin 5	Waller
Baker, Amaziah, Oct. 13, 1835	1 lea.	Austin 5	Fayette
Baker, Colbert, Nov. 23, 1832	1 lea.	Austin 2	Brazos
Baker, Daniel, D. D., May 2, 1831	1/4 lea.	Austin 2	Wharton
Baker, Isaac, June 14, 1832	1/4 lea.	DeWitt	Guadalupe
Baker, Joseph, Oct. 5, 1835	1/4 lea.	Austin 5	Waller
Baker, Joseph, Dec. 4, 1835	10 lea.	Williams, Johnson and Peebles	(?)
Baker, Larkin, June 11, 1835	1 lea.	Burnet	Cherokee
Baker, Mosely, Oct. 9, 1835	1 lea.	Zavala	Chambers
Baker, Mosely, Aug. 15, 1835	10 lea.	Williams, Johnson and Peebles	Fannin (?)
Baker, Moses, June 22, 1831	1 lea.	DeWitt	Guadalupe
Baillew, Richard, Oct. 22, 1835	1 lea.	Zavala	Orange
Balmaceda, Jose Maria, Dec. 15, 1833	1 lea.	Ximenes	Wilson
Bangs, Jose Manuel, Sept. 23, 1834	2 lea.	Lewis	Robertson
Bangs, Jose Manuel, Oct. 24, 1834	4 lea.	Lewis	Bastrop
Bankston, S. P., Aug. 22, 1835	1 lea.	Zavala	Hardin
Banuelos, Thos. and Sons-in-law, Nov. 2 5, 1834	1 1/2 lea.	Power and Hewetson	Bee
Barclay, Anderson, Feb. 18, 1835	1 lea.	Zavala	Tyler
Barela, Anastacio, Oct. 20, 1835	1 lea.	Vehlein	Angelina
Barela, See Varela			
Barfield, Roger, Nov. 25, 1835	1 lea.	Taylor	Liberty (?
Barker, Jesse, Nov. 13, 1832	1 lea.	Austin 4	Williamsor
Barker, Loman, Oct. 29, 1832	1 lea.	Austin 4	Bastrop
Barker, Martha, June 12, 1835	1 lea.	Milam	Bastrop
Barksdale, Lewis, Sept. 13, 1831	1/4 lea.	Austin 2	Fayette
Barnes, Taylor S., June 29, 1835	1/4 lea.	Burnet	Anderson
Barnett, Isaac, Oct. 16, 1835	1 lea.	Burnet	Anderson
Barnett, James, Oct. 16, 1835	1 lea.	Taylor	Liberty (?
Barnett, John S., Oct. 30, 1835	1 lea.	Taylor	Jefferson

Name and Date of Title	Amount	Colony or Commis- sioner	Present Location
Barnett, Thomas, July 10, 1824	1 lea.	Austin 1	Ft. Bend
Barnett, Thomas, May 26, 1831	1 lea.	Arciniega	Washington
Barnett, Thomas Admr., See L. McLaughlin			
Barnhill, William, Oct. 14, 1835	1 lea. 1 lab.	Smyth	Wood
Barr, William, May 28, 1798	(?)	Zepeda	Nacogdoches (?)
Barr and Davenport, Dec. 16, 1805	(?)	Procela	Angelina
Barrazo, Antonio, Aug. 3, 1835	1 lea. 1 lab.	Taylor	Houston
Barrera, Gertrudis, July 21, 1833	2 1/2 lea.	Aldrete	Goliad
Barrera, Gertrudis, Aug. 6, 1833	1 1/2 lea.	Aldrete	Goliad
Barrera, Gertrudis, Aug. 9, 1833	1 lea.	Aldrete	Goliad- Refugio
Barrera, Manuel, Nov. 29, 1833	3 lea.	Ximenes	Wilson
Barrett, William, Nov. 26, 1832	1/2 lea.	Austin 3	Brazoria
Barrett, William, June 4, 1827 and A. Harris	1 lea.	Austin 1	Ft. Bend
Barrow, John M., Aug. 10, 1835	1/4 lea.	Robertson	Milam
Barrow, Thomas H., Mch. 25, 1835	24 lab.	Robertson	McLennan
Barrow, Thomas H., June 10, 1835	1 lab.	Robertson	Falls
Barrow, Thomas H., Dec. 1, 1832	1 lea.	Austin 4	Brazos
Barrow, Solomon, Apr. 25, 1831	19 lab. and 680,000 sq. vs.	Madero	Chambers
Bartee, William, Aug. 25, 1835	1 lea.	Burnet	Cherokee
Bartels, William, Nov. 30, 1834	1/4 lea.	Power and Hewetson	Bee
Bartlett, Jesse, Oct. 19, 1832	1 lea.	Austin 2	Fayette
Bartlett, Joseph, Nov. 20, 1834	1/4 lea.	Power and Hewetson	Goliad
Bartlett, Joseph C., Feb. 9, 1836	1/4 lea.	Austin 5	Waller (?)
Bartlett, Solon, Oct. 30, 1834	1/4 lea.	Power and Hewetson	Goliad
Bartolo, Jose, Mch. 25, 1835		De Leon	Victoria
Bartolo, Jose, May 1, 1835	1/4 lea.	De Leon	DeWitt
Barton, Benjamin, Apr. 4, 1831	1/4 lea.	Austin 2	Bastrop
Barton, Elisha W., Apr. 4, 1831	1 lea.	Austin 2	Bastrop
Barton, Kimber W., July 10, 1831	1 lea.	DeWitt	DeWitt
Barton, William, Apr. 4, 1831	1 lea.	Austin 2	2/3 Bastrop 1/3 Fayette
Basquez, Augustin, Nov. 21, 1835	1 lea.	Taylor	(?)
Basquez, Gregorio, Oct. 7, 1833	11 lea.	Lessassier	Falls
Basquez, Sebastian, Sept. 10, 1835 See Vasquez	1 lea.	Taylor	Jefferson (?)
Bassett, Thomas, Nov. 23, 1835	1 lea.	Taylor	Jefferson (?)
Bastrop (de) Baron, June 8, 1824	4 lea.	Saucedo	Comal (?)
Bastrop, Town of, June 8, 1832	4 lea.	Austin 4	Bastrop
Bateman, Andrew D., Oct. 12, 1835	1 lea.	Zavala	San Augustine
Bateman, Simon, Apr. 22, 1831	1 lea.	DeWitt	2/3 Gonzales 1/3 DeWitt
Bates, Samuel, Sept. 4, 1835	1 lea.	Zavala	Angelina
Bates, Seth H., Aug. 18, 1835	24 lab.	Robertson	Falls
Bates, Seth H., Aug. 18, 1835	1 lab.	Robertson	Falls

157

Name and Date of Title	Amount	Colony or Commissioner	Present Location
Battle, Mills M., May 31, 1827	1 lea.	Austin 1	Ft. Bend
Battle, Mills M., Aug. 10, 1824	1 lea.	Austin 1	Matagorda
Berry and Williams			
Baudrand, Anthony, Feb. 6, 1836	1 lea.	Austin 5	3/4 Caldwe 1/4 Bastr (?)
Baugh, Robert G., Oct. 5, 1835	1/4 lea.	Austin 5	Fayette
Baumacher, John Andrew See Francis Dietrich			
Baxter, William, Feb. 6, 1833	1 lea.	Austin 3	Matagorda
Baylis, Daniel E., Nov. 7, 1835	1 lea.	Robertson	Williamsor (?)
Baylis, Daniel E., See Isaac Van Dorn			
Beales, Hiram, May 23, 1835	1/4 lea.	Milam	Bastrop
Bean, Pedro Elias, Aug. 13, 1828	1 lea. ·	J. M. Mora	Cherokee
Bean, Pedro Elias, Sept. 26, 1833	5 3/4 lea.	Aldrete	Liberty (?) Chambers (?)
Bean, Pedro Elias, Dec. 14, 1833	2 1/4 lea.	Aldrete	(?)
Bean, Pedro Elias, Oct. 20, 1835	1 lea.	Berry	Houston (?
Bean, William, Sept. 24, 1828	1 lea.	J. M. Mora	Smith (?)
Beard, James, Aug. 10, 1824	1 lea.	Austin 1	Ft. Bend
Beardslee, James, Mch. 31, 1831	1 lea.	Austin 2	3/4 Fayette 1/4 Wash ington
Beasley, Berry, Oct. 28, 1835	1 lea.	Vehlein	San Jacinto
Beasley, William, Jan. 25, 1836	1 lea.	Austin 5	Grimes (?)
Beasley, William, Sept. 30, 1835	1 lea.	Vehlein	Polk
Beason, Benjamin, Aug. 7, 1824	1 lea.	Austin 1	Colorado
Beaty, Edward, October 21, 1830	1 lea.	Austin 3	Jackson
Beaty, John, July 29, 1835	1 lea.	Burnet	Houston
Beaumer, Barnhart and Hendrick, Feb. 4, 1836	1 lea.	Austin 5	Bastrop (?
Becerra, Rafael, Sept. 15, 1835	1 lea.	Vehlein	5/6 Polk 1/6 Trini
Beckham, A. W., Oct. 15, 1835	1 lea.	Burnet	Houston
Bedford, Jose Ramon, June 6, 1832	1/4 lea.	DeWitt	Guadalupe
Bedford, Ramon, Sept. 5, 1835	1 lea.	Berry	Lamar
Beers, David, May 2, 1835	1 lea.	Vehlein	San Jacinto
Bega (de la), Jose Luis, May 31, 1792	(?)	Zepeda	Nacogdoche (?)
Bega (de la), Jose Luis, June 13, 1810	720,000 sq.vs.	Procela	Nacogdoche
Bega (de la), Jose Luis, June 11, 1810	1 1/2 lea.	Procela	Nacogdoche (?)
Bega (de la), Jose Luis, June 13, 1810	1 lea.	Procela	Nacogdoche
Bega (de la), Jose Luis, June 11, 1810	1 lea.	Procela	Nacogdoche (?)
See Vega			
Bela, Bentura, Oct. 22, 1835	1/3 lea.	Taylor	Hardin
Belcher, Isham G., May 27, 1828	1/4 lea.	Austin 2	Austin
Belknap, Charles, See Geo. Brown			
Bell, Jackson, Dec. 14, 1835	7 lea.	Williams, Johnson and Peebles	(?)

Name and Date of Title	Amount	Colony or Commis-sioner	Present Location
Bell, James, Dec. 8, 1835	10 lea.	Williams, Johnson and Peebles	(?)
Bell, James, Feb. 23, 1836	1/4 lea.	Austin 5	Austin (?)
Bell, James, Apr. 8, 1831	1/4 lea.	Austin 2	Fayette
Bell, James, Dec. 2, 1832	3/4 lea.	Austin 2	4/5 Walker 1/5 Grimes
Bell, James, W., Nov. 30, 1832	1 lea.	Austin 2	Burleson
Bell, Josiah H., Aug. 7, 1824	1 1/2 lea.	Austin 1	Brazoria
Bell, Josiah H., Oct. 27, 1830	1 lea.	Austin 3	Jackson
Bell, Thomas, Mch. 22, 1831	1 lea.	Austin 2	Austin
Bell, Thomas, Dec. 12, 1835	10 lea.	Williams, Johnson and Peebles	(?)
Bell, Thomas B., Aug. 16, 1824	1 lea.	Austin 1	Brazoria
Bell, Thomas H., Feb. 23, 1836	1 lea.	Austin 5	Burleson (?)
Bellows, George S., May 5, 1831	1 lea.	Austin 2	Harris
Benard, Geraseux, Mch. 16, 1835	1/4 lea.	Vehlein	Walker
Benavides, Eugenio, Jan. 5, 1833	1 lea.	De Leon	Victoria
Benavides, See Venabides			
Benham, William D., July 30, 1835	1/3 lea.	McMullen and McGloin	McMullen
Benites, Maria Manuela, Apr. 23, 1835		De Leon	
Bennett, Caleb, Nov. 13, 1834	1 lea.	Power and Hewetson	Goliad
Bennett, Charles H., Oct. 16, 1832	1 lea.	Austin 2	Burleson
Bennett, Valentine, Nov. 8, 1831	1/4 lea.	DeWitt	DeWitt
Bennett, Zimri, Nov. 29, 1834	1 lea.	Burnet	Nacogdoches
Benton, Charles, May 27, 1828	1/4 lea.	Austin 2	Austin
Berger, John, See John Burgess			
Bermea, Andres, July 29, 1835	1 lea.	Vehlein	Nacogdoches
Bermea, Pedro, Oct. 20, 1835	5 lea.	Del Moral	3 Harrison 2 Liberty
Bermea, Pedro, July 21, 1835	1/4 lea.	Burnet	Houston
Bernal, Maximo, Apr. 23, 1835		De Leon	Victoria
Berry, David, Nov. 20, 1832	1 lea.	Austin 2	Fayette
Berry, Esther, July 21, 1831	24 lab.	DeWitt	Caldwell
Berry, Esther, Sept. 20, 1831	900,500 sq. vs.	DeWitt	Gonzales
Berry, Francis, May 15, 1831	24 lab.	DeWitt	Caldwell
Berry, Francis, Aug. 23, 1831	1 lab.	DeWitt	Gonzales
Berry, John, May 2, 1831			Liberty
Berry, John F., Apr. 7, 1831	1 lea.	Austin 2	Fayette
Berry, Mandus, See Mills M. Battle			
Berry, Milly, Nov. 20, 1835	1 lea.	Smyth	(?)
Berry, Radford, Nov. 21, 1833	1/4 lea.	Austin 2	Madison
Berry, Radford, Oct. 14, 1835	3/4 lea. 1 lab.	Smyth	Lamar (?)
Berry, Thomas O., Oct. 25, 1835	1 lea.	Austin 5	Fayette
Berryman, William, Dec. 10, 1834	1 lea.	Robertson	Bell (?)
Bertram, Peter, Nov. 24, 1830	1 lea. 1 lab.	Austin 3	lea. Mata-gorda lab. Brazoria

Name and Date of Title	Amount	Colony or Commis- sioner	Present Location
Best, Humphry, Oct. 21, 1835	1 lea.	Austin 5	Lee
Best, Isaac, Aug. 19, 1824	1 lea.	Austin 1	Waller
Bettner, Charles A., Nov. 20, 1832	1/4 lea.	Austin 2	Ft. Bend
Betts, Jacob, Aug. 19, 1824	1 lea.	Austin 1	Matagorda
Bevil, John Jr., Nov. 10, 1834	1/4 lea.	Zavala	Jasper
Bevil, John, Oct. 29, 1834	1 lea.	Zavala	Jasper
Biegel, Joseph, Nov. 29, 1832	1 lea.	Austin 4	Fayette
Biggam, Francis, July 10, 1824	2 lea. 1 lab.	Austin 1	1 Brazoria 1 Wharton lab. Waller
Bigner, Frederick, Oct. 14, 1835	1/4 lea.	Zavala	Jefferson
Binns, Henry, Aug. 29, 1835	1 lea.	Zavala	Hardin
Bird, John, Oct. 14, 1831	1 lea.	Austin 2	Burleson
Bird, Thomas, May 7, 1831	1 lea.	Austin 2	Lee
Birdsell, Warren, Nov. 14, 1834	1 lea.	Vehlein	Walker
Birke, Anna, June 25, 1835	1 lea. 1 lab.	McMullen and McGloin	Bee
Bissell, Theodore, Mch. 19, 1835	1 lea.	Milam	Travis
Bittick, Jonathan, Oct. 23, 1835	7 lab. and 884,722 sq. vs.	Smyth	
Black, John S., Apr. 6, 1831	1 lea.	Austin 2	Grimes
Black, Marcus D., Apr. 6, 1831	1/4 lea.	Austin 2	Grimes
Blackman, Bennett, June 25, 1835	1 lea.	Zavala	Jefferson
Blackman, Burrell, Mch. 21, 1835	1 lea.	Vehlein	Tyler
Blackman, Joab John, July 24, 1835	1 lea.	Vehlein	Tyler
Blair, Alexander, Oct. 10, 1835	1/4 lea.	Austin 5	Burleson
Blair, George, Dec. 1, 1831	24 lab.	DeWitt	Gonzales
Blair, George, June 28, 1832	1 lab.	DeWitt	Gonzales
Blair, John, Feb. 19, 1835	1 lea.	Zavala	Jefferson
Blair, Samuel, Sept. 10, 1834	1/4 lea.	Power and Hewetson	Refugio
Blake, Bennett, Aug. 27, 1835	1 lea.	Vehlein	Montgomer
Blake, Bennett, Aug. 20, 1835	3 lea.	Williams, Johnson and Peebles	Lamar (?)
Blakey, Thomas W., Dec. 16, 1832	1 lea.	Austin 4	Brazos
Blalock, James, Feb. 22, 1836	1 lea.	Austin 5	Bastrop
Blanchard, Pliny, May 30, 1835	1 lea.	Vehlein	Houston
Blanchet, Pierre, July 7, 1835	1/4 lea.	Vehlein	Walker
Blanco, Jose Manuel, Nov. 25, 1834	1 lea.	Power and Hewetson	1/2 Goliad 1/2 Refug
Blanco, Victor, See A. F. Gutierres and Miguel Rabago			
Bland, John, June 18, 1835	1 lea.	Vehlein	Polk
Bloodgood, William, Aug. 10, 1824	1 lea.	Austin 1	3/4 Chambe 1/4 Harri
Bloodgood, William, Aug. 27, 1835	3/4 lea.	Vehlein	10 1/2 lab. Liberty 7 1/2 Chambers

Name and Date of Title	Amount	Colony or Commis-sioner	Present Location
Blossom, Hiram, Oct. 10, 1835	1 lea.	Smyth	Harrison
Blount, James H., Nov. 5, 1835	1 lea.	Vehlein	Jasper
Blunt, James, Mch. 20, 1835	1 lea.	Vehlein	Tyler
Blunt, John S., July 18, 1835	1 lea.	Vehlein	Houston
Blythe, James, Nov. 5, 1835	1 lea. 1 lab.	Taylor	Hardin
Boatwright, Amy, Oct. 24, 1835	1 lea.	Austin 5	Madison
Boatwright, Friend, Oct. 23, 1835	1 lea.	Austin 5	Lee
Boatwright, Richard, Oct. 24, 1835	1 lea.	Austin 5	Wharton
Boatwright, Thomas, Oct. 20, 1835	1 lea.	Austin 5	Madison
Boatwright, Thomas, July 27, 1824	1 lea.	Austin 1	Austin
Boden, Jean Baptiste, Sept. 12, 1835	1/3 lea.	Taylor	Houston
Boden, Juan Lorenzo, July 30, 1835	1 lea.	Vehlein	Trinity
Boden, Nicolas, June 29, 1835	1 lea.	Vehlein	Cherokee
Boden, Maria Teresa, Oct. 9, 1835	1 lea.	Vehlein	Chambers
Boden, Maria Luisa, Apr. 13, 1835 (Widow)	1 lea.	Vehlein	Trinity
Bomen, Stephen, Oct. 13, 1835	1 lea.	Taylor	Jefferson ?
Bontan, Jose Antonio, June 4, 1835	1 lea.	Burnet	Angelina
Boon, Simon, Oct. 7, 1835	1 lea.	Burnet	Henderson
Booth, Robert, May 2, 1831		Madero	Liberty
Borden, Gail, Mch. 4, 1831	1 lea.	Austin 2	Washington
Borden, Gail Jr., Mch. 29, 1831	1 lea.	Austin 2	Ft. Bend
Borden, Gail Jr., Aug. 12, 1835	10 lea.	Williams, Johnson and Peebles	(?)
Borden, John P., Nov. 20, 1832	1/4 lea.	Austin 2	Wharton
Borden, John P., Aug. 7, 1835	10 lea.	Williams, Johnson and Peebles	(?)
Borden, Paschal P., Mch. 4, 1831	1/4 lea.	Austin 2	Washington
Borden, Paschal P., Aug. 12, 1835	10 lea.	Williams, Johnson and Peebles	(?)
Borden, Thomas, See H. W. Johnson			
Borden, Thomas H., Mch. 13, 1831	1/3 lea.	Austin 2	Washington
Borden, Thomas H., Nov. 22, 1830	1/3 lea.	Austin 3	Brazoria
Boren, Matthew, Feb. 16, 1836	1 lea.	Austin 5	Madison ?
Boren, Nancy, Sept. 1, 1835	1 lea.	Robertson	Milam
Borrego, Jose Maria, Nov. 10, 1835	11 lea.	Berry	(?)
Borsoley, Maria Josefa, July 3, 1835	1 lea.	Vehlein	Cherokee
Bostic, Caleb and R. Brotherington, July 24, 1824	1 lea.	Austin 1	Matagorda
Bostick, James H., Mch. 5, 1831	1/4 lea.	Austin 2	Austin
Bostick, James H., Dec. 5, 1832	3/4 lea.	Austin 2	Bastrop
Bostick, Levi, Apr. 23, 1831	1 lea.	Austin 2	Fayette
Boulter, James, Aug. 18, 1835	1 lea.	Vehlein	Polk
Bourland, Gabriel L., July 17, 1835	1 lea.	Zavala	Sabine
Bourland, Oliver P., Sept. 21, 1835	1/4 lea.	Zavala	Sabine
Bowen, Eli A., June 20, 1835	1 lea.	Burnet	Anderson
Bowen, John, Nov. 15, 1834	1 lea.	Power and Hewetson	San Patricio

Name and Date of Title	Amount	Colony or Commissioner	Present Location
Bowen, Sylvester, Oct. 22, 1830	1 lea.	Austin 3	Jackson
Bowers, John, July 20, 1835	1/3 lea.	McMullen and McGloin	Atascosa
Bowie, James, Apr. 20, 1831	1 lea.	Austin 2	Colorado
Bowker, Elias, June 22, 1835	1/4 lea.	Zavala	San Augustin
Bowles, Benjamin, Apr. 5, 1831	1 lea.	Austin 2	Bastrop
Bowlin, Solomon, Jan. 9, 1835	1 lea.	Burnet	Anderson
Bowman, Abraham, June 20, 1831 and C. K. Reese	1 lea.	Austin 3	Matagorda
Bowman, John, Apr. 6, 1831	1 lea.	Austin 2	Grimes
Bowman, John and Henry Williams, Aug. 21, 1824	1 lea.	Austin 1	Matagorda
Bowman, Margareti C., July 4, 1835	1 lea.	Robertson	McLennan
Bowman, Samuel, Oct. 16, 1835	1 lea.	Austin 5	Grimes
Box, James E., May 9, 1835	1/4 lea.	Burnet	Houston
Box, John, July 30, 1835	1 lea.	Vehlein	Houston
Box, John A., May 8, 1831	1 lea.	Burnet	Anderson
Box, John M., June 11, 1835	1 lea.	Burnet	Houston
Box, Nelson, Mch. 15, 1835	1/4 lea.	Vehlein	Houston
Box, Robin,W. May 12, 1835	1 lea.	Burnet	Anderson
Box, Samuel C., May 8, 1835	1 lea.	Burnet	Anderson
Box, Stephen, April 6, 1835	1 lea.	Vehlein	Houston
Box, Stephen, Jr., Aug. 15, 1835	1/4 lea.	Vehlein	Houston
Box, Stillwell, Aug. 15, 1835	1 lea.	Vehlein	Houston
Box, William S., Oct. 20, 1835	1 lea.	Burnet	Cherokee
Boyd, John, Mch. 25, 1835	1 lea.	Robertson	McLennan
Boyd, John, July 13, 1835	1 lea.	Burnet	Limestone
Bracey, McLin, Jan. 7, 1833	1 lea.	Austin 4	Waller
Bradberry, Jabez, Nov. 29, 1835	1 lea. 1 lab.	Taylor	Tyler & Har
Bradley, Edward R., Aug. 10, 1824	1 lea.	Austin 1	Brazoria
Bradley, James, Feb. 15, 1836	1/4 lea.	Austin 5	Bastrop (?)
Bradley, John, July 8, 1824	1 lea.	Austin 1	Brazoria
Bradley, John M., Nov. 22, 1835	1 lea. 1 lab.	Smyth	(?)
Bradley, Mark M., Aug. 27, 1835	1 lea.	Zavala	Hardin
Bradley, Thomas, See S. T. Angier			
Brake, David, Nov. 29, 1835	1 lea.	Taylor	(?)
Branch, Humphries, Nov. 21, 1831	24 lab.	DeWitt	Guadalupe
Branch, Humphries, Nov. 29, 1831	1 lab.	DeWitt	Guadalupe
Brand, David W., Nov. 25, 1831	1/4 lea.	DeWitt	Gonzales
Bray, James and Patrick, Oct. 12,1834	1 1/4 lea.	Power and Hewetson	Goliad
Breece, Thomas H., Feb. 26, 1835	1 lea.	Zavala	Orange
Breedlove, A. W., Apr. 20, 1831	1 lea.	Austin 2	4/5 Lavaca 1/5 Colora
Breen, Charles, May 24, 1827	1 lea.	Austin 1	Brazoria
Breker, Henry, July 23, 1835	1/4 lea.	De Leon	Lavaca
Brennan, Maria, Dec. 2, 1835	1 lea.	McMullen and McGloin	Live Oak
Brewer, Green Berry, Oct. 26, 1835	1 lea.	Smyth	Freestone
Brewer, Henry, Jan. 13, 1835	1 lea.	Burnet	Nacogdoche
Brewer, William, Sept. 9, 1835	1/3 lea.	Smyth	Rusk

Name and Date of Title	Amount	Colony or Commis- sioner	Present Location
Bridge, William, Nov. 20, 1832	1 lea.	Austin 2	Washington
Bridges, John, Nov. 23, 1835	1 lea. 1 lab.	Taylor	Liberty (?)
Bridges, Ross M., Nov. 21, 1835	1 lea.	Zavala	(?)
Bridges, William B., July 24, 1824	1 lea.	Austin 1	Jackson
Brien, Isabel, Sept. 10, 1834	1 lea.	Power and Hewetson	Refugio
Brigham, Asa, Nov. 30, 1830	1 lea.	Austin 3	1/2 Brazoria 1/2 Galveston
Bright, David, July 15, 1824	1 lea. 1 lab.	Austin 1	lea. Ft. Bend lab. Austin
Brinson, Enoch, Aug. 7, 1824	1 lea.	Austin 1	Harris
Brock, Caleb, May 5, 1831	1 lea.	DeWitt	Caldwell
Brookfield, William, May 20, 1831	1 lea.	Austin 2	Fayette
Brookfield, William Chas., Oct. 26, 1835	1/3 lea.	Smyth	Harrison
Brooks, Bluford, Aug. 10, 1824	1 lea.	Austin 1	Burleson
Brooks, Geo. W., Aug. 22, 1835	1 lea.	Zavala	Hardin
Brooks, Gilbert, Aug. 17, 1835	1 lea.	Vehlein	Harris
Brookshire, Nathan, Oct. 5, 1835	1 lea.	Austin 5	1/2 Ft. Bend 1/2 Waller
Brotherson, Robert, See Caleb R. Bostic			
Brown, Alexander, May 17, 1831	1 lea.	Austin 2	Grimes
Brown, Bernard, March 23, 1835	1 lea.	De Leon	Lavaca
Brown, David., Jan. 15, 1835	1 lea.	Zavala	Jefferson
Brown, George and Charles Belknap, May 22, 1827	1 lea.	Austin 1	Ft. Bend
Brown, Henry, May 20, 1835	1 lea.	Milam	Comal
Brown, Hiram, Dec. 23, 1834	1 lea.	Zavala	Jefferson
Brown, James, Dec. 10, 1835	1 lea.	Taylor	Hardin (?)
Brown, James, Mch. 14, 1835	1 lea.	De Leon	Lavaca
Brown, James, Nov. 15, 1834	1 lea.	Power and Hewetson	Bee
Brown, Jeremiah, April 18, 1831	1 lea.	Austin 2	Lavaca
Brown, John, Aug. 19, 1824	1 lea. 1 lab.	Austin 1	lea. Harris lab. Waller
Brown, John, Mch. 30, 1830	1 lea.	Austin 3	Jackson
Brown, John, Dec. 10, 1830	1/4 lea.	Austin 3	2/3 Brazoria 1/3 Galveston
Brown, Lucretia, Oct. 16, 1835	1 lea.	Zavala	Jasper
Brown, Mesina, Nov. 2, 1835	1 lea.	Taylor	San Jacinto
Brown, Peggy (Widow, J. Frazier), May 3, 1831	1 lea.	Austin 2	Fayette
Brown, Reuben, May 20, 1835	1 lea.	Burnet	Anderson
Brown, Rosa, Sept. 25, 1834	1 lea.	Power and Hewetson	3/4 Refugio 1/4 Bee
Brown, Solomon, Apr. 16, 1828	1 lea.	Austin 2	2/3 Harris 1/3 Montgomery
Brown, William S., July 29, 1824	1 lea.	Austin 1	Washington
Browne, Samuel P., Mch. 29, 1831	1 lea.	Austin 2	Fayette
Brownrigg, George B., Nov. 23, 1835	1 lea.	Taylor	Polk (?)

Name and Date of Title	Amount	Colony or Commissioner	Present Location
Brush, Elkana and 2 sons, Oct. 30, 1834	1 1/2 lea.	Power and Hewetson	Goliad
Bryan, John W., July 17, 1835	1/4 lea.	Burnet	Anderson
Bryan, Moses Austin, Oct. 20, 1835	1/4 lea.	Austin 5	Washington
Bryan, William Joel, Jan. 29, 1836	1/4 lea.	Austin 5	Washington
Buckhanan, James, Oct. 19, 1835	1 lea.	Austin 5	Burleson
Buckner, Aylett C., July 24, 1824	1 lea.	Austin 1	Matagorda
Buckner, Aylett C., Aug. 24, 1824	2 lab.	Austin 1	Matagorda
Bueno, See Vueno			
Buentello, Tomas, Aug. 4, 1833	1 lea.	Aldrete	Goliad
Buford, Thomas Y., Sept. 4, 1835	10 lea.	Grant, Durst and Williams	Grayson (?
Bullock, Allen C., Mch. 21, 1835	1 lea.	Burnet	Leon
Bullock, James W., Jan 17, 1835	1 lea.	Zavala	Jefferson
Bundick, Samuel C., Nov. 12, 1832	1 lea.	Austin 3	Galveston
Burditt, William B., Apr. 28, 1835	1 lea.	Vehlein	Walker
Burton, John W., Apr. 8, 1835	1/4 lea.	Milam	Bastrop
Burgess, John, Aug. 10, 1835	1/4 lea.	Robertson	Hill
Burgess, John, Aug. 27, 1835	1 lea.	Vehlein	Polk
Burk, James, Nov. 25, 1834	1/4 lea.	Power and Hewetson	Bee
Burk, William, Sept. 16, 1834	1 lea.	Power and Hewetson	Bee
Burke, Benjamin, Oct. 28, 1834	1 lea.	Zavala	Tyler
Burket, David, May 10, 1832 (See David Burgett)	24 lab.	DeWitt	4/5 Lavaca 1/5 Gonza
Burket, David, Nov. 26, 1831	1 lab.	DeWitt	Gonzales
Burks, John D., Aug. 27, 1835	1 lea.	Vehlein	Polk
Burleson, Edward, Apr. 4, 1831	1 lea.	Austin 2	Bastrop
Burleson, Hopson, Oct. 16, 1835	1 lea.	Burnet	Freestone
Burleson, Jacob, Feb. 9, 1836	1 lea.	Austin 5	Burleson ?
Burleson, James, Oct. 29, 1832	1 lea.	Austin 4	Travis
Burleson, James, Oct. 3, 1835	1 lea.	Austin 5	2/3 Bastrop 1/3 Lee
Burleson, John, Oct. 30, 1832	1 lea.	Austin 4	Travis
Burleson, Jonathan, Feb. 16, 1836	1 lea.	Austin 5	Caldwell (?
Burleson, Jonathan, Dec. 4, 1832	1/4 lea.	Austin 4	Bastrop
Burleson, Joseph Sr., Oct. 8, 1835	1 lea.	Austin 5	Caldwell
Burnett, Crawford, June 17, 1831	1 lea.	Austin 2	Brazos
Burnett, Crawford, Sept. 5, 1835	1 lea.	Burnet	Cherokee
Burnett, Pumphrey, Nov. 14, 1830	1/2 lea.	Austin 3	Matagorda
Burnett, Pumphrey and A. S. Sojourner, July 24, 1824	1 lea.	Austin 1	Matagorda
Burnett, William, Mch. 25, 1831	1 lea.	Austin 2	Austin
Burney, Shadrack, Apr. 24, 1831	1/4 lea.	Madero	Chambers
Burney, William, Apr. 6, 1831	1 lea.	Austin 2	Grimes
Burnham, Jesse, Aug. 16, 1824	1 lea. 1 lab.	Austin 1	lea. Fayette lab. Color
Burnham, Jesse, Apr. 30, 1831	1 lea.	Austin 2	3/5 Colorad 2/5 Fayet
Burnham, Stephen, Sept. 12, 1835	1/3 lea.	Smyth	Cherokee

Name and Date of Title	Amount	Colony or Commis-sioner	Present Location
Burns, Arthur, July 9, 1831	1 lea.	DeWitt	DeWitt
Burns, Squire, July 10, 1831	1/4 lea.	DeWitt	DeWitt
Burrel, A. A., Sept. 2, 1835	1 lea.	Zavala	Hardin
Burroughs, James, June 15, 1835	1 lea.	Zavala	(?)
Burrus, Samuel, July 24, 1835	1/4 lea.	Vehlein	Angelina
Burrus, Thomas, Feb. 5, 1835	1 lea.	Vehlein	Polk
Burton, Isaac W., Sept. 18, 1835	1 lea.	Burnet	Henderson
Burton, John M., Mch. 24, 1831	1/4 lea.	Austin 2	Washington
Burton, John M., Nov. 21, 1832	3/4 lea.	Austin 2	Fayette
Burton, William B., Oct. 22, 1835	1 lea.	Zavala	Jefferson
Busby, William, Oct. 22, 1835	1 lea.	Vehlein	San Jacinto
Bush, John, May 13, 1835	1/4 lea.	Vehlein	Angelina
Bush, John, Dec. 5, 1835	1/3 lea.	Smyth	Upshur (?)
Bustamente, Manuel, ? ? ?	123,790 sq. vs.	?	Nacogdoches ?
Butler, Joseph, Oct. 17, 1835	1 lea.	Zavala	Jefferson
Butler, George, Nov. 5, 1835	1 lea.	Zavala	(?)
Buye, Margarita, Sept. 24, 1835	1 lea.	Taylor	Liberty
Byarle, Adam, Oct. 2, 1835	1/4 lea.	Smyth	Jasper
Bynum, William H., Feb. 9. (?)	1 lea.	Robertson	Lee
Byrd, Micajah, July 16, 1824	1 lea.	Austin 1	Washington
Byrd, Thomas, Mch. 5, 1835	1 lea.	Robertson	Falls
Byrne, John, Apr. 9, 1831	1 lea.	Austin 2	Colorado
Byrne, Mary, Oct. 7, 1834	1 lea.	Power and Hewetson	Refugio
Byrne, Matthew, July 12, 1835	1/3 lea.	McMullen and McGloin	McMullen
Cabazos, Jose Antonio, Nov. 28, 1835	7 lea. 1 lab.	Capistran	Nueces
Cabazos, Narciso, Apr. 12, 1835	1 lea.	De Leon	Calhoun
Cabazos, Narciso, Apr. 21, 1835		De Leon	Victoria
Cabrera, Fernando, Oct. 5, 1835	1 lea. 1 lab.	Berry	Louisiana (?)
Caddel, Andrew, Apr. 14, 1835	1 lea.	Zavala	San Augustine
Cadena, Jesus, Jan. 15, 1834	7 lea.	Vasquez	DeWitt and Goliad (?)
Cadena (de) Juana B., Aug. 28, 1835	1 lea.	Smyth	Rusk
Cain, James C., Nov. 26, 1835	1/3 lea.	Smyth	(?)
Calcote, James, Nov. 24, 1835	1 lea.	Taylor	Liberty
Calderon, Antonio, Nov. 5, 1835	1/2 lea.	Smyth	Wood
Caldwell, John, June 8, 1831	1 lea.	Austin 3	Wharton
Caldwell, Mathew, June 22, 1831	1 lea.	DeWitt	Lavaca
Caldwell, Pinkney, Sept. 8, 1835	3 lea.	Grant, Durst and Williams	Grayson (?)
Callahan, Moris A. and Allan Vince, Aug. 3, 1824	1 lea.	Austin 1	Harris
Callahan, John H., Oct. 19, 1835	1 lea.	Austin 5	Harris
Calvillo, Maria, Mch. 23, 1834	1 lea. 1 lab.	Seguin	Wilson
Calvit, Alexander, Aug. 3, 1824	1 lea. 2 lab.	Austin 1	1 lea. 1 lab. Brazoria 1 lab. Waller

Name and Date of Title	Amount	Colony or Commissioner	Present Location
Calvit, Frederick, Jr., Dec. 8, 1830	1 lea.	Austin 3	Brazoria
Cameron, John, Oct. 31, 1834	2 lea.	Power and Hewetson	Victoria (?)
Campbell, Cyrus, Oct. 22, 1835	1 lea.	Austin 5	Grimes
Campbell, Cyrus and Bros., Aug. 24, 1831	1 lea.	DeWitt	Guadalupe
Campbell, Daniel H., Aug. 4, 1835	1 lab.	Robertson	Falls
Campbell, Daniel H., July 14, 1835	1 lea.	Robertson	Bell
Campbell, David W., June 22, 1835	1/4 lea.	Robertson	McLennan
Campbell, Elizabeth, Apr. 7, 1831	1 lea.	Austin 2	Fayette
Campbell, James, Nov. 27, 1832	1 lea.	Austin 4	Lavaca
Campbell, Nathaniel, Nov. 4, 1835	1/4 lea.	Robertson	Williamson
Campbell, Walter, Nov. 2, 1835	1/4 lea.	Robertson	Williamson
Campbell, William, Oct. 15, 1835	1 lea.	Zavala	Tyler
Campos, Juan Vicente, vol. 29, p. 214			
Campos, Maximo, Mch. 31, 1835	1 lea.	De Leon	Calhoun
Campos, Maximo, Apr. 8, 1835		De Leon	Victoria
Camunez, Juana, Aug. 24, 1835	1 lea.	Smyth	Rusk
Canfield, Alanson, Oct. 13, 1835	1 lea.	Zavala	Sabine
Canfield, Henry, Aug. 30, 1835	1 lea.	Zavala	Sabine
Cannon, Thomas, Jan. 27, 1836	1/4 lea.	Austin 5	Burleson (?
Canon, William, Mch. 29, 1835	1 lea.	Milam	Travis
Cano, Juan, Apr. 11, 1835	1 lea.	De Leon	Calhoun
Cantu, Eustaquio, Apr. 10, 1835	1 lea.	De Leon	Calhoun
Cantu, Jesus, Nov. 5, 1831	2 lea.	Navarro	Guadalupe
Cantu, Jesus, Sept. 11, 1835	5 lea.	Berry	3 Louisiana; 2 (?)
Cantu, Jesus, Dec. 20, 1834	5 lea.	V. Flores	Lamar and Fannin (?)
Cantun, Jesus, Sept. 12, 1835	1 lea.	Robertson	McLennan
Cantun, Maria, July 19, 1835	1 lea.	Burnet	Freestone
Capeny, John, Mch. 20, 1835	1/4 lea.	De Leon	Lavaca
Caraway, Adam, Dec. 7, 1835	1 lea.	Taylor	Tyler and Liberty (?
Carbajal, Dolores, Dec. 17, 1834	1 lea.	Power and Hewetson	Goliad
Carbajal, Jose Luis, Mch. 25, 1833	1 lea.	De Leon	Victoria
Carbajal, Jose Maria Jesus, Mch. 23, 1833	1 lea. 1 lab.	De Leon	Victoria
Carbajal, Manuel, Mch. 18, 1835	1/4 lea.	De Leon	Victoria
Carbajal, Nicolas, See Dolores Carbajal			
Carbajal, Nicolas, See Gertrudis Barrera			
Cardenas (de), Francisco, Apr. 4, 1835		De Leon	Victoria
Cardenas (de), Gregorio, Apr. 24, 1835		De Leon	Victoria
Cardenas (de), Jesus, Apr. 18, 1834	11 lea.	Soto	3/4 Dimmit 1/4 Lasall
Cardon, Juan, Dec. 27, 1834	1 lea.	Robertson	Bell
Carlisle, Lawrence and James, Oct. 3, 1834	1/2 lea.	Power and Hewetson	Refugio
Carlisle, Robert, Oct. 31, 1834	1 lea.	Power and Hewetson	3/4 San Patricio 1/4 F

Name and Date of Title	Amount	Colony or Commissioner	Present Location
Carmona, Juan, Oct. 22, 1835	1 lea.	Vehlein	9/10 Trinity 1/10 Polk
Carmona, Macedonio, Aug. 27, 1835	1 lea.	Vehlein	1/4 Trinity 3/4 Polk
Carmona, Maria de los Angeles, Aug. 11, 1835	1 lea.	Smyth	Smith
Carnaghan, Mary, Sept. 10, 1835	1 lea.	Robertson	Burleson
Carnal, Patrick, Sept. 17, 1835	1/4 lea.	Vehlein	Polk
Carnes, Noah, Oct. 20, 1835	1 lea.	Austin 5	Fayette
Caro, Jose, Mch. 22, 1808	2 lea.	G. Mora	San Augustine (?)
Caro, Jose Agaton, May 30, 1835	1/4 lea.	Burnet	Smith
Caro, Jose Antonio, June 29, 1835	1 lea.	Burnet	Nacogdoches
Caro, Jose Sebastian, Dec. 11, 1835	1/3 lea.	Smyth	(?)
Caro, Pedro Jose, Aug. 7, 1835	1 lea.	Vehlein	Trinity
Caro, Tomas, Nov. 22, 1834	1 lea.	Vehlein	Angelina
Carpenter, D., See William Harris			
Carr, John P., Nov. 2, 1835	1/4 lea.	Robertson	Hill
Carreaga, Francisco, See Roman Flores			
Carriere, Joseph, Apr. 6, 1835	1 lea.	Vehlein	1/2 Liberty 1/2 Hardin
Carroll, John, Dec. 30, 1834	1/4 lea.	Burnet	Houston
Carroll, John, Dec. 3, 1831	1 lea.	McMullen and McGloin	Live Oak
Carroll, Mary, June 25, 1835	1 lea. 1 lab.	McMullen and McGloin	Bee
Carroll, Moses A., Oct. 3, 1835	1 lea.	Vehlein	Chambers
Garroll, Patrick, July 30, 1835	1 lea. 1 lab.	McMullen and McGloin	Bee
Carroll, Phillip, Oct. 14, 1835	1 lea.	Vehlein	(?)
Carroll, William, June 15, 1835	1 lea.	Zavala	Jefferson
Carson, William C., May 15, 1827	1 lea.	Austin 1	Brazoria
Carson, William H., Nov. 22, 1832	1/4 lea.	Austin 2	Fayette
Carter, Richard, Apr. 30, 1831	1 lea.	Austin 2	Brazos
Carter, Samuel, July 8, 1824	1 lea.	Austin 1	Brazoria
Carter, Wiley, Jan. 17, 1835	1/4 lea.	Robertson	Bell
Cartwright, Jesse H., Mch. 31, 1828	1 lea. 1 lab.	Austin 1	lea. Ft. Bend, lab. Lavaca
Cartwright Jesse H., Apr. 30, 1831	1/2 lea.	Austin 2	Fayette
Cartwright, John, Nov. 29, 1835	1 lea.	Smyth	Shelby and San Augustine (?)
Cartwright Matthew, July 17, 1835	1/4 lea.	Zavala	San Augustine
Cartwright, Thomas, Aug. 10, 1824	1 lea. 1 lab.	Austin 1	lea. Colorado lab. Austin
Cartwright, Thomas, Sept. 19, 1835	1 lea.	Taylor	Polk
Caruthers, Ewing, July 2, 1835	1/4 lea.	Robertson	Milam
Caruthers, John, Nov. 13, 1834	1 lea.	Vehlein	Walker
Caruthers, Thomas, Nov. 22, 1832	1 lea.	Austin 2	Brazos

Name and Date of Title	Amount	Colony or Commissioner	Present Location
Casiano, Jose, See Menchaca and als.			
Casidy, John, Nov. 24, 1834	1/4 lea.	Power and Hewetson	Bee
Casner, Isaac, Oct. 30, 1832	1 lea.	Austin 4	Bastrop
Casner, Jacob, Nov. 22, 1832	1 lea.	Austin 4	Williamso
Castanedo, Francisca, May 27, 1835	1 lea.	Vehlein	Polk
Castillo, Jose Maria, Dec. 25, 1834	1 lea.	Power and Hewetson	3/5 Bee 2/5 Refu
Castillo, Miguel, Apr. 8, 1835	1 lea.	De Leon	Calhoun
Castillo, Polito, Mch. 23, 1833	1 lea.	De Leon	Victoria
Castillo, Salvador, Nov. 6, 1835	1 lea. 1 lab.	Taylor	lea, Jaspe lab. Libe
Castleman, Andrew, May 14, 1828	1 lea.	Austin 2	Fayette
Castleman, John, Dec. 21, 1828	1 lea.	Austin 2	Fayette
Castleman, Sylvenus, July 7, 1824	2 1/2 lea. 2 lab.	Austin 1	2 lea. Wharton lea. Faye 2 lab. Au
Castro, Francisco, Sept. 7, 1835	1 lea.	Smyth	Rusk
Castro, Ygnacio and Hinsar, Heirs, Nov. 12, 1834	1 lea.	Power and Hewetson	Goliad
Castro, Maria Guadalupe, Oct. 23, 1835	1 lea.	Vehlein	Trinity
Caugran, John, Oct. 14, 1835	1/4 lea.	Zavala	Liberty
Cavero, Mariano, Feb. 6, 1836	1/4 lea.	Austin 5	Bastrop (?
Cayce, Thomas, Apr. 14, 1830	1 lea.	Austin 3	Matagorda
Cazanova (de) Ma. N.S., Oct. 15, 1835	1 lea.	Vehlein	3/4 Hardir 1/4 Polk
Cazenave, Jean Baptiste, June 13, 1835	1 lea.	Zavala	Tyler
Cerda (de la) Nepomuceno, May 3, 1792	3 1/2 lea.	Zepeda	Nacogdoch
Cervantes, Domingo, Dec. 3, 1834	1 lea.	Burnet	Nacogdoch
Cervantes, Jose, Nov. 2, 1835	1 lea. 1 lab.	Smyth	(?)
Cevallos, Julio, Aug. 28, 1835	1 lea.	Vehlein	Trinity
Chaffin, Thomas, Oct. 27, 1835	1 lea.	Burnet	Henderson
Chamar, Desario, July 16, 1835	1 lea.	Burnet	Freestone
Chamar, Maria Jacinta, July 30, 1835	23 lab. and 159,800 sq. vs.	Vehlein	Houston
Chambers, Jesse H., May 12, 1835	1/4 lea.	Burnet	Rusk
Chambers, Joseph L., Nov. 24, 1835	1 lea.	Taylor	Liberty (?
Apr. 1, 1830	1/4 lea.	Padilla	Trinity
Apr. 26, 1832	8 lea.	Chreisman	5 Falls 2 McLenna 1 Milam
Oct. 23, 1834	3 lea.	Lewis	2 Milam 1 San Jac
	5 lea.	Lewis	Falls
	600,000 sq. vs.	Lewis	Falls

Name and Date of Title	Amount	Colony or Commis-sioner	Present Location
Chambers, Thomas Jefferson, Sept. 23, 1834	8 lea.	Lewis	3/5 Ellis 2/5 Navarro
	2 lea, 11 lab. and 900,000 sq. vs.	Lewis	19/20 Chambers 1/20 Liberty
	1 lea.	Lewis	Hays
Sept. 28, 1834	4 lea.	Lewis	Robertson
Oct. 26, 1834	1/2 lea.	Lewis	Calhoun
Oct. 26, 1834	1 lea.	Lewis	Galveston
Oct. 20, 1835	8 lea.	Lewis	Travis
Chance, Joseph B., Mch. 26, 1831	1 lea.	Austin 2	3/4 Burleson 1/4 Washington
Chance, Nancy, Aug. 13, 1835	24 lab.	Robertson	Bell
Chance, Samuel, See J. H. Polley			
Chance, Samuel, May 4, 1831	2/3 lea.	Austin 2	Jackson
Chandler, David, Mch. 10, 1831	1 lea.	Austin 2	Austin
Chandler, Hugh, Oct. 16, 1835	1/4 lea.	Austin 5	Madison
Chapa, Ygnacio, Aug. 7, 1835	1 lea.	Vehlein	Trinity
Chaplin, Chichester, May 18, 1835	1 lea.	Zavala	San Augustine
Chapman, George B., Sept. 4, 1835	1/4 lea.	Robertson	Bosque
Charle, Concepcion, July 16, 1835	1 lea.	Robertson	Robertson
Charles, Isaac N., Mch. 26, 1831	1/2 lea.	Austin 2	Ft. Bend
Charles, Isaac N., See Daniel Shipman			
Chase, William, Aug. 16, 1831	1 lea.	DeWitt	Lavaca
Chavana, Antonio, Oct. 17, 1834	1 lea.	Vehlein	Angelina
Chavana, Jose Ramon, Oct. 15, 1834	1 lea.	Vehlein	17/25 Angelina 8/25 Nacogdoches
Chavana, Faustino, Oct. 22, 1835	1/3 lea.	Taylor	Hardin
Chavert, Juan Luis, Nov. 19, 1833	11 lea.	Aldrete	10/11 Limestone 1/11 Freestone
Cherry, Aaron, Sept. 5, 1835	1 lea.	Taylor	Liberty
Cherry, John, Aug. 14, 1835	1 lea.	Taylor	Liberty
Chesney, John, Oct. 30, 1835	1 lea.	Austin 5	2/3 Burleson 1/3 Lee
Chessher, Daniel, July 2, 1835	1/4 lea.	Zavala	Jasper
Chessher, James, Nov. 11, 1835	1 lea.	Zavala	(?)
Cheves, Henry, Mch. 15, 1831	1 lea.	Austin 2	1/2 Austin 1/2 Washington
Chewers, John, Mch. 26, 1835	1/4 lea.	De Leon	5 1/4 lab. Victoria 1 lab. DeWitt
Childress, Goldsby, Sept. 10, 1835	1 lea.	Robertson	5/6 Bell 1/6 Milam
Childress, Hugh M., Oct. 31, 1832	1 lea.	Austin 4	Williamson
Childress, John, Nov. 23, 1835	1 lea.	Zavala	(?)

Name and Date of Title	Amount	Colony or Commissioner	Present Location
Chiles, Lewis L., Apr. 20, 1835	1/4 lea.	Robertson	Milam
Chirino, Jose Antonio, Dec. 27, 1833	9 1/8 lea.	Ybarbo	Nacogdoch
Chirino, Jose Antonio, Mch. 11, 1835	1 7/8 lea.	Berry	(?)
Chirino, Jose Antonio, May 21, 1792	5 lea. 4 lab.	Zepeda	Nacogdoch
Chirino, Manuel, Mch. 27, 1835	1 lea.	Zavala	Jefferson
Chirino, Margarita, July 1, 1832	2 lea.	De Witt	Guadalupe
Chirino, Maria Candida, Apr. 13, 1835	5 lea. and 766,500 sq. vs.	Zavala	Nacogdoch
Chisholm, Richard H., Sept. 7, 1831	1 lea.	De Witt	De Witt
Chisum, John, Oct. 24, 1835	1/3 lea.	Smyth	Harrison
Choat, David, Aug. 12, 1835	1 lea.	Vehlein	24/25 Jeffe son 1/25 Hardin
Choat, John, Oct. 18, 1835	1 lea.	Burnet	Navarro
Choate, Moses L., Feb. 7, 1835	1 lea.	Vehlein	Polk
Choate, Redmond, Oct. 11, 1835	1 lea.	Burnet	(?)
Choate, Thomas, Jan. 18, 1832	1 lea.	Austin 3	Harris
Chonca, Cristobal, Oct. 21, 1824	1 lea.	Torres	Sabine and San Augustine (
Chreisman, Horatio, July 8, 1824	1 lea. 2 lab.	Austin 1	lea. Ft. Be lab. Aust
Chreisman, Horatio, Mch. 17, 1831	1 lea.	Austin 2	Washingtor
Chreisman, Horatio, Dec. 12, 1833	10 lea.	Williams, Johnson and Peebles	(?)
Christian, Thomas, Oct. 29, 1832	1 lea.	Austin 4	Bastrop
Chunsley, Armsted, June 28, 1835	1 lea.	Zavala	San August
Clampitt, Ezechiel, Mch. 23, 1831	1 lea.	Austin 2	Washingtor
Clampitt, Susannah, Mch. 25, 1831	1 lea.	Austin 2	Washingtor
Clapp, Elisha, Jan. 14, 1835	1 lea.	Burnet	Houston
Clapp, William C., June 23, 1831	1/4 lea.	Austin 3	Matagorda
Clare, Abraham M., Dec. 9, 1830	1 lea.	Austin 3	Jackson
Clarey, Henry, Aug. 15, 1835	24 lab.	Robertson	Coryell
Clark, Barton, Aug. 3, 1835	1 lea.	Vehlein	Houston
Clark, Benjamin, Dec. 8, 1835	1 lea. 1 lab.	Smyth	Grayson (?
Clark, David., May 7, 1831	1 lea.	Austin 2	Burleson
Clark, Eligio, July 13, 1835	1/4 lea.	Zavala	Sabine
Clark, Elijah, Nov. 4, 1835	3/4 lea.	Smyth	(?)
Clark, Ester, May 2, 1831		Madero	Liberty
Clark, James, Sept. 3, 1835	10 lea.	Grant, Durst and Williams	(?)
Clark, James, Dec. 17, 1835	1 lea. 1 lab.	Smyth	Grayson (?
Clark, James, June 8, 1835	1/4 lea.	Zavala	Sabine
Clark, John, May 2, 1831		Madero	Liberty
Clark, John, July 22, 1835	1 lea.	Zavala	Sabine
Clark, John, Sept. 5, 1834	1 lea.	Power and Hewetson	Bee
Clark, John C., July 16, 1824	1 lea.	Austin 1	Wharton
Clark, William, June 17, 1835	1 lea.	Burnet	Rusk

Name and Date of Title	Amount	Colony or Commis- sioner	Present Location
Clark, William, June (?), 1835	23 lab. and 742,000 sq. vs.	Zavala	Sabine
Clark, William, Sept. 21, 1835	1 lea.	Taylor	Orange
Clark, William F., June 21, 1835	1 lea.	Zavala	Sabine
Clarke, Anthony R., Aug. 24, 1824	1 lab.	Austin 1	Brazoria
Clarke, James, Mch. 17, 1831	1 lea.	Austin 2	Washington
Clarke, Silas, Mch. 21, 1831	1/4 lea.	Austin 2	Washington
Clarke, William C., Apr. 10, 1831	1 lea.	Austin 2	Montgomery
Clay, Nestor, Mch. 18, 1831	1 lea.	Austin 2	Washington
Clay, Nestor, Dec. 10, 1830	1 lea.	Austin 3	Jackson
Clay, Tacitus, Mch. 25, 1833	1/4 lea.	Austin 3	Jackson
Clements, Joseph D., Nov. 6, 1831	1 lea.	DeWitt	Guadalupe
Clements, Joseph D., July 11, 1835	3 lea.	Ponton	1 DeWitt 1 Guadalupe 1 Gonzales
Clover, Robert, Nov. 21, 1835	1/3 lea.	Smyth	Anderson (?)
Clifton, William, Jan. 15, 1836	1 lea.	Taylor	(?)
Clokey, Robert, Mch. 28, 1831	1 lea.	Austin 2	Washington
Clopper, E. N. and J. C. See Nicholas Clopper and Co.			
Clopper, Nicholas, Dec. 18, 1830	1 lea.	Austin 3	Matagorda
Clopper, Nicholas and Co., Dec. 16, 1828	3 lea.	Austin 2	Harris
Coats, Merit M., July 19, 1824	1 lea.	Austin 1	Waller
Cobarrubias, Jose Ma., Oct. 28, 1834	1 lea.	Power and Hewetson	9/10 Victoria 1/10 Goliad
Cobbey, William, May 5, 1831	1/4 lea.	DeWitt	Caldwell
Cobbs, James, Apr. 29, 1835	1/4 lea.	Burnet	Cherokee
Cobian (de), Guadalupe Çarreya and Faniel, Oct. 25, 1834	1 1/2 lea.	Power and Hewetson	Refugio
Cobian (de), Jose Maria and Gregorio, Oct. 30, 1834	1/2 lea.	Power and Hewetson	Refugio
Cochrane, James, Apr. 23, 1833	1/4 lea.	Austin 2	Wharton
Cochrane, James, Jan. 29, 1836	3/4 lea.	Austin 5	Austin and Washington (?)
Cochrane, Thomas, Feb. 21, 1836	1 lea.	Austin 5	Colorado (?)
Coe, Philip, May 4, 1831	1 lea.	Austin 2	Washington
Coffin, Joseph, Oct. 7, 1834	1/4 lea.	Power and Hewetson	Refugio
Coit, Daniel P., Sept. 22, 1835	1 lea.	Taylor	Liberty
Cole, Gabriel, Nov. 27, 1832	1 lea.	Austin 2	Ft. Bend
Cole, John, Mch. 24, 1831	1 lea.	Austin 2	Washington
Cole, Mary, Sept. 7, 1835	24 lab.	Robertson	Bosque
Cole, Mary, Aug. 21, 1835	1 lab.	Robertson	Falls
Cole, Reuben, Nov. 23, 1835	1 lea. 1 lab.	Taylor	(?)
Coleman, Green H., Nov. 12, 1832	1 lea.	Austin 2	Brazos
Coleman, Nicholas, Aug. 29, 1835	20 1/2 lab.	Zavala	San Augustine
Coleman, Nicholas, Oct. 3, 1835	4 1/2 lab.	Zavala	Jefferson
Coleman, R. M., Feb. 1, 1835	24 lab.	Robertson	Lee

Name and Date of Title	Amount	Colony or Commis- sioner	Present Location
Coleman, Young, Oct. 22, 1830	1 lea.	Austin 3	Jackson
Coles, John P., Aug. 19, 1824	8 1/2 lea.	Austin 1	7 1/2 lea. Washington and Burle- son 1/2 lea Washington 1/2 Brazor
Coley, Wright, Oct. 15, 1835	11 lab. and 552,500 sq. vs.	Zavala	Sabine
Collard, Elijah, Apr. 29, 1835	1 lea.	Vehlein	Montgomery
Collard, James H., Sept. 28, 1835	1/4 lea.	Vehlein	San Jacinto
Collard, Job S., May 28, 1835	1 lea.	Vehlein	Madison
Collard, Jonathan S., Sept. 27, 1835	1/4 lea.	Vehlein	San Jacinto
Collard, Samuel M., Aug. 27, 1835	1 lea.	Vehlein	Walker
Collins, Elisha M., Nov. 15, 1835	1 lea.	Zavala	Sabine (?)
Collins, Geo. J. W., Mch. 16, 1835	1 lea.	Zavala	Tyler
Collins, Stephen, Nov. 25, 1835	10 lea.	Williams, Johnson and Peebles	(?)
Collyer, James and Sons, Sept. 26, 1834	1 1/2 lea.	Power and Hewetson	Refugio
Colton, Daniel E., Apr. 21, 1831	1 lea.	Austin 2	Fayette
Colvill, Thomas, Aug. 30, 1835	1 lea.	Vehlein	Polk
Colvin, Aaron, Apr. 18, 1831	1 lea.	Austin 2	Burleson
Colvin, John, July 23, 1835	1/4 lea.	Vehlein	San Jacinto
Colwell, William, Oct. 6, 1835	1/4 lea.	Zavala	San Augustir
Conaway, Isaac S., Oct. 14, 1835	1 lea.	Vehlein	Polk
Cone, Harry H., Aug. 27, 1835	1 lea.	Vehlein	Polk
Conichi, Santiago, July 7, 1826	1 lea.	Norris	San Augustir
Conn, James, Jan. 26, 1835	1 lea.	Zavala	1/2 Jasper 1/2 Tyler
Conn, Robert, Nov. 3, 1834	1/4 lea.	Zavala	Jasper
Connell, Mathilda, Feb. 3, 1835	1 lea.	Robertson	Bell
Conner, Francis B., Mch. 14, 1835	1 lea.	Vehlein	Houston
Conner, John G., Oct. 22, 1835	1 lea.	Austin 5	3/5 Grimes 2/5 Walker
Conner, Thomas, Sept. 28, 1834	1 lea.	Power and Hewetson	Refugio
Conrad, Peter, May 31, 1827	1/4 lea.	Austin 2	Ft. Bend
Conrey, John, May 2, 1835	1 lea.	De Leon	Lavaca
Conway, John, July 5, 1835	1/3 lea.	McMullen and McGloin	Live Oak
Cook, David, Nov. 8, 1835	1/4 lea.	Burnet	Nacogdoches
Cook, James, See W. B. Dewers			
Cook, John and Isaac Hughes, Aug. 10, 1824	1 lea. 1 lab.	Austin 1	Harris
Cook, Joseph T., Feb. 2, 1835	1 lea.	Burnet	Cherokee
Cook, W. A., Mch. 14, 1835	1 lea.	Vehlein	Walker
Cook, William, Feb. 3, 1835	1/4 lea.	Robertson	Falls
Cooke, John, Apr. 4, 1831	1 lea.	Austin 2	Fayette

Name and Date of Title	Amount	Colony or Commissioner	Present Location
Cooper, Frederick, Dec. 5, 1835	1 lea.	Taylor	Tyler (?)
Cooper, James, Dec. 19, 1831	1 lea.	Austin 2	11/12 Austin 1/12 Washington
Cooper, William, See Moses Morrison			
Cooper, William, Aug. 10, 1824	1 1/2 lea. 2 lab.	Austin 1	1 1/2 lea. Waller lab. Austin
Coote, William, Feb. 4, 1835	1 lea.	Zavala	San Augustine
Copeland, Mark, July 23, 1835	1 lea.	Burnet	Leon
Cordova, Damian, Nov. 30, 1835	1 lea. 1 lab.	Smyth	Wood and Hopkins (?)
Cordova, Francisco, Aug. 26, 1835	1 lea.	Smyth	Rusk
Cordova, Joaquin, May 31, 1792	4 lea.	Zepeda	1/2 Shelby 1/2 Nacogdoches
Cordova, Jose and Bros., Apr. 26, 1810	3 1/2 lea.	De la Bega	Nacogdoches
Cordova, Miguel, See Pedro Procela			
Cornaugh, Hannah, Dec. 19, 1832	1 lea.	Austin 2	Grimes
Corner, John, May 10, 1831	1 lea.	Austin 2	Montgomery
Corner, Mary, Apr. 7, 1831	1 lea.	Austin 2	Montgomery
Corner, Thomas, May 28, 1831	1/4 lea.	Austin 2	Montgomery
Coronado, Jose, May 12, 1831	1 lea.	Madero	Liberty
Coronado, Jose, May 2, 1831		Madero	Liberty
Cortez, Miguel, Apr. 8, 1835	1 lea.	De Leon	Calhoun
Cortinas, Miguel, Oct. 29, 1835	1 lea.	Burnet	Henderson
Coryell, James, June 22, 1835	1/4 lea.	Robertson	Coryell
Corzine, Shelby, June 16, 1835	18 lab. and 628,150 sq. vs.	Zavala	Jefferson
Cotten, Goodwin B. M., Dec. 15, 1830	1 lea.	Austin 3	Matagorda
Cottle, Almond, July 12, 1831	1/4 lea.	DeWitt	Victoria
Cottle, Geo. W., Sept. 12, 1832	1 lea.	DeWitt	Fayette
Cottle, Harriet, May 1, 1831	1 lea.	DeWitt	Guadalupe
Cottle, Isaac, See Mary Ann Williams			
Cottle, Jonathan, May 1, 1831	1 lea.	DeWitt	Gonzales
Cottle, Sarah, Apr. 5, 1831	1 lea.	Austin 2	Bastrop
Cottle, Sylvenus, Oct. 8, 1835	1/4 lea.	Austin 5	Bastrop
Cotton, John, Dec. 7, 1835	1 lea.	Smyth	Upshur (?)
Coughlin, John, Sept. 2, 1834	1 lea.	Power and Hewetson	3/4 Goliad 1/4 Refugio
Counsel, J. S., June 22, 1832	1 lea.	Austin 2	Fayette
Courtney, Jeremiah, Sept. 17, 1835	1 lea.	Robertson	Falls
Covington, Hays, Dec. 30, 1834	1/4 lea.	Robertson	Burleson
Cox, Christopher G., Apr. 14, 1830	1 lea.	Austin 3	Matagorda
Cox, Euclid M., Oct. 19, 1832	1/4 lea.	Austin 2	Wharton
Cox, George W., Jan. 21, 1835	1/4 lea.	Robertson	Robertson
Cox, James, Oct. 19, 1832	1 lea.	Austin 2	Washington
Cox, James, May 28, 1832	1 lea.	Austin 2	Grimes
Cox, John S., Oct. 16, 1832	1 lea.	Austin 2	Burleson
Cox, Lewis, July 4, 1835	1 lea.	Vehlein	Walker
Cox, Thomas, Oct. 30, 1830	1 lea.	Austin 3	Calhoun

Name and Date of Title	Amount	Colony or Commissioner	Present Location
Cox, William N., Aug. 16, 1835	1 lea.	Zavala	Hardin
Cox, William R., Feb. 20, 1835	1/4 lea.	Robertson	Robertson
Coy (de los Santos) Ignacio, Oct. 15, 1835	1 lea.	Vehlein	Trinity
Coy (de los Santos) Ignacio and als., May 30, 1829	6 lea.	Padilla	Mexico (?)
Coy (de los Santos), Jose, ? ? ?	1 lea.	(?)	Nacogdoche
Coy (de los Santos) Manuel, Dec. 2, 1833	7 1/2 lea.	Aldrete	4 Liberty; 3 1/2 (?)
Coy (de los Santos) Manuel and Bros., Aug. 20, 1827	3 1/2 lea.	Chirino	Nacogdoche
Coy (de los Santos) Miguel, July 17, 1835	1 lea.	Burnet	2/3 Smith 1/3 Cherokee
Coy (de los Santos) Rafael, June 4, 1835	1 lea.	Vehlein	Houston
Crain, Phebe, Nov. 29, 1834	1 lea.	Power and Hewetson	Bee
Crain, John, Mch. 5, 1835	1 lea.	Vehlein	Walker
Crane, William, See George W. Hall			
Cravens, R. M., May 30, 1831	1 lea.	Austin 2	Fayette
Crawford, James, Nov. 13, 1832	1 lea.	Austin 4	Williamson
Creager, William, Dec. 16, 1835	1 lea. 1 lab.	Smyth	Fannin (?)
Cribbs, Gilbert, Mch. 31, 1835	1 lea.	Robertson	Milam
Crier, John, June 6, 1827	1 lea.	Austin 1	Matagorda
Crier, Kesiah, Apr. 25, 1831	1 lea.	Austin 2	Fayette
Crippin, John, Feb. 14, 1835	1 lea.	Vehlein	San Jacinto
Crissman, S., Sept. 13, 1835	1 lea.	Zavala	Polk
Crist, John, Apr. 13, 1835	1 lea.	Vehlein	Madison
Crist, Stephen, May 21, 1835	1 lea.	Burnet	Anderson
Criswell, Ann D., Mch. 25, 1835	1 lea.	Vehlein	Polk
Criswell, John J., June 15, 1831	1 lea.	Austin 3	-Matagorda
Crobb, Hilary M., Feb. 10, 1835	1 lea.	Vehlein	Walker
Cronkrite, John, June 21, 1831	1/4 lea.	Austin 2	Montgomer
Cronkrite, Lyman, June 20, 1831	1 lea.	Austin 2	Wharton
Crouch, Isaac, May 18, 1835	1 lea.	Robertson	Bosque
Crow, Levi M., June 23, 1835	1/4 lea.	Zavala	San August
Crowder, John, Nov. 23, 1835	1 lea. 1 lab.	Taylor	(?)
Crownover, Arter, Oct. 8, 1835	1 lea.	Austin 5	Madison
Crownover, John, Aug. 3, 1824	1 lea. 1 lab.	Austin 1	3/4 lea. Wharton 1/4 Mata- gorda lab. Austin
Crownover, John Sr., Oct. 8, 1835	1 lea.	Austin 5	Madison
Cruse, Squire, Mch. 14, 1835	1 lea.	Zavala	21 1/3 lab. Tyler 3 2, Jasper
Cruz, Gillermo, Sept. 35 (sic), 1835	10 lea.	Grant, Durst and Williams	(?)

Name and Date of Title	Amount	Colony or Commis-sioner	Present Location
Cruz, Juan, Apr. 10, 1835	1 lea.	Vehlein	Trinity
Cruz, Juan, Nov. 2, 1835	1/3 lea.	Taylor	Nacogdoches
Cruz, Maria Benancia, Oct. 12, 1835	1 lea.	Vehlein	Trinity
Cruz, Mariano, See Matias Pena			
Cruz, Martin, ? ? ?	22 lab. and 700,000 sq. vs.	(?)	Nacogdoches ?
Cruz (de la), Rafael, Dec. 4, 1835	1 lea. 1 lab.	Taylor	Tyler (?)
Cruz, William, May 18, 1835	1 lea.	Vehlein	1/2 Houston 1/2 Trinity
Cude, Timothy, Sept. 15, 1835	1 lea.	Taylor	Montgomery
Cummings, Mishack, June 19, 1835	1 lea.	Zavala	Sabine
Cummins, James, July 7, 1824	6 lea. 1 lab.	Austin 1	Colorado
Cummins, James, Nov. 18, 1831	2 lea.	Arciniega	Colorado
Cummins, James, Aug. 16, 1824	6 lea.	Austin 1	5 Austin 1 Brazoria
Cummins, John, July 21, 1824	1 lea.	Austin 1	Brazoria
Cummins, John H., Jan. 5, 1835	1 lea.	Vehlein	4/5 Walker 1/5 San Jacinto
Cummins, John H., July 29, 1834	1 lea.	Flores	Houston
Cummins, Maria, Nov. 20, 1830	1 lea.	Austin 3	Matagorda
Cummins, Moses, May 3, 1831	1 lea.	Austin 2	Burleson
Cummins, Rebecca, July 21, 1824	1 lea. 2 lab.	Austin 1	lea. Brazoria lab. Waller
Cummins, William, July 21, 1824	1 lea.	Austin 1	Brazoria
Cunningham, Allen U., Oct. 21, 1835	1 lea.	Taylor	Liberty (?)
Cunningham, Colvin, Nov. 4, 1835	1/4 lea.	Robertson	(?)
Cunningham, David A., July 23, 1835	1/4 lea.	Zavala	Jefferson
Cunningham, John C., Apr. 6, 1831	1 lea.	Austin 2	3/4 Bastrop 1/4 Fayette
Cunningham, L. C., Aug. 1, 1835	1/4 lea.	Milam	Bastrop
Cunningham, Robert, Mch. 4, 1833	1 lea.	Austin 4	Colorado
Curd, Isaiah, Oct. 12, 1835	1 lea.	Austin 5	Brazos
Curbiero, Maria Feliciana, See Durum	1 lea.	Austin 5	
Curhiel, Maria Josefa, Sept. 16, 1835	1 lea.	Robertson	McLennan
Curry, David, July 28, 1835	1/4 lea.	Robertson	Milam
Curry, James A., Feb. 24, 1835	1 lea.	Zavala	Sabine
Curry, Thomas, July 28, 1835	1 lea.	Robertson	Milam
Curry, Willie, July 13, 1835	1 lea.	Burnet	3/4 Freestone 1/4 Lime-stone
Curtis, Charles, Jan. 12, 1835	1/4 lea.	Robertson	Bell
Curtis, Elijah, Apr. 5, 1831	1/4 lea.	Austin 2	Bastrop
Curtis, Hinton, Aug. 10, 1824	1 lea.	Austin 1	Matagorda
Curtis, James, Feb. 20, 1835	1/4 lea.	Milam	Hays
Curtis, James, Sr., Aug. 3, 1824	1 lea.	Austin 1	Burleson
Curtis, James, Jr., Aug. 19, 1824	1 lea.	Austin 1	Brazos
Curtis, Washington, Apr. 5, 1831	1/4 lea.	Austin 2	Bastrop
Cushing, Theophilus, June 4, 1835	1 lea.	Zavala	Tyler
Cutts, David, Sept. 10, 1835	1 lea.	Zavala	Polk
Colonization Law, v. 55, p. 100			

Name and Date of Title	Amount	Colony or Commis-sioner	Present Location
Commissioners, v. 55, p. 24			
Dabney, John H., Nov. 19, 1832	1 lea.	Austin 2	Colorado
Dale, Benjamin, Oct. 30, 1834	1 lea.	Power and Hewetson	5/6 San Pa-tricio 1/6 Bee
Daley, John, Oct. 10, 1834	1/4 lea.	De Leon	DeWitt
Daly, John, Nov. 20, 1834	1/4 lea.	Power and Hewetson	Goliad
Damken, Gerit, Feb. 5, 1836	1/4 lea.	Austin 5	Bastrop (?)
Daniels, Williamson, Oct. 17, 1832	1 lea.	Austin 2	Lavaca
Dargan, W. L., Oct. 15, 1835	1 lea.	Taylor	Liberty (?)
Darling, Socrates, Feb. 1 3, 1836	1 lea.	Austin 5	Bastrop (?)
Darneill, Ansell, Aug. 27, 1835	1/4 lea.	Robertson	McLennan
Darneill, Napoleon, Aug. 20, 1835	1/4 lea.	Robertson	McLennan
Darst, Jacob C., Apr. 24, 1831	24 lab.	DeWitt	Guadalupe
Darst, Jacob C., July 1, 1831	1 lab.	DeWitt	Lavaca
Davenport, J. B. B., Sept. 18, 1835	4 lea.	Berry	Upshur
Davenport, See Barr and Davenport			
David, Luis, Nov. 21, 1835	1 lea.	Taylor	Hardin
Davidson, John, Nov. 28, 1835	1 lea. 1 lab.	Taylor	(?)
Davidson, Robert, Dec. 30, 1834	24 lab.	Robertson	Bell
Davidson, Samuel, July 21, 1824	1 lea.	Austin 1	Brazos
Davidson, Uriah, Aug. 24, 1835	1 lea.	Zavala	Hardin
Davila, Miguel, Jan. 30, 1836	11 lea.	Aldrete	10 Grayson 1 Hopkins
Davila, Miguel, Oct. 18, 1833	11 lea.	Lessassier	6 Milam 3 Bell 2 Wil liamson
Davis, Alfred B., July 24, 1835	1/4 lea.	Burnet	Anderson
Davis, Brinkley, Mch. 25, 1835	1 lea.	Robertson	Limestone
Davis, Caldwalder, May 13, 1835	1 lea.	Zavala	Sabine
Davis, Daniel, May 1, 1831	1 lea.	DeWitt	5/6 DeWitt 1/6 Gonza
Davis, Edward B., Aug. 27, 1835	1/4 lea.	Vehlein	Polk
Davis, Eljas K., Aug. 28, 1835	1 lea.	Taylor	Liberty
Davis, George W., Sept. 6, 1831	1 lea.	DeWitt	DeWitt
Davis, James C., June 30, 1831	1/4 lea.	DeWitt	Lavaca
Davis, Jesse K., May 15, 1832	1/4 lea.	DeWitt	Guadalupe
Davis, John, Dec. 10, 1830	1 lea.	Austin 3	Jackson
Davis, John, Mch. 18, 1835	1 lea.	Vehlein	17 lab. San Jacinto 8 lab. Walke
Davis, John, Oct. 28, 1831	1/4 lea.	DeWitt	Lavaca
Davis, Joseph, Mch. 16, 1831	1 lea.	Austin 2	Washington
Davis, Joshua, Aug. 9, 1834	5 1/4 lea.	Power and Hewetson	Refugio
Davis, Kinchen W., May 28, 1832	1 lea.	Austin 2	Ft. Bend
Davis, Luis, Sept. 28, 1835	1 lea.	Vehlein	Liberty
Davis, Nancy (Widow), Feb. 27, 1835	1 lea.	Zavala	Orange
Davis, Samuel, Apr. 7, 1835	1/4 lea.	Zavala	Orange
Davis, Thomas, See Daniel H. Millburn			

Name and Date of Title	Amount	Colony or Commis- sioner	Present Location
Davis, Thomas K., Feb. 19, 1836	1 lea.	Austin 5	Brazoria (?)
Davis, William, Oct. 14, 1835	1 lea.	Burnet	Houston
Davis, William, Apr. 7, 1835	1/4 lea.	Zavala	Orange
Davis, William, Nov. 29, 1835	1 lea. 1 lab.	Taylor	(?)
Davis, William M., Mch. 26, 1835	1 lea.	Zavala	(?)
Davis, Zachariah, July 19, 1831	1 lea.	DeWitt	Lavaca
Day, James, Aug. 25, 1835	1 lea.	Robertson	Williamson
Dean, John M., Sept. 12, 1835	1 lea.	Zavala	4155 acres Polk 273 acres Trinity
Dean, Sophia, Feb. 19, 1835	1 lea.	Zavala	Jefferson
Dearduff, William, Nov. 5, 1831	1/4 lea.	DeWitt	DeWitt
Deark, Delily, Oct. 23, 1835	1 lea.	Zavala	Newton
Debard, Elijah J., Jan. 8, 1835	1 lea.	Burnet	Smith
Decker, Isaac, Mch. 17, 1835	1 lea.	Milam	Travis
Deckrow, Daniel, See Thomas McCoy			
Decrow, Thomas, Apr. 5, 1831	1/4 lea.	Austin 2	Bastrop
Deel, (Widow Reed) Sarah, Nov. 20, 1832	1 lea.	Austin 3	Harris
Defee, William, Feb. 13, 1835	2/3 lea.	Zavala	Sabine
Invalid, 1 Texas 721, 8 Texas 226			
Delapplain (?), Feb. 17, 1836	1 lea.	Austin 5	(?)
Delgado, Jose, Dec. 15, 1833	1 lab.	Ximenes	Bexar
Delgado, Juan, Feb. 10, 1836	1 lea.	Austin 5	Austin (?)
Delgado, Juan, Miguel, Nepomuceno and Pedro, Nov. 26, 1831	4 lea.	McMullen and McGloin	San Patricio
Delgado, Maria Josefa, Mch. 25, 1835	1 lea.	Robertson	Milam
Delgado, Miguel, Nov. 9, 1833	1 lea. 1 lab.	Aldrete	Louisiana (?)
Demos, Charles, Aug. 3, 1824	1 lea.	Austin 1	Matagorda
Demos, Peter, July 24, 1824	1 lea.	Austin 1	Matagorda
Dempsey, Francis W., Dec. 18, 1830	1 lea.	Austin 3	Matagorda
Denman, Obediah, Sept. 24, 1835	1/3 lea.	Smyth	Jasper
Denmon, Obediah, July 27, 1835	1/4 lea.	Zavala	Jasper
Denson, Jesse, May 4, 1831	1 lea.	Austin 2	1/2 Harris 1/2 Waller
Denton, Abraham, May 15, 1832	1/4 lea.	DeWitt	Gonzales
Denton, John, Oct. 23, 1830	1/4 lea.	Austin 3	Jackson
Denton, Samuel, ? ? ?	1 lea.	Austin 4	Burleson
Denton, William, Oct. 21, 1835	1 lea.	Zavala	Hardin (?)
Deveny, John, Nov. 19, 1835	1 lea.	Taylor	(?)
Dever, John, May 2, 1831		Madero	Liberty
Dever, Thomas, May 2, 1831		Madero	Liberty
Dever, Thomas, May 11, 1831	1/4 lea.	Madero	Liberty
Dever, William, Mch. 31, 1831	1/4 lea.	Austin 2	Washington
Dever, William, Apr. 17, 1831	3/4 lea.	Austin 2	Brazos
Devereux, Andrew, Oct. 30, 1834	1/4 lea.	Power and Hewetson	Goliad
Devers, Elizabeth, June 21, 1831	1 lea.	Austin 2	Fayette
Devore, Jesse, June 20, 1835	1 lea.	Vehlein	Liberty
Dewees, W. B., Apr. 28, 1831	1/2 lea.	Austin 2	Colorado

Name and Date of Title	Amount	Colony or Commissioner	Present Location
Dewees, Wm. Blufford and			
James Cook, Aug. 3, 1824	1 lea.	Austin 1	Colorado
DeWitt, Eliza, Apr. 15, 1831	1 lea.	DeWitt	Gonzales
Aug. 11, 1831	621,250 sq. vs.	DeWitt	Gonzales
Aug. 9, 1831	880,000 sq. vs.	DeWitt	Gonzales
DeWitt, Green, Aug. 13, 1831	1 lea.	DeWitt	Guadalupe
Nov. 18, 1831	1 lea.	DeWitt	DeWitt
May. 12, 1832	2 lab.	DeWitt	Guadalupe
Dec. 4, 1831	1 lea.	DeWitt	Gonzales
Dec. 10, 1831	1 lea.	DeWitt	Gonzales
Dec. 5, 1831	1 lea.	DeWitt	Guadalupe
Sept. 15, 1832	1 lab.	DeWitt	Gonzales
DeWitt, James C., Dec. 1, 1835	1 lea. 1 lab.	Taylor	Walker (?)
DeWitt, Joseph, Oct. 20, 1832	1 lea.	Austin 2	Burleson
Dias, Agustin, Nov. 26, 1835	1/3 lea.	Smyth	(?)
Dias, Juan Garza, Apr. 17, 1836	4 lea.	Ramirez	Webb
Dias, Maria Gertrudis, Oct. 9, 1835	1 lea.	Vehlein	Chambers
Dias, Vicente, Nov. 20, 1835	1 lea. 1 lab.	Smyth	Navarro (?)
Dickerson, Waller, Nov. 30, 1835	10 lea.	Williams, Johnson and Peebles	(?)
Dickinson, Almerion, May 5, 1831	1 lea.	DeWitt	Caldwell
Dickinson, Edward, Nov. 26, 1831	1/4 lea.	DeWitt	Gonzales
Dickinson, John, Aug. 19, 1824	1 lea.	Austin 1	3/4 Galvest 1/4 Harris
Dickinson, Lemuel, May 7, 1831	1 lea.	Austin 2	Burleson
Dietrich, Francis, Baumacher and			
Langenheim, Nov. 24, 1834	3/4 lea.	Power and Hewetson	Bee
Dikes, George P., July 28, 1835	1 lea.	Vehlein	Polk
Dikes, John M., June 20, 1835	1/4 lea.	Vehlein	Polk
Dikes, Lovic, Sept. 21, 1835	10 lea.	Grant, Durst and Williams	(?)
Dikes, Levi B., May 23, 1835	1 lea.	Vehlein	Polk
Dikes, Lovick P., ? ? 1835	1 lea. 1 lab.	Smyth	Hopkins
Dikes, Mark W., Oct. 9, 1835	1/4 lea.	Burnet	Anderson
Dikes, Miles G., Aug. 23, 1831	1/4 lea.	DeWitt	Caldwell
Dikes, Wesley, Oct. 16, 1835	1 lea.	Zavala	21 1/2 lab. Jefferson 3 1/2 Orar
Dill, James, July 26, 1828	4 lea.	Madero	Cherokee
Dillard, Abraham, Mch. 20, 1831	1/4 lea.	Austin 2	Washington
Dillard, John J., Dec. 10, 1830	1 lea.	Austin 3	Wharton
Dillard, Nicholas, Aug. 16, 1824	1 lea.	Austin 1	Brazoria
Dillard, William, Mch. 25, 1835	1 lea.	Robertson	McLennan
Dilliard, John B., Dec. 12, 1835	4 lab. and 840,000 sq. vs.	Smyth	San Augusti
Dimery, Allen, Apr. 20, 1835	1 lea.	Burnet	Leon

Name and Date of Title	Amount	Colony or Commis- sioner	Present Location
Dimitt, Philip, Nov. 3, 1834	1 1/4 lea.	De Leon	Victoria
Dimitt, Philip, Nov. 10, 1834	2 lea.	De Leon	Victoria
Dimitt, Philip, Dec. 24, 1829	1 1/4 lea.	Austin 3	Calhoun
Dinsmore, John, Apr. 23, 1833	1/4 lea.	Austin 2	Wharton
Dinsmore, Silas, Jr., Apr. 18, 1832	1 lea.	Austin 3	Matagorda
Dixon, Robert H., Oct. 17, 1835	1 lea.	Taylor	Jefferson (?)
Dobie, William, Nov. 19, 1832	1/4 lea.	Austin 3	Harris
Doharty, George, Mch. 3, 1835	1 lea.	Robertson	Bell
Dominguez, Jose Alfonso, Oct. 21, 1835	1 lea.	Vehlein	(?)
Dominguez, Sixto, Oct. 9, 1835	9 lab.	Austin 5	Austin (?)
Donaho, Daniel, Sept. 3, 1835	1 lea.	Vehlein	Liberty
Donaho, Moses, Sept. 7, 1835	1 lea.	Vehlein	Liberty
Donaho, William, Sept. 3, 1835	1 lea.	Vehlein	Liberty
Donahoe, Daniel, Dec. 4, 1835	1 lea.	Zavala	Hardin
Donahoe, Willis, Oct. 21, 1835	1 lea.	Zavala	Hardin
Donahoe, Willis, Nov. 7, 1835	1 lea.	Zavala	Hardin
Donaldson, Daniel T., Nov. 21, 1832	1/4 lea.	Austin 2	Lavaca
Donoho, Charles, Apr. 12, 1831	1 lea.	Austin 2	Waller
Donoho, Isaac, July 8, 1836	1/4 lea.	Austin 5	Waller (?)
Donoho, Mortimer, July 8, 1836	1/4 lea.	Austin 5	Waller (?)
Donovan, Amos, Apr. 13, 1835	1 lea.	Vehlein	Trinity
Dorr, John M., Oct. 10, 1835	1 lea. 1 lab.	Smyth	Harrison
Dorr, John M., Sept. 3, 1835	1 lea.	Grant, Durst and Williams	(?)
Dorsett, John, Nov. 18, 1835	1 lea.	Zavala	Jefferson (?)
Dorsett, Theodore, May 4, 1831	1 lea.	Madero	Liberty
Dorsey, John, Feb. 9, 1836	1/4 lea.	Austin 5	Montgomery ?
Dortolan, Bernardo, Mch. 28, 1797	4 lea.	Zepeda	Nacogdoches ?
Dottery, Bryant, Mch. 8, 1831	1 lea.	Austin 2	Austin
Dougherty, Patrick, Oct. 29, 1835	1 lea. 1 lab.	Smyth	Harrison
Douglass, James, Nov. 28, 1834	1 lea.	Power and Hewetson	Bee
Douglass, John, Feb. 16, 1835	1 lea.	De Leon	Lavaca
Douglass, Samuel C., Oct. 22, 1832	1 lea.	Austin 2	Austin
Dowlearn, Patrick, July 25, 1831	1/4 lea.	DeWitt	DeWitt
Downer, Erasmus D., Jan. 18, 1832	1/4 lea.	Austin 3	Matagorda
Downey, Patrick, Sept. 16, 1834	1 lea.	Power and Hewetson	3/4 Bee 1/4 Refugio
Downey, Patrick, R. T., John and James, Nov. 25, 1834	1 1/4 lea.	Power and Hewetson	Refugio
Doyle, Festus, June 28, 1835	1 lea. 1 lab.	McMullen and McGloin	Live Oak
Doyle, James, July 31, 1835	1 lea.	Milam	Bastrop
Drake, James, July 19, 1835	9 lab. and 364,371 sq. vs.	Zavala	Jefferson
Dry, Daniel, Nov. 27, 1835	1 lea. 1 lab.	Smyth	(?)
Dry, John, Nov. 27, 1835	1 lea. 1 lab.	Smyth	(?)
Dry, John F., Nov. 26, 1835	1 lea. 1 lab.	Smyth	(?)
Dry, Paul, Nov. 4, 1835	1 lea. 1 lab.	Smyth	(?)

Name and Date of Title	Amount	Colony or Commissioner	Present Location
Duel, Lewis, Oct. 26, 1835	1 lea.	Vehlein	Walker
Duff, James C., Feb. 5, 1836	1 lea.	Austin 5	Fayette (?)
Dugan, Cataline, Oct. 28, 1834	1 lea.	Power and Hewetson	Goliad
Duggins, Alexander, Dec. 9, 1834	1 lea.	Robertson	Bell
Duke, Thomas M., July 24, 1824	1 lea.	Austin 1	Matagorda
Duke, Thomas M., Nov. 29, 1830	1 lea.	Austin 3	Matagorda
Dunbar, Lavinia, May 1, 1835	1 lea.	De Leon	DeWitt
Dunbar, Lavinia, Apr. 24, 1835		De Leon	Victoria
Duncan, Benjamin, June 28, 1831	1/4 lea.	DeWitt	Gonzales
Duncan, Elisha, Aug. 30, 1835	1 lea.	Zavala	Hardin
Duncan, George H., Feb. 15, 1836	10 lea.	Grant, Durst and Williams	(?)
Duncan, George H., Dec. 5, 1835	1 lea.	Smyth	Harrison (?
Duncan, Meredith, July 25, 1835	1 lea.	Vehlein	2/3 Harris 1/3 Liber
Duncan, Meredith, May 2, 1831		Madero	Liberty
Duncan, Sarah Ann, June 16, 1835	1 lea.	Vehlein	Cherokee
Duncan, William, Apr. 25, 1831	1 lea.	Madero	Liberty
Duncan, William, May 2, 1831		Madero	Liberty
Dunkin, Jacob, May 16, 1835	1/4 lea.	Vehlein	Angelina
Dunlavy, William, Dec. 16, 1835	10 lea.	Williams, Johnson and Peebles	(?)
Dunman, Joseph, Apr. 24, 1831	1 lea.	Madero	Liberty
Dunn, Andrew, Mch. 30, 1835	1 lea.	Milam	Hays
Dunn, Andrew, Feb. 15, 1835	1 lea.	Robertson	Milam
Dunn, James, July 31, 1835	1/4 lea.	Robertson	Robertson
Dunn, James, Dec. 24, 1834	1 lea.	Robertson	Robertson
Dunn, John, Oct. 8, 1834	1 lea.	Power and Hewetson	Refugio
Dunn, Mathew, Dec. 8, 1834	1/4 lea.	Robertson	Milam
Duran, Jose Maria, Oct. 10, 1835	1 lea.	Vehlein	3/4 Chambe 1/4 Jefferson
Duran, Maria Feliciana Curbier, Nov. 7, 1807 Set aside by Sp. Ct. Dec. Misc. Deed 110	2 lea.	V. Flores	Bexar (?)
Duran, Vicente, Dec. 28, 1833	1 lea. 1 lab.	Ximenes	Guadalupe
Durbin, Bazil, Oct. 22, 1830	1/4 lea.	Austin 3	Jackson
Durcy, Francisco, Nov. 9, 1835	6 lea.	Berry	Upshur (?)
Durst, Abraham, May 6, 1831	1 lea.	Austin 2	Brazoria
Durst, John, Apr. 3, 1834	5 lea.	Aldrete	3 1/2 Hous 7 lab. Nacogdoc 4/5 lab. Houston 1 Anderson

Name and Date of Title	Amount	Colony or Commissioner	Present Location
Durst, John, May 9, 1832	8 lea. 23 lab.	Chirino	6 1/4 Cherokee, 2 1/2 Nacogdoches 1/2 Angelina
Durst, Jose, May 18, 1833	2 lea.	Ybarbo	1 Rusk 1 Nacogdoches
Durst, Luis Orlando, Sept. 20, 1835	2 lea.	Grant, Durst and Williams	Lamar (?)
Duty, George, July 19, 1824	1 lea.	Austin 1	Fayette
Duty, Joseph, July 19, 1824	1 lea.	Austin 1	Colorado
Duty, Joseph, Oct. 30, 1832	1/2 lea.	Austin 4	Travis
Duty, Mathew, Oct. 29, 1832	1/2 lea.	Austin 4	Travis
Duty, Solomon, Heirs of, Oct. 30, 1832	1/2 lea.	Austin 4	Bastrop
Duty, Thomas, Aug. 3, 1835	1/3 lea.	McMullen and McGloin	Bee
Duty, William, June 26, 1835	1/4 lea.	Milam	1/2 Travis 1/2 Bastrop
Dweyer, Jeremiah, Nov. 10, 1830	1 lea.	Austin 3	Matagorda
Dweyer, Simon, June 25, 1835	1 lea. 1 lab.	McMullen and McGloin	Bee
Dwight, G. E., Aug. 15, 1835	1 lea.	Robertson	Coryell
Dyer, Clement C., Aug. 10, 1824	1 lea.	Austin 1	Colorado
Dyer, Clement C., Aug. 24, 1824	1 1/2 lab.	Austin 1	Waller
Dyson, James, Mch. 13, 1835	1 lea.	Zavala	Orange
Dyson, William, Feb. 13, 1835	1 lea.	Zavala	Orange
Earle, Thomas, July 7, 1824	1 lea. 1 lab.	Austin 1	Harris
Early, Mary Ann, Mch. 29, 1831	1 lea.	Austin 2	Washington
Earnest, Felix B., Oct. 22, 1830	1/4 lea.	Austin 3	Jackson
Easley, Daniel, Feb. 21, 1835	1 lea.	Zavala	Jefferson
Easley, John, Sept. 29, 1835	1/4 lea.	Robertson	Lee
Eason, Ashley D., Mch. 18, 1835	1/4 lea.	Robertson	Robertson
Eastland, Nicholas, Feb. 16, 1836	1 lea.	Austin 5	Bastrop (?)
Eastland, W. H., Feb. 16, 1836	1 lea.	Austin 5	Bastrop (?)
Easton, Harmon, Mch. 18, 1835	1/4 lea.	Robertson	Falls
Eaton, Benjamin, May 16, 1827	1 lea.	Austin 2	Austin
Eaton, Richard, Dec. 22, 1834	2 1/2 lab.	Robertson	Robertson
Eaton, Richard, Sept. 17, 1835	22 1/2 lab.	Robertson	Limestone
Eaton, Stephen, Oct. 24, 1835	1 lea.	Zavala	Jefferson
Eaton, Stephen H., Sept. 17, 1835	1 lea.	Robertson	Robertson
Eaton, William J., Jan. 25, 1832	1/4 lea.	Austin 3	Matagorda
Ebberly, Jacob, Nov. 7, 1832	1 lea.	Austin 4	Williamson (?)
Eblin, John, June 10, 1831	1 lea.	Austin 2	Fayette
Edens, John, Apr. 20, 1835	1 lea.	Burnet	Houston
Edinburgh, Christopher, June 12, 1835	1 lea.	Vehlein	Walker
Edwards, Amos, Nov. 14, 1830	1 lea.	Austin 3	Galveston
Edwards, Charles, Apr. 30, 1831	1 lea.	Austin 2	Bastrop
Edwards, Daniel F., Sept. 7, 1835	1 lea.	Zavala	Angelina

Name and Date of Title	Amount	Colony or Commissioner	Present Location
Edwards, Gustavus E., Aug. 19, 1824	1 lea.	Austin 1	Wharton
Edwards, Haden, Feb. 16, 1835	11 lea.	Bowie	7 Rusk; 4 Panola
Edwards, Haden H., Oct. 28, 1835	1/3 lea.	Smyth	Gregg
Edwards, John H., Apr. 13, 1831	1 lea.	Austin 2	3/5 Harris 2/5 Mont gomery
Edwards, John T., Apr. 16, 1831	1/4 lea.	Austin 2	Ft. Bend
Edwards, Monroe, Feb. 10, 1835	1 lea.	Robertson	Milam
Egleston, Horatio, July 16, 1835	1 lea.	Milam	Blanco
Egleston, S. V. R., Feb. 21, 1835	1 lea.	Milam	2/3 Hays 1/3 Trav
Elam, John, Aug. 7, 1824	1 lea.	Austin 1	Washingto
Elder, Robert, Aug. 24, 1824	1 lab.	Austin 1	Walker
Eldridge, Thomas, Apr. 1, 1835	1/4 lea.	Robertson	McLennan
Elguezabal, Valentin, Nov. 28, 1833	5 lea.	Aldrete	Red River, Lamar, Bowie (?
Elizondo, Andres and Antonio, Dec. 15, 1835	3 lea.	Falcon	Mexico (?)
Elizondo, Jose Nicolas, Oct. 14, 1835	11 lea.	Berry	10 Hunt; 1 Harrison
Elizondo, Manuel, Oct. 22, 1835	11 lea.	Berry	(?)
Ellery, Joseph, Aug. 23, 1835	1 lea.	Zavala	Hardin
Ellin, James W., Mch. 24, 1835	1 lea.	Milam	(?)
Elliot, F. P., Aug. 27, 1835	1 lea.	Zavala	Hardin
Elliot, Nicholas, Sept. 6, 1835	1 lea.	Zavala	(?)
Elliot, Peter S., Aug. 17, 1835	1 lea.	Burnet	Freestone
Elliot, William, Jan. 12, 1835	1 lea.	Burnet	Anderson
Elliot, William, Mch. 22, 1829	1 lea.	Ybarbo	Rusk
Ellis, Alfred, Aug. 27, 1835	1 lea.	Zavala	Hardin
Ellis, Benjamin F., Aug. 27, 1835	1/4 lea.	Vehlein	Polk
Ellis, George, Aug. 17, 1835	1 lea.	Vehlein	Harris
Ellis, Joseph L., Aug. 27, 1835	1/4 lea.	Vehlein	Polk
Elua, Felipe, Dec. 12, 1833	1 lea.	Ximenes	
Elum, Raines, Feb. 1, 1835	1/4 lea.	Robertson	Milam
Emanuel, Albert, Nov. 25, 1835	1 lea.	Vehlein	Polk (?)
Emanuel, Albert, Jan. 28, 1836	10 lea.	Grant, Durst and Williams	(?)
Emmons, C. B., July 7, 1835	1/4 lea.	Robertson	McLennan
Engledon, Creed S., July 13, 1835	1 lea.	Burnet	Limestone
Engledon, John, June 18, 1835	1 lea.	Burnet	Cherokee
English, George, July 29, 1835	1/4 lea.	Zavala	Sabine
English, James, Oct. 17, 1835	1/4 lea.	Zavala	Newton
Enrique, Rafael, Nov. 6, 1812		Herrera	(?)
Equis, Geronimo, ? ? ?	1 lab. and 690,000 sq. vs.	?	Nacogdoch
Equis, Maria Trinidad, Oct. 9, 1835	1 lea.	Burnet	Henderson
Erath, George B., July 25, 1835	1/4 lea.	Robertson	Burleson
Erie, Santiago, Nov. 21, 1834	1 1/4 lea.	Vehlein	Angelina
Ernst, Frederick, Apr. 16, 1831	1 lea.	Austin 2	Austin

Name and Date of Title	Amount	Colony or Commissioner	Present Location
Escalera, Jose Maria, Apr. 25, 1835		De Leon	Victoria
Escalera, Jose Maria, Apr. 25, 1835		De Leon	Victoria
Escalera, Jose Maria, Apr. 2, 1833	1/4 lea.	De Leon	Victoria
Escalera, Jose Maria, Mch. 20, 1833	1 lea.	De Leon	Victoria
Escalera, Juan Nepomuceno, Mch. 20, 1833	1 lea.	De Leon	Victoria
Escobar, Jose Luis, Sept. 30, 1835	11 lea.	Berry	(?)
Escobedo, Bartolo, June 22, 1835	1 lea.	Vehlein	Polk
Esnaurizar, Antonio Maria, Nov. 10, 1831	11 lea.	Navarro	8 1/2 Guadalupe; 2 Comal 3/4 Hays
Esparza, Alejandro, Mch. 26, 1835	1 lea.	De Leon	1/2 Calhoun 1/2 Victoria
Esparza, Pedro Jose, ? ? ?	15 lab.	?	Nacogdoches
Estrada, Maria Gertrudis, Aug. 11, 1835	1 lea.	Smyth	Smith
Estrada, Yginia, See Heirs of Huizar			
Evans, Holden, Apr. 11, 1831	1 lea.	Austin 2	Brazos
Evans, John S., Apr. 6, 1831		Austin	1/2 Colorado 1/2 Wharton
Evans, Musgrove, Feb. 13, 1836	1 lea.	Austin 5	Bastrop (?)
Evans, Vincent L., Feb. 4, 1836	1 lea.	Austin 5	Bastrop (?)
Everett, William, May 12, 1831	1 lea.	Madero	Liberty
Everitt, Richard, July 30, 1835	1 lea. 1 lab.	McMullen and McGloin	Live Oak
Everitt, Stephen H., Feb. 28, 1835	1 lea.	Zavala	Jasper
Ewing, Alexander, Oct. 3, 1835	1/4 lea.	Austin 5	Fayette
Ewing, Edly, Oct. 5, 1835	1 lea.	Burnet	Anderson
Bwing, George, Nov. 10, 1830	1 lea.	Austin 3	Jackson
Ewing, James L., Oct. 11, 1835	1 lea.	Vehlein	Nacogdoches
Ewing, Wilson, Oct. 14, 1835	1 lea.	Burnet	Anderson
Ewing, Wilson, Oct. 29, 1835	1 lea. 1 lab.	Smyth	Harrison
Eyles, Henry Robert, Nov. 20, 1834	1 lea.	Power and Hewetson	Bee
Fadden, John, July 14, 1835	1/3 lea.	McMullen and McGloin	McMullen
Fadden, Patrick, July 30, 1835	1 lea. 1 lab.	McMullen and McGloin	3/4 McMullen 1/4 Live Oak
Fagan, Nicholas, James and John, Sept. 22, 1834	1 1/2 lea.	Power and Hewetson	Refugio
Fairchild, Philo, Apr. 4, 1831	1 lea.	Austin 2	Ft. Bend
Falcon, Blas Maria, Nov. 18, 1834	5 1/2 lea.	Fernandez	Nueces (?)
Falcon, Jose, May 28, 1835	1 lea.	Zavala	Tyler
Falcon, Josefa Perez, May 2, 1835	1 lea.	Burnet	Rusk
Falcon, Juan, Apr. 24, 1835	1 lea.	Vehlein	Polk
Falenash, Charles, Aug. 19, 1824	1 lea.	Austin 1	Burleson

Name and Date of Title	Amount	Colony or Commis- sioner	Present Location
Faliepe, John, Jan. 24, 1836	1 lea.	Taylor	(?)
Faliepe, Joseph, Jan. 18, 1836	1 lea.	Taylor	(?)
Fan, Eli, Feb. 10, 1836	1 lea.	Austin 5	Madison (?)
Farias, Francisco, Oct. 5, 1835	1 lea.	Navarro	Bexar
Farias, Policarpo, Nov. 18, 1834	2 lea.	Capistran	Nueces
Farley, Massilon, Nov. 1, 1835	1 lea.	Robertson	Milam
Farmer, Alexander, Nov. 23, 1831	1 lea.	Austin 3	Galveston
Faulk, John R., Sr., July 6, 1835	1 lea.	Vehlein	Liberty
Faulkenberry, David, Mch. 18, 1835	1 lea.	Robertson	Limestone
Felder, Charles A., Aug. 28, 1835	1 lea.	Zavala	Hardin
Fennel, John, Sept. 13, 1832	1/4 lea.	DeWitt	DeWitt
Fenton, David, July 29, 1824	1 lea.	Austin 1	Matagorda
Ferguson, Alston, Jan. 5, 1835	1 lea.	Burnet	Cherokee
Ferguson, G. W., Nov. 25, 1835	1 lea.	Taylor	Liberty (?)
Ferguson, John, June 11, 1835	1 lea.	Zavala	(?)
Ferguson, John, Jan. 3, 1835	1 lea.	Burnet	2/3 Anderso 1/3 Hendei son
Ferguson, Joseph, Jan. 5, 1835	1 lea.	Burnet	Anderson
Ferguson, Warwick, Oct. 15, 1835	1 1/4 lea.	Burnet	1/3 Smith 2/3 Hendei son 1/4 Cherokee
Fernandez, Juan, Feb. ?, 1833	1 lea.	De Leon	Jackson
Fernandez, Juan, Apr. 10, 1835		De Leon	Victoria
Fernandez Onafree, Sept. 22, 1835	11 lea.	Berry	Panola, Hun Grayson (
Fernet, A. L., and J. Varin, Oct. 29, 1834	2 lea.	Power and Hewetson	Victoria
Field, Isaiah, June 12, 1835	1 lea.	Vehlein	Liberty
Fields, John F., Aug. 24, 1824	1 lab.	Austin 1	Brazoria
Fin, Santiago, Nov. 15, 1796	?	Zepeda	Sabine or Shelby (?)
Fischback, Isaac H., Dec. 15, 1835	1 lea. 1 lab.	Smyth	Lamar (?)
Fisher, James, July 19, 1824	1 lea.	Austin 1	Burleson
Fisher, James, Dec. 12, 1834	1 lea.	Robertson	Robertson
Fisher, Job., Aug. 10, 1835	1/4 lea.	Robertson	Robertson
Fisher, John, Aug. 10, 1835	1/4 lea.	Robertson	Robertson
Fisher, John, Aug. 14, 1835	1 lea.	Zavala	Tyler
Fisher, Reuben, Feb. 10, 1836	1 lea.	Austin 5	Fayette (?)
Fisher, Reuben, Sept. 5, 1835	1 lea.	Robertson	Milam
Fisher, Samuel R., Aug. 16, 1835	1 lea.	Zavala	3/5 Hardin 2/5 Tyler
Fisher, Samuel Rhoads, Dec. 2, 1830	1 lea.	Austin 3	Matagorda
Fisher, Samuel Rhoads, Oct. 29, 1832	2 lea.	Austin 3	Matagorda
Fisher, William, July 4, 1835	24 lab.	Robertson	Bosque
Fisk, Greenleaf, Nov. 7, 1835	1 lea.	Robertson	Williamson
Fitch, Jabes, July 12, 1835	1/4 lea.	Burnet	Anderson
Fitzgerald, Daniel, July 10, 1824	1 lea.	Austin 1	Ft. Bend
Fitzgibbens, John, Dec. 11, 1828	1 lea.	Austin 2	Austin
Fitzgibbins, William, Mch. 29, 1835	24 lab.	Robertson	Limestone
Fitzgivens, William, Apr. 6, 1831	1 lea.	Austin 2	Grimes

Name and Date of Title	Amount	Colony or Commissioner	Present Location
Fitzsimmons, Patrick and Sons, Sept. 26, 1834	1 1/2 lea.	Power and Hewetson	1 San Patricio 1/2 Refugio
Flack, Elisha, Apr. 13, 1831	1/4 lea.	Austin 2	Wharton
Flanakin, Isaiah, July 19, 1824	2 lab.	Austin 1	Austin
Fleming, Peter, Mch. 15, 1835	1 lea.	Robertson	Hill
Flemings, Joseph, Jan. 18, 1836	1 lea.	Taylor	(?)
Fletcher, Joshua, Feb. 26, 1831	1 lea.	Austin 2	4/5 Washington 1/5 Fayette
Flores, Antonio, Oct. 16, 1834	1 lea.	Vehlein	Angelina
Flores, Felix, Aug. 11, 1835	1 lea.	Smyth	Smith
Flores, Francisco, Mch. 23, 1834	5 lea. 1 lab.	Seguin	Wilson
Flores, Gaspar, Sept. 25, 1835	6 lea.	Navarro	2/3 Wilson 1/3 Karnes
Flores, Geronimo et als., May 21, 1829	10 lea. 1/2 lab.	Padilla	Mexico (?)
Flores, Jose, May 4, 1792	4 lea.	Zepeda	Nacogdoches (?)
Flores, Juan, Aug. 7, 1835	1 lea.	Vehlein	Trinity
Flores, Juan, See Santiago Serna			
Flores, Manuel, Dec. 15, 1835	1 lea.	Berry	. Fannin (?)
Flores, Maria Tinolia, Sept. 22, 1835	1 lea. 1 lab.	Smyth	Upshur
Flores, Martin, Nov. 6, 1835	1 lea. 1 lab.	Taylor	lea. Jasper lab. Liberty
Flores, Roman and Franco. Carreaga, Mch. 4, 1829	14 lea.	Padilla	Mexico (?)
Flores, Vital, Nov. 22, 1833	5 lea.	Aldrete	Louisiana (?)
Flores, Vital, Dec. 14, 1833	6 lea.	Aldrete	5 San Jacinto 1 Walker
Flores, Vital, July 15, 1829	1 lea.	Ybarbo	Nacogdoches
Flowers, Elisha, July 19, 1824	1 lea. 1 lab.	Austin 1	lea. Matagorda lab. Colorado
Foirman, Abraham, Nov. 14, 1835	1 lea.	Taylor	Jasper (?)
Fokes, Abigail, Nov. 2, 1835	1 lea.	Robertson	Milam
Foley, George, July 10, 1831	1/4 lea.	DeWitt	Lavaca
Foote, Robert, Oct. 5, 1835	1/4 lea.	Burnet	Limestone
Forbes, John, May 6, 1835	1 lea.	Vehlein	Houston
Forbes, John, Oct. 1, 1835	11 lea.	Bowie	Rusk (?)
Ford, James, Apr. 11, 1831	1 lea.	Austin 2	Walker
Ford, William W., Oct. 17, 1832	1/4 lea.	Austin 2	Montgomery
Fordhran, Charles, May 18, 1831	1/4 lea.	Austin 2	Colorado
Foster, Isaac, Aug. 10, 1824	1 lea.	Austin 1	24/25 Matagorda 1/25 Brazoria
Foster, James, Nov. 22, 1832	1 lea.	Austin 4	Burleson
Foster, John, July 15, 1824	2 1/2 lea. 3 lab.	Austin 1	Ft. Bend
Foster, John R., Nov. 26, 1832	1/4 lea.	Austin 3	Jackson
Foster, John R., Dec. 16, 1835	10 lea.	Williams, Johnson and Peebles	Grayson (?)

Name and Date of Title	Amount	Colony or Commissioner	Present Location
Foster, Moses A., June 22, 1832	1 lea.	Austin 2	Brazos
Foster, Randolph, July 16, 1824	1 lea.	Austin 1	3/4 Ft. Bez 1/4 Walke
Fox, Michael, Nov. 25, 1834	1 lea.	Power and Hewetson	Bee
Fraisier, Suzannah, June 4, 1835	10 lab. and 811,597 sq. vs.	Zavala	Orange
Francis, Sebastian, Oct. 10, 1835	1 lea.	Smyth	Grayson
Frazer, Harmon, Oct. 23, 1835	1 lea.	Vehlein	Tyler
Frazier, James, See David Shelby			
French, John J., June 26, 1835	1 lea.	Zavala	Jefferson
French, Joseph, Feb. 8, 1835	24 lab.	Robertson	McLennan
Friar, Daniel B., Nov. 27, 1832	1 lea.	Austin 4	Washington
Friar, Daniel B., Feb. 20, 1835	24 lab.	Robertson	Milam
Frier, Enoch, Oct. 11, 1835	1 lea.	Burnet	Navarro
Frost, David, Nov. 21, 1832	1/4 lea.	Austin 2	5/6 Washinton 1/6 Burleson
Frost, Robert B., Mch. 25, 1835	1/4 lea.	Robertson	Limestone
Frost, Samuel, Dec. 22, 1834	1 lea.	Robertson	Milam
Frost, Samuel, Apr. 1, 1835	1 lab.	Robertson	Limestone
Frost, William, June 8, 1835	1 lea.	Burnet	Anderson
Fuente (de la), Jose Felix, Apr. 6, 1835	1 lea.	De Leon	Calhoun
Fuente, Jose Maria, Sept. 30, 1835	11 lea.	Berry	(?)
Fulcher, Francis, May 14, 1835	1 lea.	Vehlein	Madison
Fulcher, Jacob, Nov. 24, 1835	1 lea. 1 lab.	Taylor	Jefferson
Fulcher, John, Sept. 12, 1835	1 lea.	Robertson	Bell
Fulcher, Joshua, Nov. 21, 1835	1 lea.	Smyth	Panola (?)
Fullenwider, Peter H., Oct. 20, 1835	1 lea.	Austin 3	Madison
Fuller, Benjamin F., July 16, 1835	1 lea.	Zavala	San August
Fuller, E. M., Sept. 12, 1835	1 lea.	Smyth	Harrison
Fuller, Franklin, Oct. 12, 1835	1 lea.	Smyth	Harrison
Fuller, Samuel, Apr. 20, 1831	1 lea.	Austin 2	Lavaca
Fullerton, Henry, Dec. 22, 1834	1 lea.	Robertson	Robertson
Fulshear, Benjamin, Apr. 24, 1831	1/4 lea.	DeWitt	1/2 DeWitt 1/2 Gonzales
Fulshear, Benjamin and Graves, June 3, 1831	1 lea.	Navarro	Guadalupe
Fulshear, Churchill, Apr. 24, 1831	1 lea.	DeWitt	DeWitt
Fulshear, Churchill, July 16, 1824	1 lea.	Austin 1	Ft. Bend
Fulshear, Graves, Apr. 24, 1831	1/4 lea.	DeWitt	DeWitt
Fulton, Marcus L., Oct. 24, 1835	1/4 lea.	Austin 5	Brazos
Fulton, Samuel, Apr. 9, 1831	1 lea.	Austin 2	Grimes
Fuqua, Benjamin, June 14, 1832	1/4 lea.	DeWitt	Guadalupe
Fuqua, Silas, June 16, 1832	1 lea.	DeWitt	Caldwell
Furnash, John, Mch. 30, 1831	1/4 lea.	Austin 2	Austin
Gafford, Clardey, Aug. 1, 1835	1 lea.	Robertson	McLennan
Gafford, Jefferson, July 31, 1835	1/4 lea.	Robertson	Robertson
Gafford, John, Sept. 10, 1835	22 lab.	Robertson	Milam

Name and Date of Title	Amount	Colony or Commis- sioner	Present Location
Gafford, John, Sept. 10, 1835	2 lab.	Robertson	Falls
Gafford, Stephen, July 30, 1835	1 lea.	Robertson	Robertson
Gage, Burleson, Sept. 20, 1835	1 lea.	Milam	Comal (?)
Gage, Moses, Oct. 8, 1835	1 lea.	Austin 5	Caldwell
Gage, Reuben, Sept. 25, 1835	1 lea.	Milam	Bastrop
Gagne, Jean Baptiste, May 25, 1835	1 lea.	Burnet	Rusk
Gaines, James, Apr. 3, 1830	1 lea.	Padilla	Sabine
Gaines, Thompson C., June 20, 1835	1 lea.	Zavala	Hardin
Galan, Norberto, Sept. 29, 1833	1 lea.	Aldrete	Goliad
Galan, Tomas and Antonio, Oct. 4, 1834	1 1/4 lea.	Power and Hewetson	Refugio
Galban, Estevan, Apr. 9, 1835		De Leon	Victoria
Galban, Jose, Apr. 24, 1833	1 lea.	De Leon	Victoria
Galban, Jose Maria, Oct. 30, 1834	1 lea.	Power and Hewetson	Victoria
Galbruith, George, May 13, 1831	1/4 lea.	Austin 2	Harris
Galindo, Andres, Apr. 5, 1834		De Leon	Victoria
Galindo, Ygnacio, Sept. 15, 1835	11 lea.	Berry	(?)
Galindo, Ygnacio, Apr. 13, 1833	11 lea.	Lessassier	9/10 McLennan 1/10 Falls
Gallaher, Edward, May 21, 1827	1/4 lea.	Austin 2	Wharton
Gallardo, Pedro, Oct. 30, 1834	1 lea.	Power and Hewetson	Victoria
Gallardo, Pedro, Mch. 21, 1833	1 lea.	De Leon	Jackson
Gallion, John, June 19, 1835	1 lea.	Zavala	Sabine
Galoway, Peter, Apr. 15, 1835	1 lea.	Zavala	San Augustine
Gamez, Jose Maria, Aug. 4, 1835	1 lea.	Vehlein	Trinity
Garancio, Eufrazio, Apr. 25, 1835		De Leon	Victoria
Garcia, Atanacio, Mch. 23, 1835	1/4 lea.	Milam	Bastrop
Garcia, Casimiro, Nov. 23, 1835	1 lea.	Zavala	Liberty (?)
Garcia, Cleto, Apr. 10, 1835	1 lea.	De Leon	Calhoun
Garcia, Desiderio, Mch. 23, 1833	1 lea.	De Leon	Victoria
Garcia, Diego, Apr. 26, 1835	1 lea.	De Leon	Victoria
Garcia, Diego, Mch. 12, 1835	1 lea.	De Leon	Victoria
Garcia, Florentine, Apr. 26, 1835	1 lea.	De Leon	Calhoun
Garcia, Gregorio, June 20, 1835	1 lea.	Zavala	Hardin
Garcia, Jose, Nov. 15, 1835	1 lea.	Zavala	Tyler (?)
Garcia, Jose Antonio, Oct. 22, 1835	11 lea.	Del Moral	(?)
Garcia, Manuel, Apr. 12, 1816	2 lea.	Enriquez	Webb (?)
Garcia, Maria, Mch. 21, 1835		De Leon	Victoria
Garcia, Florentina, Mch. 20, 1835		De Leon	Victoria
Garcia, Pedro, Apr. 10, 1835	1 lea.	De Leon	Calhoun
Garcia, Rafael, Mch. 21, 1835	5 lea.	De la Fuente	Starr
Garcia, Rafael, May 22, 1829	7 lea. 2 lab.	Fernandez	Cameron
Garcia, Pedro, Apr. 17, 1836	4 lea.	Ramirez	Hidalgo
Garcia, Rosalia, Apr. 9, 1835		De Leon	Victoria
Garcia, Valentin, Apr. 3, 1835		De Leon	Victoria
Garcia, Valentin, Jan. 5, 1833	4 lea.	De Leon	Jackson
Garcia, Valentin, Apr. 4, 1835	1 lea. 9 lab.	De Leon	Calhoun
Garcia, Valentin, Sept. 27, 1834	3 lea. 16 lab.	De Leon	Victoria

Name and Date of Title	Amount	Colony or Commissioner	Present Location
Garcia, Valentin, Sept. 7, 1834	3 lea. 16 lab.	De Leon	Victoria
Garcia, Ysidro, Mch. 31, 1835	5 lea.	De la Fuente	Starr
Garner, Arthur, Sept. 30, 1835	1 lea.	Vehlein	San Jacinto
Garner, Edward, Aug. 3, 1835	1/3 lea.	McMullen and McGloin	Atascosa
Garner, James, June 30, 1835	1 lea. 1 lab.	McMullen and McGloin	McMullen
Garner, James A., Sept. 30, 1835	1/4 lea.	Vehlein	San Jacinto
Garner, James S., Sept. 30, 1835	1 lea.	Vehlein	Polk
Garner, Reden, July 9, 1835	1 lea.	Burnet	Freestone
Garner, Thomas H., July 8, 1835	1 lea.	Burnet	Leon
Garnett, William, Mch. 11, 1835	1/4 lea.	Robertson	Milam
Garrett, Alse, Apr. 20, 1835	1 lea.	Burnet	Leon
Garrett, Charles, July 15, 1824	1 lea. 1 lab. and 440,000 sq. vs.	Austin 1	lea. Brazos lab. Walle
Garrett, Claiborne, Dec. 3, 1832	1/4 lea.	Austin 2	Grimes
Garrett, Eli, June 3, 1835	1/4 lea.	Burnet	Nacogdoche
Garrett, Jacob, Nov. 9, 1835	1 lea.	Zavala	San August
Garrett, Milton, May 15, 1835	1/4 lea.	Vehlein	Angelina
Garrett, Thomas B., Mch. 12, 1835	1 lea.	Vehlein	Liberty
Garvin, John E., May 5, 1831	1/4 lea.	DeWitt	Gonzales
Garza (de la), Alejandro, Oct. 20, 1834	2 lea.	Lewis	Brazos
Garza (de la), Alejandro, Oct. 22, 1834	3 lea.	Lewis	Ellis
Garza (de la), Andres, June 25, 1832	3 lea.	Garcia	Starr
Garza (de la), Baltazar, ? ? ?	1 lab. and 539,650 sq. vs.	?	Nacogdoche (?)
Garza, Carlos and Rafael, Oct. 28, 1834	1 1/4 lea.	Power and Hewetson	Victoria
Garza, Cayetano, Nov. 15, 1834	1 lea.	Power and Hewetson	San Patrici
Garza, Dionisio, June 27, 1832	4 1/5 lea.	Garcia	Starr
Garza, Jesus, Apr. 5, 1834	4 lea.	Aldrete	7/8 Angeli 1/8 Cherokee
Garza, Joaquin, Mch. 24, 1834	1 lea.	McMullen and McGloin	Atascosa
Garza, Jose Antonio, Apr. 15, 1824	2 lea.	Saucedo	Bexar
Garza, Manuel, Oct. 1, 1835	1 lea.	Berry	2/3 Graysc 1/3 Cooke
Garza, Jose Maria, Nov. 4, 1833	11 lea.	Aldrete	5 Montgome 3 1/4 San Jacinto 2 Walker
Garza, Juan, July 4, 1835	1 lea. 1 lab.	McMullen and McGloin	San Patrici

Garza, Juan and Jose, See Santiago Serna

Name and Date of Title	Amount	Colony or Commissioner	Present Location
Garza, Juan Nepomuceno, ? ? ?	10 lea.	?	Hidalgo
Garza, Julian, Mch. 9, 1833		De Leon	Victoria
Garza, Julian de la, his wife, Maria Antonia, Nov. 15, 1834	2 3/4 lea.	Power and Hewetson	San Patricio
Garza, Manuel, May 22, 1829	6 lea. 7 lab.	Fernandez	Cameron (?)
Garza, Maria Antonia, Mch. 18, 1835		De Leon	Victoria
Garza, Maria Antonia, Apr. 24, 1835		De Leon	Victoria
Garza, Maria Jacinta, for her son, Antonio Gorcoschea, Oct. 23, 1834	1 lea.	Power and Hewetson	San Patricio
Garza, Patricio, July 31, 1835		De Leon	Victoria
Garza, Patricio, June 15, 1835	5 lab.	De Leon	Victoria
Garza, Pedro, Mch. 13, 1834	11 lea.	Vasquez	DeWitt (?)
Garza, Roman, May 7, 1831	11 lea.	Madero	1/2 Houston 1/2 Leon
Gates, John, Oct. 3, 1835	1 lea.	Vehlein	(?)
Gates, Samuel, July 8, 1824	1 lea.	Austin 1	Washington
Gates, Samuel, May 7, 1831	1 lea.	Austin 2	Lee
Gates, William, July 16, 1824	2 lea.	Austin 1	Washington
Gates, William, June 20, 1835	1 lea.	Burnet	Cherokee
Gay, Thomas, June 8, 1831	1/4 lea.	Austin 2	Ft. Bend
Gay, Thomas, Nov. 24, 1832	3/4 lea.	Austin 2	Fayette
Gazley, Thomas J., Mch. 1, 1831	1 lea.	Austin 2	Bastrop
Gedruf, Lefroy, June 20, 1835	1 lea.	Zavala	6/7 Liberty 1/7 Hardin
Gee, Alfred, Oct. 19, 1835	1 lea.	Austin 5	Madison
Gee, Eason, June 20, 1835	1 lea.	Burnet	2/3 Smith 1/3 Cherokee
Geiger, Jacob H., May 2, 1831		Madero	Liberty
Gengle, Pedro, May 6, 1792	2,840 sq. vs.	Zepeda	Nacogdoches
George, Freeman, July 7, 1824	1 lea. 1 lab.	Austin 1	lea. Matagorda lab. Waller
George, James, June 28, 1831	1 lea.	DeWitt	Caldwell
George, John, July 29, 1835	1 lea.	Vehlein	Trinity
Gerish, James Sr., Jan. 27, 1835	1 lea.	Zavala	Jefferson
Gerish, James Jr., Feb. 17, 1835	1 lea.	Zavala	Jefferson
Gervais, Sinclair D., Mch. 26, 1835	1 lea.	Milam	Hays
Ghalleher, David, Feb. 1, 1835	1 lea.	Robertson	Milam
Gholson, Albert G., July 3, 1835	1/4 lea.	Robertson	Falls
Gholson, Samuel, Apr. 25, 1835	1 lea.	Robertson	McLennan
Gholston, Samuel, Feb. 9, 1835	1 lab.	Robertson	Falls
Gibbs, Zacheus, Feb. 2, 1835	1 lea.	Burnet	Cherokee
Gibson, Absalom, Dec. 30, 1834	1 lea.	Burnet	Cherokee
Gibson, Absalom, Nov. 30, 1835	10 lea.	Williams, Johnson and Peebles	(?)
Gibson, James, June 12, 1832	24 lab.	DeWitt	22 Gonzales 2 Fayette
Gibson, James, Aug. 11, 1831	1 lab.	DeWitt	Gonzales
Gibson, Jesse, June 10, 1835	1 lea.	Burnet	Anderson

Name and Date of Title	Amount	Colony or Commissioner	Present Location
Gibson, Samuel, Nov. 4, 1835	1 lea.	Taylor	Jefferson (?
Gil, Carlos, Apr. 17, 1834	5 lea.	Aldrete	(?)
Gilbert, John, June 5, 1835	1 lea.	Zavala	Sabine
Gilbert, Preston, June 4, 1827	1 lea.	Austin 1	Colorado
Gilbert, Sarah, June 11, 1827	1 lea.	Austin 1	Wharton
Gilchrist, Charles, Nov. 20, 1835	1 lea.	Zavala	Jasper (?)
Gill, John P., May 13, 1831	1/4 lea.	Austin 2	2/3 Washington 1/3 Fayette
Gillan, Michael, June 22, 1831	1 lea.	De Witt	Caldwell
Gillet, J., (heirs of), Mch. 27, 1831	1 lea.	Austin 2	Grimes
Gilliland, Daniel, Aug. 3, 1824	1 lab.	Austin 1	Austin
Gilliland, Daniel, Apr. 26, 1831	1 lea.	Austin 2	Colorado
Gilliland, Elam W., July 6, 1835	1 lea.	Burnet	Leon
Gilliland, James, Oct. 15, 1832	1 lea.	Austin 4	Travis
Gistman, David, Nov. 29, 1835	1 lea.	Taylor	(?)
Givens, Charles C., Aug. 12, 1835	10 lea.	Williams, Johnson and Peebles	Hunt (?)
Givens, Charles C., Dec. 11, 1828	1/4 lea.	Austin 2	Washington
Glass, George, Nov. 25, 1835	1 lea. 1 lab.	Smyth	(?)
Glass, George M., Nov. 22, 1835	1 lea.	Taylor	Jefferson (?
Glass, Peter, Nov. 4, 1835	1 lea. 1 lab.	Smyth	(?)
Glass, William, Nov. 28, 1835	1 lea. 1 lab.	Taylor	Jefferson (?
Glenn (widow) Sally, Nov. 4, 1834	1 lea.	Zavala	Jasper
Goguet, Estevan, See Pedro de Lara			
Golightly, John, Oct. 13, 1835	1 lea.	Taylor	Jefferson (?
Golightly, T. J., Nov. 3, 1835	1/4 lea.	Vehlein	San Jacinto
Goliher, Matthew, Oct. 28, 1835	1 lea.	Burnet	Henderson
Gomez, Maximo, Dec. 20, 1834	1 lea.	Power and Hewetson	5/6 Bee 1/6 Refugi
Gomez, Jose Maria, Aug. 4, 1835	1 lea.	Vehlein	
Gomez, Yrineo, Jan. 15, 1848	5 lea.	Flores	Hidalgo
Gonzales, Antonio, Sept. 8, 1835	11 lea.	Berry	(?)
Gonzales (Hidalgo) Francisco, Oct. 13, 1834	1 lea.	Power and Hewetson	Victoria
Gonzales, Jose Antonio (y Valdes), Apr. 22, 1834	4 lea.	Aldrete	(?)
Gonzales, Jose Antonio (y Valdes), Mch. 4, 1834	3 lea.	Vasquez	Karnes
Gonzales, Jose Antonio (y Valdes), Jan. 30, 1834	2 lea.	Vasquez	Karnes (?)
Gonzales, Jose Antonio (y Valdes), vol. 28 p. 18			De Witt
Gonzales, Feliciano, Oct. 13, 1835	1 lea.	Berry	Lamar
Gonzales, Juan, Apr. 18, 1834	11 lea.	Soto	Kinney
Gonzales, Juan, Oct. 15, 1834	1 lea.	Power and Hewetson	Victoria
Gonzales, Maria Sinforosa, May 9, 1835	1 lea.	Burnet	Rusk
Gonzales, Pedro, Apr. 24, 1835		De Leon	Victoria

Name and Date of Title	Amount	Colony or Commissioner	Present Location
Gonzales, Pedro, July 30, 1835	1/4 lea.	De Leon	Calhoun
Gonzales, Romano, May 12, 1835	1/4 lea.	Burnet	Rusk
Gonzales, Santiago, Apr. 11, 1835	1 lea.	De Leon	Calhoun
Gonzales, Simon, Apr. 24, 1835		De Leon	Victoria
Gonzales, Town of, Aug. 25, 1832	4 lea.	DeWitt	Gonzales
Good, Edward, July 6, 1835	1 lea.	Zavala	Jasper
Goodrich, B. B., July 22, 1835	1 lea.	Vehlein	Walker
Goodwin, Henry, Oct. 15, 1835	1 lea.	Zavala	Newton
Goodwin, Robert, Oct. 15, 1835	1 lea.	Zavala	Newton
Goodwin, Shearly, Oct. 18, 1835	1 lea.	Zavala	Newton
Gorbet, Chester, July 19, 1824	1 lea.	Austin 1	Brazoria
Gorden, Elizabeth, Apr. 11, 1831	1 lea.	Austin 2	Washington
Gordian, Antonio, Oct. 1, 1835	1 lea. 1 lab.	Taylor	(?)
Gorham, William, Nov. 21, 1832	1/4 lea.	Austin 2	Fayette
Gortari, Elijio, Aug. 30, 1831	1 lea.	Navarro	Guadalupe
Gortari, Elijio, Feb. 23, 1834	1 lea. 1 lab.	Bustillo	Bexar
Gortari, Vicente, Dec. 28, 1833	1 lea.	Ximenes	Guadalupe
Goscazcohechea, Antonio, Oct. 23, 1834	1 lea.	Power and	San Patricio
(See Maria Jacinta de la Garza)		Hewetson	(?)
Goss, Thomas, Oct. 15, 1835	1 lea.	Burnet	Anderson
Gossett, Elijah, Feb. 7, 1835	1 lea.	Burnet	Houston
Gossett, James L., July 24, 1835	1 lea.	Burnet	Houston
Gouldrich, Michael, Aug. 24, 1824	1 lab.	Austin 1	Galveston
Gove, Humphry N., Dec. 15, 1832	1/4 lea.	Austin 3	Matagorda
Gragg, John, Dec. 16, 1835	1 lea. 1 lab.	Smyth	Lamar (?)
Gragg, Moses, May 28, 1835	1 lea.	Vehlein	Houston
Graham, Andrew, Nov. 19, 1832	1 lea.	Austin 2	Bastrop
Graham, John H., Nov. 7, 1835	1 lea.	Zavala	Angelina
Graham, Sam L., Oct. 26, 1835	1/4 lea.	Zavala	Tyler
Graham, Walter B., Oct. 26, 1835	1/4 lea.	Zavala	Angelina
Grande, Jose de Jesus, vol. 29, p. 195			
Grande, Jose de Jesus, Dec. 13, 1833	3 lea.	Aldrete	3/5 Freestone 2/5 Anderson
Grange, Marcelo, Oct. 15, 1835	1 lea.	Zavala	Jefferson
Grantham, Mathew F., Dec. 7, 1832	1/4 lea.	Austin 2	Austin
Grasmeyer, F. W., Apr. 4, 1831	1/4 lea.	Austin 2	Bastrop
Graves, Heirs of Richard, Nov. 15, 1830	1 lea.	Austin 3	Matagorda
Graves, Thomas A., Nov. 10, 1835	1/4 lea.	Robertson	Milam
Gray, Allen G., Sept. 16, 1835	1 lea.	Zavala	(?)
Gray, Daniel, Feb. 4, 1836	1 lea.	Austin 5	Bastrop (?)
Gray, Joshua, Feb. 5, 1836	1/4 lea.	Austin 5	Bastrop (?)
Gray, Mayberry B., Oct. 13, 1835	1/4 lea.	Austin 5	Washington
Gray, Pleasant, July 12, 1835	1 lea.	Vehlein	Walker
Gray, Thomas, Feb. 4, 1836	1/4 lea.	Austin 5	Bastrop (?)
Gray, Thomas and J. H. Moore, Aug. 16, 1824	1 lea. 1 lab.	Austin 1	lea. Brazoria lab. Colorado
Gray, Thomas Fairfax, Feb. 27, 1836	1 lea.	Austin 5	Lavaca (?)
Grayham, John M., Aug. 26, 1835	1 lab.	Robertson	Falls
Grayham, John M., July 5, 1831	1 lea.	Robertson	Falls
Grayson, Peter Wm., July 22, 1831	1 lea.	Austin 3	Matagorda

Name and Date of Title	Amount	Colony or Commis- sioner	Present Location
Green, Amos, May 2, 1831	1 lea.	Madero	Liberty
Green, Amos, May 2, 1831		Madero	Liberty
Green, Benjamin, Oct. 27, 1831	1 lea.	Austin 5	Fayette
Green, Benjamin M., Aug. 28, 1831	1 lea.	Taylor	Liberty (?
Green, Fitz H., Aug. 26, 1831	1/3 lea.	Taylor	Hardin
Green, Fitz M., May 2, 1831		Madero	Liberty
Green, Patrick, Jan. 8, 1833	1 lea.	Austin 3	1/2 Jacksc 1/2 Mata gorda
Green, Reason, Aug. 26, 1835	1 lea.	Taylor	Liberty
Green, Reason, May 2, 1831		Madero	Liberty
Greenville, Benjamin, Oct. 23, 1835	1 lea.	Austin 5	Fayette
Greenwood, Elizabeth, May 7, 1831	1 lea.	Austin 2	Burleson
Greenwood, Franklin J., Apr. 7, 1831	1 lea.	Austin 2	Grimes
Greenwood, Garrison, Mch. 5, 1835	1 lea.	Burnet	Houston
Greenwood, Joel, May 13, 1831	1 lea.	Austin 2	Grimes
Greeson, Isaac, Oct. 12, 1835	1 lea.	Burnet	Henderson
Gregg, Darius, Apr. 6, 1831	1/4 lea.	Austin 2	Grimes
Gregory, John, Nov. 4, 1835	1 lea.	Vehlein	Houston
Griffin, Moses, July 29, 1835	1 lea.	Robertson	Bell
Griffith, Henry, Apr. 25, 1831	1 lea.	Madero	Chambers
Griffith, Henry, May 10, 1831	1 lea.	Austin 2	Wharton
Griffith, Noah, Apr. 11, 1831	1 lea.	Austin 2	Montgome¤
Grigsby, Joseph, Nov. 6, 1834	1 lea.	Zavala	Jefferson
Grigsby, Nathaniel, Oct. 28, 1834	1/4 lea.	Zavala	Jasper
Grillet, Cleri, Oct. 22, 1835	1 lea. 1 lab.	Taylor	Harrison
Grimes, Frederick, Mch. 9, 1831	1/4 lea.	Austin 2	1/2 Austin 1/2 Wash ington
Grimes, George, Mch. 16, 1831	1 lea.	Austin 2	Austin
Grimes, Jesse, Apr. 6, 1831	1 lea.	Austin 2	Grimes
Grisset, John, Nov. 23, 1835	1 lea. 1 lab.	Taylor	Orange
Gritten, Edward, July 28, 1835	1/4 lea.	Milam	Bastrop
Gritten, Edward, July 28, 1835	1 lea.	Milam	Travis
Groce, Elizabeth, July 8, 1835	1 lea.	Burnet	Anderson
Groce, Jared E., July 29, 1824	10 lea.	Austin 1	5 Brazoria 3 Grimes 2 Waller
Groce, Jared E. Jr., Jan. 29, 1836	1 lea.	Austin 5	Waller (?)
Groce, Leonard K., Apr. 21, 1831	1 lea.	Austin 2	Grimes
Gross, Larkin, May 28, 1835	1 lea.	Zavala	Sabine
Guajardo, Bacilio, Apr. 25, 1835		De Leon	Victoria
Guajardo Pascual, Apr. 12, 1835	1 lea.	De Leon	Calhoun
Guerrero, Francisco, Aug. 30, 1827	8 lea. 24 lab. 449,550 sq. vs.	Mora	San August
Guerrero, Maria Guadalupe, Apr. 25, 1835		De Leon	Victoria
Guild, Alfred R., Feb. 16, 1833	1/4 lea.	Austin 4	Burleson
Guild, Alfred R., June 15, 1835	1 lea.	Aldrete	Burleson
Guthrie, Robert, July 19, 1824	1 lea.	Austin 1	Jackson
Gutierres, Alberto, Aug. 9, 1833	4 lea.	Aldrete	3 1/2 Karn 1/2 Golia

Name and Date of Title	Amount	Colony or Commis- sioner	Present Location
Gutierres, Antonio Ramon, Oct. 1, 1835	1 lea. 1 lab.	Taylor	(?)
Gutierres, Francisco, Oct. 8, 1835	1 lea.	Taylor	(?)
Gutierres, Valentin, Apr. 8, 1835		De Leon	Victoria
Hadden, John, July 29, 1834	1 lea.	Austin 1	Colorado
Hadley, Joshua, May 7, 1831	1 lea.	Austin 2	Grimes
Hadley, Joshua, Feb. 25, 1835	1 lea.	Robertson	Limestone
Hady, Samuel C., Aug. 19, 1824	1 lea.	Austin 1	Waller
Hagan, John, Aug. 25, 1835	1 lea.	Burnet	Houston
Hagerty, Thomas J., Sept. 17, 1835	1 lea.	Vehlein	Liberty
Haggard, James, May 21, 1835	1 lea.	Milam	Bastrop
Haggard, William H., May 23, 1835	1 lea.	Milam	Hays
Haile, Jonas J., Aug. 25, 1835	1 lea.	Burnet	Houston
Halderman, Jesse, Dec. 3, 1832	1/4 lea.	Austin 4	Washington
Haley, John, Feb. 25, 1835	23 lab. and 198,750 sq. vs.	Zavala	Sabine
Hall, Briton, June 20, 1835	1 lea.	Zavala	Jasper
Hall, Elisha, Nov. 12, 1830	1 lea.	Austin 3	Matagorda
Hall, George B., See Samuel T. Angier			
Hall, George H. and als., Nov. 20, 1834	1 lea.	Power and Hewetson	Goliad
Hall, Hudson, Oct. 27, 1835	1/3 lea.	Smyth	Harrison
Hall, James, Nov. 6, 1835	1 lea.	Robertson	Milam
Hall, James, Jan. 3, 1835	1 lea.	Burnet	Anderson
Hall, James, Jr., Apr. 26, 1831	1 lea.	Austin 2	Waller
Hall, James, 3rd, May 7, 1831	1 lea.	Austin 2	Burleson
Hall, John, July 10, 1824	2 lea. 2 lab.	Austin 1	lea. Brazoria lab. Waller
Hall, John, Apr. 25, 1831	1/4 lea.	Austin 2	Waller
Hall, Sarah, Oct. 31, 1834	1 lea.	Power and Hewetson	Goliad
Hall, Solomon, Feb. 5, 1836	1 lea.	Austin 5	2/3 Gonzales 1/3 Caldwell ?
Hall, Warren D. C., Dec. 2, 1830	1 lea.	Austin 3	Brazoria
Hall, Warren D. C., June 24, 1831	1 lea.	Austin 3	2/3 Harris 1/3 Brazoria
Hall, William, July 10, 1824	1 lea.	Austin 1	Ft. Bend
Hall, William A., Dec. 3, 1832	1 lea.	Austin 4	Fayette
Hallmark, Geo. W., Aug. 15, 1835	1 lea.	Vehlein	Houston
Ham, Caiaphas K., Nov. 23, 1832	1/4 lea.	Austin 2	Austin
Hamblin, Paschal, Oct. 10, 1835	1 lea.	Austin 5	Montgomery
Hamilton, David, May 9, 1827	1 lea.	Austin 1	Wharton
Hamilton, Francis, Oct. 12, 1835	1 lea.	Smyth	Grayson
Hamilton, James, June 12, 1835	1 lea.	Burnet	Cherokee
Hamilton, Josiah F., Apr. 6, 1831	1 lea.	Austin 2	Wharton
Hamilton, Walter F., Apr. 30, 1831	1 lea.	Austin 2	Fayette
Hampton, Alexander, Aug. 30, 1835	1 lea.	Zavala	Hardin
Hampton, Lowry T., Apr. 10, 1835	1 lea.	Vehlein	Polk
Hanks, Bird L., Dec. 24, 1832	1 lea.	Austin 4	Washington
Hanks, Elijah F., Oct. 15, 1835	1 lea.	Zavala	Tyler
Hanks, Wyatt, Nov. 5, 1834	1 lea.	Zavala	Jasper

Name and Date of Title	Amount	Colony or Commissioner	Present Location
Hanley, James, Sept. 17, 1835	1 lea.	Vehlein	Trinity
Hannor, Jesse, Sept. 12, 1835	1 lea.	Robertson	McLennan
Hansley, Sarah, July 5, 1835	24 lab.	Robertson	Bosque
Hansley, Sarah, Aug. 21, 1835	1 lab.	Robertson	Falls
Harbor, Joseph, Dec. 11, 1828	1 lea.	Austin 2	Washington
Hardin, Augustine B., May 11, 1831	1/2 lea.	Madero	Liberty
Hardin, Benjamin Watson, May 11, 1831	1 lea.	Madero	Liberty
Hardin, Benjamin W., May 2, 1831		Madero	Liberty
Hardin, Ennis, May 27, 1835	1 lea.	Robertson	Bosque
Hardin, Franklin, May 12, 1831	1/4 lea.	Madero	Liberty
Hardin, Milton A., June 17, 1835	1/4 lea.	Vehlein	Polk
Hardin, Samuel H., Apr. 25, 1831	1/2 lea.	Austin 2	Waller
Hardin, William, Apr. 23, 1831	1 lea.	Austin 2	Harris
Hardin, William, Sept. 16, 1835	1 lea.	Vehlein	San Jacinto
Hardin, Zara, May 2, 1831		Madero	Liberty
Hardison, John, Oct. 10, 1835	1 lea. 1 lab.	Smyth	Grayson
Hardy, William, Apr. 16, 1831	1 lea.	Austin 2	Lavaca
Harland, Isaiah, Feb. 20, 1835	1 lea.	Robertson	Falls
Harmon, Elijah D., Nov. 7, 1835	1 lea.	Robertson	Williamson
Harmon, John, Mch. 12, 1835	1 lea.	Robertson	McLennan
Harmon, John, May 21, 1835	1 lea.	Zavala	Orange
Harper, Benjamin J., Mch. 4, 1835	1 lea.	Vehlein	Polk
Harper, Henry, Oct. 13, 1835	1 lea.	Smyth	Harrison
Harrington, Arabella, Mch. 22, 1831	1 lea.	Austin 2	Washington
Harris, Abner, See William Barrett			
Harris, Anthony, Mch. 19, 1835	1/4 lea.	Zavala	Orange
Harris, David, Aug. 19, 1824	1 lea.	Austin 1	Harris
Harris, David, Oct. 20, 1832	1 lea.	Austin 3	Harris
Harris, Edward C., June 26, 1835	1 lea.	Burnet	Anderson
Harris, Isaac, June 25, 1832	1 lea.	Austin 4	Bastrop
Harris, James, Oct. 10, 1835	1 lea.	Smyth	Harrison
Harris, John, Oct. 16, 1832	1/4 lea.	Austin 2	Grimes
Harris, John R., Aug. 16, 1824	1 lea.	Austin 1	Harris
Harris, William, July 10, 1824	1 lea.	Austin 1	Brazoria
Harris, William, Dec. 18, 1830	2/3 lea.	Austin 3	Brazoria
Harris, William, May 10, 1831	1 lea.	Madero	Liberty
Harris, William and D. Carpenter, Aug. 16, 1824	1 lea.	Austin 1	Harris
Harris, William E., Feb. 7, 1835	1 lea.	Robertson	Milam
Harris, William J., July 21, 1824	1 lab.	Austin 1	Harris
Harris, William P., Dec. 10, 1832	1 lea.	Austin 3	Harris
Harris, William and Robert Wilson, Jan. 13, 1832	1 lea.	Austin 3	Harris
Harris, William and Robert Wilson, June 13, 1832	2 lea.	Austin 2	Harris
Harrison, George, Aug. 16, 1824	1 lea.	Austin 1	Brazoria
Harrison, Henry, Nov. 2, 1830	1/4 lea.	Austin 3	Matagorda
Harrison, Henry, Dec. 16, 1830	1/2 lea.	Austin 3	Matagorda
Harrison, John, Nov. 2, 1835	1/4 lea.	Vehlein	Cherokee
Harrison, T. J., Aug. 26, 1835	1 lea.	Zavala	Hardin
Hart, Elizabeth, Dec. 29, 1834	1 lea.	Power and Hewetson	San Patrici

Name and Date of Title	Amount	Colony or Commissioner	Present Location
Hart, Felix and Son, Nov. 22, 1834	1 1/4 lea.	Power and Hewetson	Bee
Hart, Gustavus, July 17, 1835	1/4 lea.	Zavala	Sabine
Hart, John and Sons, Nov. 10, 1834	1 3/4 lea.	Power and Hewetson	San Patricio
Hart, Timothy and Mother, Nov. 20, 1834	1 1/4 lea.	Power and Hewetson	Bee
Harvey, Blasingame W., Feb. 20, 1835	1 lea.	Zavala	San Augustine
Harvey, William, July 20, 1824	1 lea.	Austin 1	Austin
Hatch, Sylvenus, Mch. 30, 1830	1 lea.	Austin 3	Jackson
Hatfield, Basil M., Oct. 23, 1835	1 lea.	Austin 5	3/4 Lee 1/4 Washington
Haughy, Bridget, June 25, 1835	1 lea. 1 lab.	McMullen and McGloin	Live Oak
Haven, Eben, June 24, 1831	1 lea.	DeWitt	Victoria
Hawkins, Edmond St. John, May 16, 1831	1/4 lea.	Austin 2	Fayette
Hawkins, Isaac K., Oct. 18, 1832	1/4 lea.	Austin 2	Washington
Hawkins, William S., May 18, 1835	1/4 lea.	Robertson	Limestone
Hawkins, William W., Nov. 20, 1832	1/4 lea.	Austin 2	2/3 Burleson 1/4 Washington
Hawley, Joel Edwin, June 22, 1835	1 lea.	Zavala	Hardin
Haworth, Absalom B., Feb. 15, 1835	1 lea.	Robertson	Milam
Hayes, Jacob, Apr. 8, 1831	1 lea.	Austin 2	Grimes
Hayes, Stephen, July 8, 1835	1 lea. 1 lab.	McMullen and McGloin	2/3 Live Oak 1/3 Atascosa
Hayes, Thomas and Son, Nov. 27, 1834	1 1/4 lea.	Power and Hewetson	Bee
Haynes, Thomas S., Aug. 16, 1824	1 lea.	Austin 1	Brazos
Hayney, John W., Oct. 20, 1835	1 lea.	Berry	(?)
Hayslitt, Samuel, Oct. 19, 1835	1 lea.	Austin 5	Caldwell
Hazel, Seth, Oct. 14, 1835	1 lea.	Smyth	Grayson (?)
Head, James H., Mch. 18, 1835	1 lea.	Robertson	Limestone
Health, William, June 7, 1835	1/4 lea.	Vehlein	Houston
Heard, Jeremiah, Nov. 29, 1830	1 lea.	Austin 3	Jackson
Heard, John M., Dec. 10, 1830	1 lea.	Austin 3	Jackson
Heard, Thomas H. P., Dec. 10, 1830	1 lea.	Austin 3	Jackson
Heard, William, Nov. 24, 1830	1 lea.	Austin 3	Jackson
Hearn, Robert, Patrick and James, Oct. 24, 1834	1 1/4 lea.	Power and Hewetson	Refugio
Heart, John, Dec. 3, 1831	1 lea.	McMullen and McGloin	San Patricio ?
Heath, Richard, May 24, 1831	1/4 lea.	DeWitt	Lavaca
Heffernan, James, June 30, 1835	1 lea. 1 lab.	McMullen and McGloin	Bee

Name and Date of Title	Amount	Colony or Commis- sioner	Present Location
Heffernan, John, June 25, 1835	1 lea. 1 lab.	McMullen and McGloin	Live Oak
Hely, Michael, July 30, 1835	1 lea. 1 lab.	McMullen and McGloin	1/2 Live Oa 1/2 McMullen
Henderson, Francis, Nov. 12, 1832	1 lea.	Austin 2	Brazos
Henderson, Peter M., Aug. 2, 1835	1 lea.	Zavala	Hardin
Henesey, Thomas, July 30, 1835	1/3 lea.	McMullen and McGloin	Atascosa
Henrie, Arthur, May 16, 1835	1 lea.	Vehlein	Trinity
Henrie, John M., Mch. 30, 1835	1/4 lea.	Zavala	Orange
Henriquez, Maria Gertrudis, May 13, 1835	1 lea.	Burnet	Smith
Henry, Harvey M., Aug. 28, 1835	1 lea.	Vehlein	San Jacinto
Henry, Hugh, Dec. 22, 1834	1 lea.	Robertson	Robertson
Henry, John, May 5, 1831	1 lea.	DeWitt	Caldwell
Henry, Maurice, Dec. 13, 1832	1/4 lea.	Austin 3	Brazoria
Henry, Patrick, July 10, 1835	1/3 lea.	McMullen and McGloin	Live Oak
Henry, Robert, Dec. 22, 1834	1 lab.	Robertson	Robertson
Henry, Robert, Dec. 22, 1834	24 lab.	Robertson	Robertson
Henry, Thomas, July 30, 1835	1 lea.	McMullen and McGloin	Live Oak
Henry, Walter, July 20, 1835	1/3 lea.	McMullen and McGloin	Live Oak
Hensley, Andrew J., Aug. 7, 1835	1/4 lea.	Robertson	Robertson
Hensley, Charles, Aug. 7, 1835	1/4 lea.	Robertson	Robertson
Hensley, Harmon, Mch. 16, 1831	1 lea.	Austin 2	Brazoria
Hensley, James, Aug. 3, 1824	1 lea. 1 lab.	Austin 1	lea. Brazori lab. Austin
Hensley, John M., Nov. 10, 1832	1 lea.	Austin 2	Fayette
Hensley, William R., Apr. 20, 1831	1 lea.	Austin 2	Lavaca
Hereford, Charles, Oct. 11, 1835	1 lea.	Zavala	San Augustin
Hermans, Cornelius P., Sept. 26, 1834	1 lea.	Power and Hewetson	Refuigo
Hernandez, Andres, Apr. 12, 1758	4 lea. 5 lab.	?	3/4 Karnes 1/4 Wilson
Hernandez, Franco. Ricardo, Dec. 3, 1833	1 lea.	Ximenes	Bexar
Hernandez, Jose Maria, May 1, 1835	1 lea.	De Leon	Victoria
Hernandez, Manuel and Bros., Nov. 28, 1834	2 lea.	Power and Hewetson	Refugio
Herrald, Dennis, June 22, 1835	1 lea.	Robertson	Falls
Herrera, Francisco, Dec. 24, 1833	1 lea. 1 lab.	Ximenes	Wilson
Herrera, Ignacio, Mch. 20, 1834	1 lea. 1 lab.	McMullen and McGloin	Atascosa

Name and Date of Title	Amount	Colony or Commissioner	Present Location
Herrera, Manuel, July 6, 1835	1 lea.	Vehlein	Walker
Herrera, Miguel, June 3, 1835	1 lea.	Zavala	Tyler
Herrin, Moses, Oct. 13, 1835	1 lea.	Burnet	Limestone
Herring, William, Nov. 23, 1835	1 lea. 1 lab.	Taylor	Jasper (?)
Hertz, Joseph, May 22, 1835	1/4 lea.	Burnet	Anderson
Hewetson, James, Nov. 19, 1834	1 1/4 lea.	Power and Hewetson	Refugio
Hews (heirs of William), Nov. 15, 1834	1 lea.	Power and Hewetson	Refugio
Heynie, John, ? ? ?	1 lea.	Robertson	Robertson (?)
Hibbins, John, Dec. ?, 1832	1 lea.	Austin 4	Lavaca (?)
Hidalgo, Eusebio, Apr. 8, 1835		De Leon	Victoria
Hidalgo, Eusebio, Apr. 8, 1835	1 lea.	De Leon	Calhoun
Hidalgo, Francisco Gonzales, Oct. 3, 1834		Power and Hewetson	Victoria
Hidalgo, See Ydalgo			
Higgins, John, Nov. 23, 1835	1 lea. 1 lab.	Taylor	(?)
Highsmith, Ahijah M., Apr. 5, 1831	1 lea.	Austin 2	Bastrop
Highsmith, Samuel, May 1, 1831	24 lab.	DeWitt	Guadalupe
Highsmith, Samuel, Aug. 4, 1831	937,100 sq. vs.	DeWitt	Gonzales
Hill, Ezra, Feb. 12, 1836	1 lea.	Austin 5	Lavaca (?)
Hill, Francis, Aug. 3, 1835	1/4 lea.	Vehlein	Houston
Hill, Henry P., July 14, 1835	1 lea.	Milam	Travis
Hill, Jacob, Sept. 6, 1835	1 lea.	Zavala	Hardin
Hill, Thomas, July 14, 1831	1 lea.	Austin 2	Austin
Hill, William, Aug. 11, 1831	1 lea.	DeWitt	Gonzales
Hill, William C. J., Jan. 25, 1836	1 lea.	Austin 5	Grimes (?)
Hillebrant, Christian, Aug. 5, 1835	1 lea.	Taylor	Jefferson
Hillhouse, John, Nov. 3, 1835	1 lea. 1 lab.	Smyth	(?)
Hillis, John, Nov. 9, 1835	1 lea.	Taylor	(?)
Hinch, Samuel, Mch. 31, 1831	1 lea.	Austin 2	Washington
Hinds, Gerren, May 10, 1831	1 lea.	DeWitt	Caldwell
Hinds, James, May 25, 1831	1 lea.	DeWitt	Caldwell
Hines, Allen, Nov. 28, 1835	1 lea.	Smyth	Harrison (?)
Hines, James A., Apr. 7, 1830	1/4 lea.	Padilla	Sabine
Hines, William, Mch. 13, 1835	1 lea.	Zavala	Liberty (?)
Hinkson, John, Nov. 13, 1830	1/4 lea.	Austin 3	Jackson
Hiroms, Samuel C., July 25, 1831	1 lea.	Austin 3	Harris
Hiroms, Samuel C., Apr. 30, 1835	1 lea.	Vehlein	Polk
Hobdy, Joses, Feb. 18, 1835	1 lea.	Zavala	San Augustine
Hodge, Alexander, Apr. 12, 1828	1 lea.	Austin 1	Ft. Bend
Hodge, Archibald, Apr. 8, 1831	1 lea.	Austin 2	Montgomery
Hodge, James, Apr. 8, 1831	1 lea.	Austin 2	Montgomery
Hodge, John, Mch. 21, 1831	1 lea.	Austin 2	11/12 Austin 1/12 Washington
Hodge, Robert, July 14, 1831	1 lea.	Austin 2	Ft. Bend
Hodge, William (Heirs of), Apr. 23, 1831	1 lea.	Austin 2	Walker
Hodges, Joseph, Mch. 16, 1835	1 lea.	Vehlein	Houston
Hodges, Nathaniel, Dec. 9, 1835	1 lea.	Taylor	(?)
Hodges, Newell C., Mch. 12, 1835	1 lea.	Burnet	Houston
Hodges, William H., May 4, 1831	1 lea.	Madero	Chambers

Name and Date of Title	Amount	Colony or Commissioner	Present Location
Hoffman, David, Oct. 22, 1835	1 lea. 1 lab.	Smyth	Sabine
Hoffman, David A., Mch. 3, 1832	1 lea.	Austin 3	Jackson
Hogan, Josiah, Dec. 20, 1834	1 lea.	Robertson	Falls
Hoggart, James, Jan. 18, 1835	1 lea.	Zavala	Chambers
Hoit, Samuel, Nov. 15, 1830	1 lea.	Austin 3	Matagorda
Hoket, Edward W., June 3, 1835	1 lea.	Burnet	Cherokee
Holcomb, John D., Oct. 20, 1835	1/4 lea.	Austin 5	Brazos
Holden, Thomas, Nov. 22, 1834	1 lea.	Power and Hewetson	Bee
Holderman, David, May 25, 1835	1/4 lea.	Milam	Bastrop (?)
Holland, Francis, Aug. 10, 1834	1 lea.	Austin 1	Grimes
Holland, James, Apr. 7, 1831	1/4 lea.	Austin 2	Grimes
Holland, P., Sept. 26, 1835	1 lea.	Zavala	Tyler (?)
Holland, William, Aug. 10, 1824	1 lea.	Austin 1	Grimes
Holliman, Kinchen, Aug. 10, 1824	1 lea.	Austin 1	Ft. Bend (?
Hollingsworth, James, Oct. 28, 1831	1/4 lea.	Austin 2	Burleson
Holly, William, See Geo. H. Hall			
Holman, Isaac, Aug. 5, 1835	1 lea.	Burnet	Freestone
Holman, John W., Oct. 12, 1835	1/4 lea.	Vehlein	Nacogdoche
Hood, Joseph L., Dec. 23, 1834	1 lea.	Robertson	Bell
Hope, James, July 10, 1824	1/4 lea. 2 lab.	Austin 1	Brazos
Hope, Prosper, Adolphus heirs, or Richard, Dec. 11, 1828	1/2 lea.	Austin 2	Washington
Hopkins, Daniel, Nov. 23, 1835	1 lea.	Taylor	Jefferson an Jasper (?
Hopkins, James E., Dec. 17, 1835	1 lea. 1 lab.	Smyth	Lamar (?)
Horne, Charles S., Oct. 4, 1835	1 lea.	Zavala	(?)
Hornsby, Reuben, Oct. 30, 1832	1 lea.	Austin 4	Travis
Horton, Alexander, Feb. 24, 1835	1/4 lea.	Zavala	Jefferson
Horton, Susannah, Feb. 24, 1835	1 lea.	Zavala	Jefferson
Horton, Wade, Dec. 5, 1835	1/3 lea.	Taylor	(?)
Hotchkiss, Archibald, Sept. 18, 1835	1 lea.	Taylor	Jefferson
Hotchkiss, Augustin, Nov. 21, 1834	1 lea.	Zavala	San Augusti
Hotchkiss, Augustus, Sept. 12, 1835	1 lea.	Taylor	Madison
Houjoa, Antony, Feb. 15, 1835	1/4 lea.	Austin 5	Ft. Bend (?
Houlihan, John, June 25, 1835	1 lea. 1 lab.	McMullen and McGloin	3/4 Live Oa 1/4 Atasc
Houghteling, James, Nov. 19, 1835	1/3 lea.	Smyth	Upshur (?)
House, George, Nov. 22, 1831	1 lea.	Austin 3	1/2 Jackson 1/2 Whart
House, Joseph, Apr. 11, 1831	1 lea.	Austin 2	2/3 Harris 1/3 Montgomery
House, William, July 6, 1831	1/4 lea.	DeWitt	Caldwell
Houston, Sam, May 5, 1835	1,836,291 sq. vs.	Burnet	Nacogdoche
Houston, Samuel, June 9, 1833	1 lea.	Austin 3	Calhoun
Howard, James L., Oct. 15, 1835	1/4 lea.	Zavala	Newton
Howard, John, Nov. 25, 1835	1 lea.	Zavala	San Augusti ?

Name and Date of Title	Amount	Colony or Commissioner	Present Location
Howard, John, July 21, 1835	10 lea.	Grant, Durst and Williams	Grayson (?)
Howard, William P., Sept. 12, 1835	10 lea.	Grant, Durst and Williams	Lamar (?)
Howard, William, Nov. 29, 1835	1 lea.	Taylor	Jefferson (?)
Hoye, Catalina, July 20, 1835	1/3 lea.	McMullen and McGloin	Atascosa
Hubert, Mathew, Oct. 22, 1835	1 lea.	Vehlein	San Jacinto
Hudson, Charles, July 29, 1824	1 lea.	Austin 1	Wharton
Hudson, Obadiah, Mch. 31, 1831	1 lea.	Austin 2	9/10 Washington 1/10 Fayette
Huejas, Maria Falcona, May 9, 1835	1 lea.	Burnet	Rusk
Huff, George, Aug. 19, 1824	1 1/2 lea.	Austin 1	2/3 Wharton 1/3 Ft. Bend
Huff, John, July 10, 1824	1 lea.	Austin 1	Wharton
Huff, William T., Oct. 10, 1835	1 lea.	Austin 5	Burleson
Huffman, David, Oct. 25, 1834	1 lea.	Vehlein	Polk represented on map Jan. 16/92
Hughart, Edward, June 21, 1832	1/4 lea.	DeWitt	Gonzales
Hughes, Hiram, Oct. 13, 1835	1/4 lea.	Zavala	San Augustine
Hughes, Isaac, See John Cook			
Hughes, James, June 6, 1832	1/4 lea.	DeWitt	3/4 Gonzales 1/4 DeWitt
Hughes, Walter, Nov. 9, 1835	1 lea.	Zavala	Sabine
Hughs, Alexander, Nov. 28, 1835	1 lea. 1 lab.	Taylor	Tyler (?)
Hughson, James, Jan. 17, 1832	1 lea.	Austin 3	Calhoun
Huizar, Antonio, Oct. 9, 1835	1 lea. 1 lab.	Berry	Grayson
Huizar, Heirs of Jeronimo, Nov. 12, 1834	1 lea.	Power and Hewetson	Goliad
Huling, Thomas B., July 30, 1835	1 lea.	Zavala	Jasper
Humble, John, Nov. 20, 1835	1 lea.	Smyth	Henderson
Humon, Samuel, Dec. 9, 1834	1 lea.	Robertson	Bell
Humphries, James, Dec. 4, 1835	1 lea. 1 lab.	Smyth	(?)
Humphries, Pelham, Feb. 14, 1835	1 lea.	Zavala	Jefferson
Hunt, Charles S., May 15, 1835	1/4 lea.	Zavala	Angelina
Hunt, Hershell H., Oct. 22, 1831	1/4 lea.	Austin 3	Jackson
Hunt, Nathaniel, Nov. 24, 1834	1 lea.	Zavala	San Augustine
Hunt, William R., Feb. 23, 1832	1 lea.	Austin 2	Colorado
Hunter, Daniel H. M., July 20, 1831	1/4 lea.	Austin 3	3/4 Brazoria 1/4 Harris
Hunter, Eli, July 24, 1824	1 lea.	Austin 1	Wharton
Hunter, Elijah, Aug. 21, 1835	1 lea.	Zavala	Hardin
Hunter, Johnson, Aug. 10, 1824	1 lea.	Austin 1	Harris
Hunter, Johnson, Nov. 14, 1832	1 lab.	Austin 2	Waller
Hunter, Joseph, Vol. 27, p. 139	1 lea.	Taylor	(?)
Hunter, Ralph, Oct. 10, 1835	1 lea.	Burnet	Henderson

Name and Date of Title	Amount	Colony or Commissioner	Present Location
Huntingdon, J., Oct. 7, 1835	1 lea.	Burnet	3/4 Hender son 1/4 Anderson
Hurd, Norman, June 16, 1835	1 lea.	Zavala	Tyler
Hurtado, Manuel, Sept. 19, 1835	11 lea.	Del Moral	(?)
Huston, Almanzor, Feb. 14, 1835	1 lea.	Zavala	Jefferson
Hyden, Nathaniel, Oct. 14, 1835	1 lea.	Zavala	San August
Hynes, Peter and John, Sept. 9, 1834	1 1/4 lea.	Power and Hewetson	Refugio
Ibarbo, Juan, Jose and Bros., Aug. 25, 1835	11 lea.	Procela	Louisiana (
Ibarbo, Juan Jose and Bros., May 5, 1834	10 lea. 23 1/2 lab.	Flores	Nacogdoche ?
Iiams, John, Aug. 7, 1824 See Jiams	1 lea.	Austin 1	Chambers
Ingersoll, John W., Aug. 27, 1835	1 lea.	Vehlein	Walker
Ingram, Ira, Nov. 13, 1830	1 lea.	Austin 3	Matagorda
Ingram, Ira, Aug. 24, 1824	1 lab.	Austin 1	Waller
Ingram, John, May 29, 1827	1/4 lea.	Austin 2	Fayette
Ingram, Seth, Nov. 13, 1830	1 lea.	Austin 3	Matagorda
Ingram, Seth, July 29, 1824	2 lea. 1 lab.	Austin 1	2 lea. Whar lab. Austi
Irion, Robert A., June 13, 1835	1 lea.	Vehlein	5/12 Hardi 4/12 Polk 3/12 Libe
Irion, Robert A., Aug. 15, 1835	10 lea.	Williams, Johnson and Peebles	(?)
Irons, John, July 16, 1824	1 lea.	Austin 1	Waller
Irvine, Robert B., Sept. 7, 1835	1/4 lea.	Zavala	Hardin
Isaacks, Elijah, June 20, 1835	1 lea.	Zavala	Jasper
Isaacks, Samuel, July 15, 1824	1 lea. 1 lab.	Austin 1	Ft. Bend
Isaacks, William, Nov. 26, 1834	1 lea.	Zavala	Sabine
Isles, Perry B., Apr. 6, 1831	1 lea.	Austin 2	Bastrop
Ives, Abraham, Nov. 17, 1835	1 lea.	Smyth	(?)
Ives, Amasa, May 16, 1831	1 lea.	Austin 2	Austin
Ives, David, Apr. 23, 1835		De Leon	Victoria
Jack, Patrick C., Apr. 6, 1831	1/4 lea.	Austin 2	Grimes
Jack, Spencer H., Apr. 20, 1833	1/4 lea.	Austin 2	Lavaca
Jack, Spencer H., Sept. 20, 1835	10 lea.	Williams, Johnson and Peebles	Hunt (?)
Jack, William H., Mch. 19, 1831	1 lea.	Austin 2	Fayette
Jack, William H., Oct. 3, 1835	1 lea.	Austin 3	Galveston
Jackson, Alexander, July 16, 1824	2 lea.	Austin 1	Wharton
Jackson, Elisha D., Mch. 21, 1831	1 lea.	Austin 2	Washington

Name and Date of Title	Amount	Colony or Commis-sioner	Present Location
Jackson, Humphrey, Aug. 16, 1824	1 lea. 1 lab.	Austin 1	Harris
Jackson, Isaac, Aug. 7, 1824	1 lea.	Austin 1	Grimes
Jackson, Isaac, Mch. 19, 1831	1 lea.	Austin 2	Washington
Jackson, Isaac, Mch. 21, 1831	1 lea.	Austin 2	Washington
Jackson, Stephen, June 10, 1835	1 lea.	Zavala	Hardin
Jackson, Thomas, May 1, 1831	24 lab.	DeWitt	Gonzales
Jackson, Thomas, May 10, 1831	1 lab.	DeWitt	Gonzales
Jackson, Thomas J., Aug. 5, 1835	1 lea.	Burnet	Rusk
Jackson, Thomas R., Mch. 28, 1835	1 lea.	Milam	Hays
Jacobs, John, Oct. 26, 1835	1/4 lea.	Burnet	(?)
Jacobs, William, Sept. 12, 1835	1 lea.	Zavala	Polk
Jameison, Isaac, Apr. 7, 1831	1 lea.	Austin 2	Washington
James, Angus J., May 5, 1831	1/4 lea.	Austin 2	Ft. Bend
James, John, Oct. 25, 1834	1 lea.	Power and Hewetson	Refugio
James, Phineas, May 1, 1831	1 lea.	DeWitt	Gonzales
James, Thomas, Oct. 16, 1835	1 lea.	Austin 5	Brazos
Jameson, George, Sept. 14, 1835	1 lea.	Zavala	Polk
Jamison, Thomas, Nov. 29, 1830	1/2 lea.	Austin 3	Matagorda
Jamison, Thomas, See Thomas J. Tone			
Janey, John, Aug. 11, 1835	1/3 lea.	Smyth	Nacogdoches
Jaques, Adaline, May 6, 1835	1 lea.	Burnet	Leon
Jaques, Benjamin F., Oct. 29, 1830	1 lea.	Austin 3	Matagorda
Jeffry, Edward, Apr. 28, 1831	1/4 lea. and 147,600 sq. vs.	Austin 2	Ft. Bend
Jenkins, Edward, Apr. 4, 1831	1 lea.	Austin 2	Bastrop
Jett, John, Feb. 11, 1835	1 lea.	Zavala	Orange
Jett, Stephen, Feb. 18, 1835	1 lea.	Zavala	Orange
Jiams, John, Aug. 7, 1824	1 lea.	Austin 1	Chambers
Johns, William, May 2, 1831		Madero	Liberty
Johns, Williams, Mch. 3, 1835	1 lea.	Vehlein	Polk (?)
Johnson, Alvey R., Sept. 21, 1835	1 lea.	Smyth	Gregg
Johnson, Candler, June 26, 1835	1 lea.	Zavala	Angelina
Johnson, Francis W., Mch. 28, 1831	1 lea.	Arciniega	Fayette
Johnson, Frank, Mch. 14, 1835	1 lea.	Burnet	Houston
Johnson, Henry A., June 16, 1835	1/4 lea.	Vehlein	Houston
Johnson, Henry W., et als., July 29, 1824	1 lea.	Austin 1	11/25 Brazoria 1/25 Matagorda
Johnson, Isaac, Nov. 23, 1835	1 lea. 1 lab.	Taylor	(?)
Johnson, James, Nov. 18, 1835	1 lea.	Zavala	San Augustine ?
Johnson, John, Oct. 6, 1835	1 lea.	Vehlein	Trinity
Johnson, John, Sept. 30, 1835	10 lea.	Grant, Durst and Williams	(?)
Johnson, John D., Aug. 20, 1835	1 lea.	Zavala	Jasper
Johnson, John S., Oct. 16, 1835	1 lea.	Zavala	(?)
Johnson, William, Apr. 24, 1835	1 lea.	Burnet	Leon
Johnston, Achilles S. E., May 18, 1835	1 lea.	Zavala	Sabine
Johnston, Elizabeth, June 20, 1835	1 lea.	Vehlein	Polk
Johnston, Hugh B., May 3, 1831	1 lea.	Madero	Liberty

Name and Date of Title	Amount	Colony or Commissioner	Present Location
Johnston, Hugh B., May 2, 1831		Madero	(?)
Johnston, Joseph S., Apr. 30, 1835	1/4 lea.	Zavala	Jefferson
Johnston, William, July 25, 1835	1/4 lea.	Zavala	Angelina
Jones, Benjamin F., Oct. 22, 1835	1 lea. 1 lab.	Smyth	lea. Jasper lab. Newtc
Jones, Crawford, Nov. 26, 1835	1 lea. 1 lab.	Smyth	(?)
Jones, Henry, July 8, 1824	1 lea.	Austin 1	Ft. Bend
Jones, Isaac, Aug. 27, 1835	1 lea.	Vehlein	San Jacinto
Jones, James W., Aug. 10, 1824	1 lea. 1 lab.	Austin 1	lea. Wharto lab. Ft. Be
Jones, Jesse T., Feb. 3, 1835	1 lea.	Burnet	Cherokee
Jones, John, May 31, 1827	1/4 lea.	Austin 2	Ft. Bend
Jones, John, Apr. 16, 1831	1 lea.	Austin 2	11/12 Faye 1/12 Aust
Jones, John, July 10, 1831	1/4 lea.	DeWitt	Jackson
Jones, John H., Oct. 17, 1832	1 lea.	Austin 2	Brazos
Jones, Joseph P., Dec. 11, 1834	1 lea.	Robertson	Milam
Jones, Lewis, Nov. 17, 1835	1 lea. 1 lab.	Smyth	(?)
Jones, Oliver, Aug. 10, 1824	1 lea. 1 lab.	Austin 1	lea. 23/25 Brazoria 2/25 Mata gorda lab. Austin
Jones, Randal, July 15, 1824	1 lea. 1 lab.	Austin 1	1/2 lea. Ft. Bend 1 Wharton 1 Ft. Bend
Jones, Silas, June 10, 1831	1 lea.	Austin 2	Fayette
Jones, Simon, Oct. 20, 1835	1 lea.	Austin 5	Madison
Jones, Stephen, Apr. 19, 1831	1 lea.	Austin 2	Brazos
Jones, Stephen, Nov. 25, 1835	1 lea.	Zavala	San Augusti and Jaspe
Jones, Timothy, Oct. 24, 1835	1 lea.	Austin 5	Grimes
Jones, Wiley M. C., July 17, 1835	1 lea.	Burnet	Freestone
Jones, William, Oct. 15, 1835	1 lea.	Zavala	Jasper
Jordan, James, May 15, 1835	1 lea.	Burnet	Smith
Jordan, James, June 3, 1835	1 lea.	Vehlein	Walker
Jordan, John, Jan. 8, 1835	1 lea.	Burnet	Cherokee
Jordan, Joseph, June 10, 1835	1 lea.	Burnet	Anderson
Jordan, Levi, Feb. 4, 1835	1 lea.	Burnet	Cherokee
Juarez, Encarnacion, Aug. 3, 1835	1 lea. 1 lab.	Taylor	Houston
Juarez, Victoriano, July 4, 1835	1 lea. 1 lab.	McMullen and McGloin	San Patrici
Jurdin, Elizabeth, July 4, 1835	1 lea. 1 lab.	McMullen and McGloin	Live Oak
Kanaff, A., Nov. 23, 1835	1 lea.	Berry	Navarro (?
Keating, John, Oct. 10, 1834	1 lea.	Power and Hewetson	Refugio
Keating, John and Michael, Oct. 9, 1834	1/2 lea.	Power and Hewetson	Bee

Name and Date of Title	Amount	Colony or Commissioner	Present Location
Keep, Edward S., Feb. 20, 1835	1 lea.	Milam	2/3 Comal 1/3 Hays (?)
Keep, Imla, July 24, 1824	1 lea.	Austin 1	Brazoria
Kegans, James, Mch. 23, 1831	1 lea.	Austin 2	Washington
Kegans, Maria, Dec. 3, 1832	1 lea.	Austin 2	Brazos
Kehoe, Peter, Dec. 29, 1834	1 lea.	Power and Hewetson	(?)
Keller, Francis, Mch. 3, 1830	1 lea.	Austin 3	Jackson
Keller, Francis G., May 6, 1831	1 lea.	Austin 2	Jackson
Keller, John C., June 4, 1827	1 lea.	Austin 1	Matagorda
Kellog, Albert G., June 8, 1835	1/4 lea.	Zavala	San Augustine
Kelly, Charles, Sept. 27, 1834	1/4 lea.	Power and Hewetson	3/4 Refugio 1/4 Bee
Kelly, John, July 19, 1824	2 lab.	Austin 2	Brazos
Kelly, John, Sept. 27, 1834	1/4 lea.	Power and Hewetson	Bee
Kelly, John, Mch. 5, 1831	1 lea.	Austin 2	Waller
Kendrick, Isaac, June 3, 1835	1 lea.	Burnet	Cherokee
Kennard, Antony D., Nov. 22, 1832	1 lea.	Austin 2	Grimes
Kennard, William S., July 6, 1835	1 lea.	Burnet	3/5 Sabine 2/5 Newton
Kennedy, Samuel, July 7, 1824	1 lea. 1 lab.	Austin 1	lea. Ft. Bend lab. Austin
Kennedy, Sarah, Apr. 25, 1831	1 lea.	Austin 2	Ft. Bend
Kenelly, Samuel, Apr. 28, 1831	1 lea.	Austin 2	Colorado
Kenney, Louisiana, See Louisiana Morton			
Kenney, Samuel, Feb. 8, 1835	1/4 lea.	Robertson	Robertson
Kenney, Thomas, Feb. 20, 1835	1 lea.	Robertson	Lee
Kennon, Alfred, July 19, 1824	1 lea.	Austin 1	Burleson
Kent, Andrew, June 28, 1831	1 lea.	DeWitt	Lavaca
Kent, Joseph, June 10, 1832	1/4 lea.	DeWitt	DeWitt
Kerby, John, June 7, 1835	1 lea.	Burnet	Nacogdoches
Kerr, James, July 8, 1831	1 lea.	DeWitt	Lavaca
Kerr, James, May 6, 1827	1 lea.	Austin 1	Jackson
Kerr, Lucy, June 2, 1832	1 lea.	Austin 2	Fayette
Kerr, Peter and William, Aug. 10, 1824	1 lea.	Austin 1	Washington
Killely, Mark, July 30, 1835	1 lea. 1 lab.	McMullen and McGloin	Live Oak
Kimball, George C., Nov. 28, 1831	1/4 lea.	DeWitt	Caldwell
Kimble, Helena, See James Dill			
Kimbro, William, Sept. 17, 1835	1 lea.	Burnet	Anderson
Kincheloe, Lewis, Oct. 5, 1835	1/4 lea.	Austin 5	Austin
Kincheloe, William, July 8, 1824	2 lea.	Austin 1	Wharton
King, Edward, Oct. 8, 1835	1 lea.	Vehlein	3/5 Harris 2/5 Liberty
King, Gray B., Dec. 15, 1835	10 lea.	Williams, Johnson and Peebles	(?)
King, Gray B., Sept. 20, 1835	1 lea. 1 lab.	Smyth	Wood

Name and Date of Title	Amount	Colony or Commissioner	Present Location
King, Gray B., Mch. 5, 1835	1 lea.	Austin 4	Madison
King, John G., Apr. 24, 1831	1 lea.	DeWitt	Guadalupe
Kingston, Wm. and Peter Powell, Mch. 8, 1827	1 lea.	Austin 1	Matagorda
Kinkead, John, Mch. 31, 1831	1/4 lea.	Austin 2	Burleson
Kivlan, Maria Brigida, Dec. 5, 1831	1 lea.	McMullen & McGloin	Live Oak
Kirkham, Spencer, May 4, 1835	1 lea.	Vehlein	Liberty
Kirkmare, James, Nov. 4, 1835	1 lea. 1 lab.	Smyth	(?)
Kistler, Frederic, July 11, 1832	1 lea.	DeWitt	Gonzales
Klekamp, John B., Feb. 3, 1836	1 lea.	Austin 5	Caldwell
Knight, James, May 9, 1831	1 lea.	Madero	Liberty
Knight, James, May 2, 1831		Madero	Liberty
Knight, James and W. C. White, July 15, 1824	1 lea. 1 lab.	Austin 1	Ft. Bend
Knight, James and W. C. White, Apr. 4, 1831	1 lea.	Austin 2	Bastrop
Knight, Salathiel F., Oct. 19, 1835	1 lea.	Austin 5	Fayette
Knox, George, Nov. 21, 1835	1 lea. 1 lab.	Taylor	(?)
Kokernot, David L., July 23, 1835	1 lea.	Vehlein	1/2 Harris 1/2 Liber
Korn, Jesse, July 23, 1835	1 lea.	Burnet	Freestone
Kuykendall, Abraham, Sept. 27, 1835	1 lea.	Zavala	Nacogdoche
Kuykendall, Abner, July 7, 1824	1 lea.	Austin 1	lea. Ft. Bei 1/2 lea. Washingt lab. Aust
Kuykendall, Abner, Apr. 24, 1831	1 lea.	Austin 2	Lee
Kuykendall, Abner, May 9, 1831	1 lea.	Austin 2	Burleson
Kuykendall, Adam, Aug. 15, 1835	10 lea.	Williams Johnson and Peebles	(?)
Kuykendall, Brazilla, Aug. 7, 1824	1 lab.	Austin 1	Austin
Kuykendall, Brazilla, Apr. 27, 1828	1/4 lea. and 1/4 lab.	Austin 2	Austin
Kuykendall, Brazilla, Feb. 5, 1836	3/4 lea.	Austin 5	Washington (?)
Kuykendall, Elizabeth M., May 1, 1828	1 lea.	Austin 2	Austin
Kuykendall, Gibson, May 27, 1828	1 lea.	Austin 2	1/4 Austin 3/4 Washington
Kuykendall, Gibson, Aug. 10, 1835	10 lea.	Williams Johnson and Peebles	(?)
Kuykendall, Joseph, July 8, 1824	1 lea.	Austin 1	Ft. Bend
Kuykendall, Robert, July 16, 1824	2 lea.	Austin 1	Wharton
Kuykendall, Thornton P., Feb. 5, 1836	1/4 lea.	Austin 5	Washington (?)
Kuykendall, William, Apr. 29, 1828	1/4 lea. 1/4 lab.	Austin 2	Austin
Kuykendall, William, Aug. 12, 1835	10 lea.	Williams, Johnson and Peebles	(?)

Name and Date of Title	Amount	Colony or Commissioner	Present Location
Labaume, Jose, Nov. 21, 1834	1 lea.	Vehlein	Angelina
Labaume, Jose, July 1, 1832	6 lea.	Madero	1/2 Guadalupe 1/2 Gonzales
Lacy, John, Nov. 23, 1835	1 lea.	Taylor	(?)
Lacy, John S., Oct. 15, 1835	1 lea.	Zavala	Sabine
Lacy, Martin, Jan. 3, 1835	1 lea.	Burnet	Cherokee
Lacy, Peter, Nov. 23, 1835	1 lea. 1 lab.	Taylor	(?)
Lacy, William D., Mch. 28, 1831	1/4 lea.	Austin 2	Fayette
Ladd, William J., May 22, 1835	1/4 lea.	Burnet	Nacogdoches
Lafferty, Benija, June 22, 1835	1 lea.	Burnet	Smith
La Flore, Joseph, Apr. 15, 1833	1/4 lea.	Austin 3	Galveston
Leakey, Joel, May 28, 1827	1 lea.	Austin 1	1/2 Washington 1/2 Austin
Leakey, Joel, Apr. 2, 1831	1 lea.	Austin 2	1/2 Washington 1/2 Austin
Leakey, Joel, Apr. 23, 1831	1/2 lea.	Austin 2	1/3 Washington 2/3 Austin
Leakey, William, June 27, 1835	1 lea.	Zavala	5/6 San Augustine 1/6 Sabine
Lambert, Walter, Nov. 27, 1834	1/4 lea.	Power & Hewetson	2/3 Refugio 1/3 Bee
Lampkin, John, Nov. 21, 1835	1 lea.	Taylor	(?)
Lancaster, Archibald, Oct. 20, 1835	1/4 lea.	Zavala	Hardin
Lance, Jacob, Feb. 15, 1836	1 lea.	Austin 5	Bastrop (?)
Landrum, John, Apr. 10, 1831	1 lea.	Austin 2	Grimes
Landrum, William, Apr. 10, 1831	1 lea.	Austin 2	Montgomery
Landrum, Zacharia, Apr. 10, 1831	1 lea.	Austin 2	Montgomery
Lane, John S., Sept. 22, 1835	1 lea.	Zavala	Sabine
Lang, Edward, Aug. 31, 1835	1 lea.	Robertson	Williamson
Langdon, L.R., Sept. 10, 1835	1 lea.	Zavala	(?)
Langenheim, William, See Francis Dietrich			
Langford, Alfred, Sept. 17, 1835	1 lea.	Zavala	(?)
Lanier, Benjamin, June 20, 1835	1 lea.	Vehlein	Tyler
Lankford, Mary, Nov. 8, 1835	1 lea.	Zavala	(?)
Lara, Pedro, See Vicente Micheli			
Lara, Pedro, See Barr & Davenport			
Laramore, John, Oct. 29, 1835	1 lea.	Smyth	Upshur
La Riviera, Juan, Mch. 5, 1835	1 1/4 lea.	Burnet	Houston
Larrison, Allen, Mch. 12, 1831	1/4 lea.	Austin 2	Austin
Larrison, Daniel, May 16, 1835	1 lea.	Vehlein	Madison
Lary, Samuel, Oct. 11, 1835	1 lea.	Vehlein	Madison
Laso, Carlos, Feb. 18, 1833	1 lea.	De Leon	Jackson
Lastley, James, Oct. 12, 1835	1 lea.	Austin 5	Burleson
Latham, Enoch, Oct. 6, 1835	1/4 lea.	Austin 5	Ft. Bend
Latham, James, June 18, 1835	1 lea.	Burnet	Rusk
Latham, Jeremiah, Oct. 12, 1835	1 lea.	Burnet	Navarro
Latham, Lewis, Nov. 16, 1835	1 1/4 lea.	Burnet	9/10 Liberty 1/10 Harris ?

Name and Date of Title	Amount	Colony or Commissioner	Present Location
Latham, Lewis, Oct. 15, 1835	1 1/4 lea.	Vehlein	9/10 Libert 1/10 Harr
Latham, Martin, Oct. 5, 1835	1 lea.	Burnet	Navarro
Latham, William, Feb. 13, 1836	1/4 lea.	Austin 5	Bastrop (?)
Lattin, Adolphus D., July 7, 1835	1 lea.	Burnet	Anderson
Laughlin, William, Apr. 11, 1831	1/4 lea.	Austin 2	Grimes
Lavery, William, Dec. 25, 1834	1 lea.	Power & Hewetson	Goliad
Lavigne, Bautista Tessier, July 25, 1835	1 lea.	Vehlein	Angelina
Lavigne, Polonio, Nov. 26, 1835	1/3 lea.	Smyth	(?)
Lawhon, John C., Mch. 10, 1835	1 lea.	Zavala	Jefferson
Lawlor, Joseph P., Sept. 13, 1832	1/4 lea.	DeWitt	Gonzales
Lawlor, Martin, Nov. 20, 1834	1/4 lea.	Power & Hewetson	Goliad
Lawrence, Adam, Mch. 10, 1831	1/4 lea.	Austin 2	Washington
Lawrence, David, Mch. 4, 1831	1 lea.	Austin 2	Washington
Lawrence, Martin B., Feb. 6, 1836	1 lea.	Austin 5	Burleson (?
Lawrence, Mary, Dec. 11, 1832	1 lea.	Austin 4	Brazos
Lawrence, Richard, Apr. 4, 1831	1/4 lea.	Austin 2	Bastrop
Lawrence, Samuel, Mch. 26, 1831	1 lea.	Austin 2	Burleson
Lawrence, Samuel, Jan. 28, 1836	1 lea.	Austin 5	Washington
Lawson, George P., Sept. 21, 1835	1 lea.	Zavala	(?)
Lazarin, Jean Simon, Sept. 17, 1835	1 lea.	Taylor	Polk
Lazarin, Marcelino, Sept. 17, 1835	1 lea. 1 lab.	Smyth	Cooke
Lazarin, Maria Felipe, Sept. 12, 1835	1 lea.	Taylor	Jefferson
Leach, Rachel, Oct. 27, 1835	1 lea.	Burnet	Navarro
Leach, William, June 12, 1832	1/4 lea.	DeWitt	Guadalupe
League, Hosea H., May 25, 1827	1 lea.	Austin 1	Matagorda
Leal, Antonio, See Edmond Quirk			
Leal, Francisco, July 20, 1835	1 lea. 1 lab.	McMullen & McGloin	Live Oak
Leal, Jose, Oct. 26, 1833	6 lea.	Lessassier	Milam
Leal, Luis, July 30, 1835	1/3 lea.	McMullen & McGloin	Live Oak
Lee, Abner, Jr., Jan. 2, 1832	1 lea.	Austin 2	Brazos
Lee, Abner, Sr., Nov. 23, 1832	1 lea.	Austin 2	Brazos
Lee, Hiram, Mch. 16, 1831	1/4 lea.	Austin 2	Washington
Lee, Isaac, Mch. 15, 1831	1 lea.	Austin 2	Washington
Lee, Isaac, Aug. 13, 1835	1 lea.	Smyth	Rusk
Lefton, Jerusa, Nov. 3, 1835	1 lea.	Berry	Louisiana (
Lefton, Lewis, July 31, 1835	1 lea.	Berry	Fannin
Legarreta, Ramon de, Jan. 15, 1804	5 lea.	Ugarte	(?)
Legrand, Edwin P., May 25, 1835	1 lea.	Zavala	Jasper
Lejarza (de), Agustin Martinez, July 5, 1834	2 lea.	Woods	1 1/3 Trini 2/3 Polk
Lejarza (de), Agustin Martinez, July 5, 1834	1 lea.	Woods	Polk (?)
Lejarza (de), Agustin Martinez, July 5, 1834	19 lab. & 713,000 sq. vs.	Woods	Liberty

Name and Date of Title	Amount	Colony or Commissioner	Present Location
Lejarza (de), Agustin Martinez, July 5, 1834	5 lab. & 286,400 sq. vs.	Woods	Hardin
Lejarza (de), Agustin Martinez, July 5, 1834	1 lea.	Woods	1/3 Polk 2/3 Trinity
Leon (de), Agapito, Apr. 2, 1833	1 lea.	De Leon	Victoria
Leon (de), Felix, Apr. 9, 1835		De Leon	Victoria
Leon (de), Felix, Apr. 21, 1835		De Leon	Victoria
Leon (de), Felix, Jan. 25, 1833	1 lea.	De Leon	Victoria
Leon (de), Fernando, Sept. 28, 1834		De Leon	Victoria
Leon (de), Fernando, Sept. 26, 1834	1 lea.	De Leon	Victoria
Leon (de), Francisco, Apr. 12, 1835	1/4 lea.	De Leon	Calhoun
Leon (de), Guadalupe, Mch. 20, 1835		De Leon	Victoria
Leon (de), Jesusa, Sept. 22, 1834	1 lea.	Power & Hewetson	Refugio
Leon (de), Juan Francisco, Mch. 25, 1835		De Leon	Victoria
Leon (de), Maria de Jesus, Apr. 23, 1835		De Leon	Victoria
Leon (de), Maria de Jesus, See Rafael Manchola			
Leon (de), Maria de Jesus, Oct. 7, 1833	2 lea.	De Leon	Golaid
Leon (de), Maria de Jesus, Oct. 14, 1833	2 lea.	De Leon	Golaid
Leon (de), Maria del Refugio, Apr. 23, 1835		De Leon	Victoria
Leon (de), Martin, Dec. 1, 1833		De Leon	Victoria
Leon (de), Martin, Jan. 25, 1833	5 lea.	De Leon	Victoria
Leon (de), Silvestre, Mch. 4, 1833		De Leon	Victoria
Leon (de), Silvestre, Apr. 2, 1833	1 lea.	De Leon	Victoria
Leone, Donato, Feb. 7, 1835	1 lea.	Vehlein	Angelina
Lessassier, Luke, Apr. 30, 1831	1 lea.	Austin 2	Washington
Lessassier, Luke, Oct. 29, 1830	1 lea.	Austin 3	Matagorda
Lessley, Leman D., Aug. 30, 1835	1 lea.	Zavala	Hardin
Lester, Josiah, Mch. 18, 1831	1 lea.	Austin 2	Washington
Leverenz, Lubble, Feb. 3, 1835	1 lea.	Austin 5	Bastrop (?)
Lewis, Barbara C., Jan. 15, 1835	1 lea.	Burnet	Cherokee
Lewis, Franklin, Mch. 29, 1831	1 lea.	Austin 2	Fayette
Lewis, Henry K., Nov. 8, 1830	1 lab. & 388,100 sq. vs.	Austin 3	Harris
Lewis, Henry K., Nov. 28, 1832	5 lab.	Austin 2	Harris
Lewis, Ira R., June 15, 1831	1 lea.	Austin 3	Galveston
Lewis, John E., Nov. 22, 1832	1/4 lea.	Austin 4	Fayette
Lewis, Patsey, July 23, 1835	4 lab. & 889,857 sq. vs.	Zavala	San Augustine
Lewis, Washington, Oct. 22, 1835	1 lea.	Burnet	Anderson
Lewis, Willey, Nov. 3, 1835	1 lea. 1 lab.	Smyth	(?)

Name and Date of Title	Amount	Colony or Commissioner	Present Location
Lewis, William W., July 15, 1835	1 lea.	Robertson	Milam
L'Hermit, Jose Miguel, Mch. 25, 1833	1/4 lea.	De Leon	Victoria
L'Hommedieu, Charles W., June 23, 1831	1/4 lea.	Austin 3	Galveston
Liberty, Town of, vol. 44, p. 72			
Liddle, James, Dec. 8, 1835	1 lea.	Taylor	(?)
Liego, Maria del Carmen, July 3, 1835	1 lea.	Vehlein	Cherokee
Liendo, Jose Justo, Aug. 22, 1833	5 lea.	Lessassier	1 lea. Lee 4 7/8 Mila 1/8 Willian son
Liendo, Jose Justo, Oct. 28, 1833	5 lea.	Lessassier	Waller
Liendo, Jose Justo, May 2, 1834	1 lea.	Aldrete	(?)
Lightfoot, William, Sept. 13, 1835	10 lea.	Williams, Johnson & Peebles	Fannin (?)
Lightfoot, Wilson T., Apr. 4, 1831	1/4 lea.	Austin 2	Bastrop
Lillard, Lewis F., Oct. 17, 1835	1 lea.	Taylor	Jefferson (?
Lilley, Armstead J., Jan. 24, 1836	1 lea.	Taylor	(?)
Lindley, Jonathan, July 17, 1835	1/4 lea.	Vehlein	Polk
Lindley, Samuel, Aug. 27, 1835	1 lea.	Vehlein	3/4 Montgo ery 1/4 Walke
Lindly, Joseph, Apr. 6, 1835	1 lea.	Vehlein	Montgomery
Lindsay, James, See Clopper, Nichols & Co.			
Lindsay, James, Nov. 29, 1830	1/4 lea.	Austin 2	Harris
Lindsey, Benjamin, Feb. 21, 1835	1 lea.	Zavala	Sabine
Lindsey, Isaac, Aug. 10, 1835	1 lea.	Burnet	Anderson
Lindsey, John, Mch. 13, 1835	1 lea.	Vehlein	Polk
Lindsey, Mary Ann, Apr. 22, 1835	1 lea.	Milam	Travis
Lindsey, Owen, July 6, 1835	1/4 lea.	Zavala	5/6 Sabine 1/6 San Augustine
Lindsey, Thomas, July 23, 1835	1/4 lea.	Zavala	Sabine
Liney, Patsey, Nov. 20, 1835	1 lea.	Zavala	Jasper (?)
Linn, Edward, Apr. 7, 1835		De Leon	Victoria
Linn, Edward, May 1, 1835	1/4 lea.	De Leon	Victoria
Linsey, Benjamin, Aug. 19, 1824	1 lea.	Austin 1	3/5 Matagoi 2/5 Bra- zoria (?)
Linville, Richard, June 30, 1835	1 lea.	Zavala	Newton
Lippincott, Elizabeth, May 19, 1827	1 lea.	Austin 2	Ft. Bend
Little, John, May 21, 1828	1 lea. 1 lab.	Austin 1	Lea. Austin. Lab. Ft. B
Little, John, Jan. 5, 1835	1 lea.	Burnet	Anderson
Little, Walter, Nov. 15, 1835	1 lea.	Vehlein	(?)
Little, William, July 10, 1824	1 lea. 1 lab.	Austin 1	Ft. Bend
Litton, Adison, Mch. 23, 1835	1 lea.	Milam	Bastrop
Living, Eleanor, Dec. 8, 1831	1 lea.	Austin 2	Lavaca
Lockhart, Andrew, Sept. 14, 1831	1 lea.	DeWitt	Dewitt
Lockhart, Byrd, Apr. 30, 1831	1 lea.	DeWitt	Gonzales
Lockhart, Byrd, June 27, 1833	1 lea.	Patrick	Gonzales
Lockhart, Byrd, July 8, 1831	1 lea.	Navarro	Caldwell

Name and Date of Title	Amount	Colony or Commissioner	Present Location
Lockhart, Byrd, Apr. 5, 1835	1 lea.	Navarro	Gonzales
Lockhart, Byrd, Nov. 25, 1831	1 lea.	Navarro	3/4 Lavaca 1/4 Gonzales
Lockhart, Byrd B., May 25, 1831	1/4 lea.	DeWitt	Dewitt
Lockhart, Charles, May 10, 1831	1 lea.	DeWitt	Dewitt
Lockhart, John B., Dec. 2, 1831	1/4 lea.	DeWitt	Dewitt
Lockhart, Samuel, July 9, 1831	1 lea.	DeWitt	Dewitt
Lockhart, Washington, Sept. 10, 1831	1/4 lea.	DeWitt	Dewitt
Lockhart, William B., Sept. 17, 1832	1/4 lea.	DeWitt	Gonzales
Logan, Greenberry, Dec. 22, 1831	1/4 lea.	Austin 3	Brazoria
Logan, John, Apr. 16, 1831	1 lea.	Austin 2	Fayette
Logan, Ornan, Feb. 14, 1836	10 lea.	Grant, Durst & Williams	(?)
Logan, William G., Apr. 30, 1835	1 lea.	Vehlein	San Jacinto
Logan, William M., Nov. 7, 1835	1/4 lea.	Vehlein	San Jacinto
Lomas, Lewis, Mch. 30, 1831	1 lea.	Austin 2	Bastrop
Lomas, Lewis, Feb. 12, 1835	1 lea.	Robertson	Milam
Long, Jacob, Nov. 23, 1832	1 lea.	Austin 2	Burleson
Long, Jane H., Apr. 30, 1827	1 lea. 1 lab.	Austin 1	Lea. Ft. Bend Lab. Waller
Longbotham, Robert B., July 24, 1835	1 lea.	Burnet	1/2 Limestone 1/4 Navarro 1/4 Freestone
Longoria, Juan Antonio, Feb. 9, 1835	1 lea.	Vehlein	Angelina
Longorio, Antonio, July 17, 1832	4 lea.	Elizondo	Nueces
Looney, Joseph K., Nov. 10, 1830	1/4 lea.	Austin	Jackson
Lopez, Esteban, Sept. 3, 1834	1 lea.	Power & Hewetson	Refugio
Lopez, Guadalupe, Dec. 4, 1835	1 lea. 1 lab.	Taylor	Jefferson (?)
Lopez, Ignacio, May 16, 1835	1 lea.	Vehlein	Houston
Lopez, Jose Leonisio, Aug. 7, 1835	1 lea.	Vehlein	Trinity
Lopez, Luterio, Sept. 11, 1835	1 lea.	Vehlein	2/3 Jefferson 1/3 Chambers
Lopez, Manuel, Apr. 18, 1835		De Leon	Victoria
Lopez, Manuel, Apr. 9, 1835	1 lea.	De Leon	Calhoun
Lopez, Manuel & Mariano, Sept. 15, 1835	11 lea.	Berry	Fannin
Lopez, Manuel & Mariano, Dec. 14, 1835	11 lea.	Berry	(?)
Losoya, Domingo, Mch. 20, 1834	1 lea.	McMullen & McGloin	Bexar
Loupy, Armand Victor, Nov. 26, 1835	1 lea.	Power & Hewetson	3/5 San Patricio 2/5 Bee
Lout, Pinckney, Feb. 27, 1835	1 lea.	Zavala	Orange
Love, Samuel, July 23, 1831	1 lea.	Austin 3	Matagorda
Low, Eli, June 9, 1835	1 lea.	Zavala	Sabine
Low, Garret, Nov. 2, 1835	1/4 lea.	Robertson	McLennan
Low, Issac, June 20, 1835	11 lab. & 56,008 sq. vs.	Zavala	Sabine

Name and Date of Title	Amount	Colony or Commis- sioner	Present Location
Loyd, Peterson L., Oct. 2, 1835	1/4 lea.	Robertson	Robertson
Lucas, John, Nov. 20, 1835	1 lea.	Zavala	San Augustin
Lucas, Robert, Oct. 11, 1835	1 lea.	Zavala	Tyler
Luce, William, Jan. 21, 1835	1 lea.	Burnet	Smith
Lucobichi, Jose, June 20, 1803	4 lea.	Flores	Angelina
Lumbrera, Aniseta, Sept. 21, 1835	1 lea. 1 lab.	Smyth	Upshur
Lumpkin, William M., June 8, 1835	1 lea.	Burnet	Nacogdoche
Luna, Gertrudis, July 25, 1835	1 lea.	Burnet	Freestone
Luna (de la), Manuel, Mch. 20, 1834	1 lea.	McMullen & McGloin	Bexar
Lusk, Levi, Dec. 9, 1835	1 lea.	Taylor	Jefferson (?
Lymon, Warren, Aug. 20, 1835	1 lea.	Robertson	Milam
Lynch, James, July 16, 1824	1 lea.	Austin 1	Washington
Lynch, Nathaniel, Aug. 19, 1824	1 lea.	Austin 1	Harris
Lynch, Stephen, Dec. 15, 1835	1 lea. 1 lab.	Smyth	(?)
Lyon, James M., July 16, 1835	23 lab. 600,000 sq. vs.	Burnet	Freestone
Lytle, John W., Jan. 23, 1833	1 lea.	Austin 3	Galveston
Mabbit, Lenard H., Oct. 29, 1834	1/4 lea.	Zavala	Tyler
Mackey, Naomi, June 4, 1835	17,302,291 sq. vs.	Zavala	Sabine
Mackey, Ruth, Dec. 8, 1832	1 lea.	Austin 2	Bastrop
Madden, James, Oct. 13, 1835	1 lea.	Burnet	Anderson
Maden, Isaac, June 16, 1831	1/4 lea.	Austin 2	Lavaca
Maginnies, John, May 4, 1835	1 lea.	Vehlein	Polk
Magano, Jacinto, Aug. 15, 1835	1 lea.	Taylor	Angelina
Main, Mickam, July 6, 1835	1 lea.	Burnet	Anderson
Maldonado, Basilio, Apr. 8, 1835	1 lea.	De Leon	Calhoun
Malley, Julianna, Aug. 19, 1835	1 lea.	Taylor	1/2 Harris 1/2 Libert
Malone, John, ? ? ?	1 lea.	Power & Hewetson	Refugio
Malone, John, Oct. 15, 1835	1/4 lea.	Burnet	Cherokee
Managhan, George F., May 1, 1831	1/4 lea.	DeWitt	Gonzales
Mancha, Antonio, Dec. 22, 1832	14 lab.	Austin 2	Austin
Mancha, Maria Bonita, July 26, 1835	1 lea.	Vehlein	Trinity
Manchaca, Jose Antonio, Sept. 27, 1833	11 lea.	Lessassier	8 lea. Falls 3 McLenna
Manchola, Rafael, July 10, 1834 (See Maria de Jesus de Leon)	2 lea.	De Leon	Victoria
Manlove, Bartholomew, Apr. 22, 1835	1 lea.	Milam	Bastrop
Mann, Levi, Oct. 11, 1835	1/4 lea.	Zavala	(?)
Manning, Stephen, May 29, 1835	1 lea.	Vehlein	Walker
Manso, Camilio, Mch. 14, 1835		De Leon	Victoria
Manso, Leonardo, Mch. 3, 1835		De Leon	Victoria
Manso, Leonardo, Sept. 26, 1834	1 lea.	De Leon	Jackson
Mansola, Juan Bautista, Aug. 15, 1835	1/3 lea.	Smyth	Rusk
Mansolo, Anastacio, Aug. 30, 1831	1 lea.	Navarro	Guadalupe
Mansolo, Tomas, Apr. 28, 1810	1 1/2 lea.	Torres	Angelina
Manwaring, William, Apr. 30, 1835	1/4 lea.	Burnet	Nacogdoche

Name and Date of Title	Amount	Colony or Commis- sioner	Present Location
Marchand, Marcos, Dec. 30, 1834	1 1/4 lea.	Power & Hewetson	(?)
Mardez, Abner, Sept. 12, 1835	1 lea.	Vehlein	Polk
Mariotini, Mary A.O., Nov. 23, 1835	1 lea.	Burnet	Rusk (?)
Marlin, John, Feb. 2, 1835	1 lea.	Robertson	Falls
Marlin, William, Feb. 2, 1835	1/4 lea.	Robertson	Falls
Marmon, Manuela, Aug. 5, 1835	1 lea.	Vehlein	Trinity
Marquez, Manuel, Apr. 4, 1835		De Leon	Victoria
Marquez, Manuel, June 30, 1835	1 lea.	De Leon	1/2 Victoria 1/2 Jackson
Marquez, Maria C., Dec. 15, 1833	11 lea.	Aldrete	3/4 Robertson 1/4 Leon
Marsh, Shubael, July 8, 1824	1 lea.	Austin 1	Brazoria
Marsh, Shubael, Dec. 14, 1831	1/2 lea.	Austin 3	Brazoria
Marshall, Isaac, Oct. 18, 1832	1/4 lea.	Austin 2	Austin
Marshall, Samuel B., Oct. 2, 1835	1 lea.	Burnet	Leon
Martin, Daniel, Nov. 18, 1835	1 lea.	Smyth	Rusk (?)
Martin, Eliza, May 2, 1831		Madero	Liberty
Martin, James, May 12, 1831	1 lea.	Madero	Liberty
Martin, James, May 2, 1831		Madero	Liberty
Martin, John, May 19, 1828	1/4 lea. & 1/4 lab.	Austin 2	Austin
Martin, John F., May 11, 1831	1/4 lea.	Austin 2	Brazos
Martin, Joshua W., Jan. 17, 1832	1/4 lea.	Austin 2	Colorado
Martin, Josiah C., May 2, 1831		Madero	Liberty
Martin, Laurence, Nov.,8, 1831	1/4 lea.	Austin 2	Lavaca
Martin, Neal, Apr. 13, 1835	1 lea.	Vehlein	Montgomery
Martin, Phillip, May 26, 1835	1 lea.	Burnet	Anderson
Martin, Wiley, July 29, 1834	1 lea.	Austin 1	Brazoria
Martin, Wiley, May 7, 1831	1 lea.	Austin 2	Ft. Bend
Martin, William S., May 13, 1831	1/4 lea.	Austin 2	Brazos
Martínez, Carlos, June 7, 1788	15 lea.	Cazorla	Karnes
Martinez, Dionisio, Not Titled			
Martinez, Dionisio, Mch. 20, 1834	1 lea.	McMullen & McGloin	Bexar
Martinez, Francisco, May 18, 1835	1 lea.	Vehlein	1/2 Houston 1/2 Trinity
Martinez, Jose Dolores, Nov. 28, 1833	11 lea.	Aldrete	5 lea. San Jacinto 5 Liberty 1 Chambers
Martinez, Jose Maria, May 23, 1835	1 lea.	Burnet	Rusk
Martinez, Juana, Dec. 4, 1835	1 lea.	Zavala	Orange (?)
Martinez, Marcelino, Oct. 18, 1835	3 lea.	Lessassier	2 lea. Mc- Lennan 1 Falls
Martinez, Marcelino, Apr. 8, 1834	1 lea.	Lessassier	Robertson
Mascoro (Rios) Maria Engracia, Nov. 23, 1835	1 lea.	Zavala	Jefferson (?)
Mason, James Y., Nov. 20, 1835	1 lea.	Smyth	Panola (?)
Mason, Peter, Oct. 17, 1835	1 lea.	Taylor	Liberty
Masters, Henry, Jan. 28, 1835	1 lea.	Vehlein	Houston

Name and Date of Title	Amount	Colony or Commissioner	Present Location
Masters, Jacob, Sr., Feb. 14, 1835	1 lea.	Burnet	Houston
Masters, Jacob, Jr., Feb. 14, 1835	1 lea.	Burnet	Houston
Mathew, John, Oct. 26, 1835	1 lea.	Smyth	3/4 Rusk 1/4 Gregg
Mathews, Charles M., Dec. 26, 1834	1 lea.	Robertson	1/2 Burlesc 1/2 Milan
Mathews, Robert, May 28, 1831	1/4 lea.	Austin 2	Brazos
Mathews, William A., May 5, 1831	1/4 lea.	DeWitt	Gonzales
Mathis, John, Dec. 11, 1830	1/4 lea.	Austin 3	Jackson
Mathis, William, July 19, 1824	1 lea.	Austin 1	Brazos
Maxlen, Samuel, Jan. 15, 1836	1 lea.	Taylor	Liberty (?)
May, George, June 20, 1835	1 lea.	Burnet	Rusk
May, James, May 2, 1835	1/4 lea.	De Leon	3/5 Dewitt 2/5 Lavac
May, John, Sr., May 2, 1835	1 lea.	De Leon	2/3 Lavaca 1/3 Dewit
May, Joseph, May 4, 1835	1/4 lea.	De Leon	Dewitt
Mayfield, John E., Sept. 16, 1835	1 lea.	Vehlein	Liberty
Mayhan, Francis, July 31, 1835	1 lea.	Robertson	Falls
Mayo, John, Nov. 27, 1835	1 lea.	Taylor	(?)
Mayo, William, Nov. 23, 1835	1 lea. 1 lab.	Taylor	Jefferson (?
Mays, Andrew, Feb. 12, 1836	1 lea.	Austin 5	Bastrop (?)
Mays, Thomas H., Apr. 4, 1831	1/4 lea.	Austin 2	Bastrop
Mayun, Ignacio, Apr. 10, 1835		De Leon	Victoria
Means, Hugh, Oct. 15, 1835	1 lea.	Vehlein	Liberty
Means, William, May 15, 1835	1 lea.	Zavala	(?)
Medford, William, Oct. 5, 1835	1 lea.	Austin 5	Bastrop
Medina, Juan Antonio, July 16, 1800		De la Bega	Nacogdoche
Medina, Juan Jose, Nov. 20, 1835	1 lea.	Vehlein	Polk (?)
Medina, Pedro, July 22, 1835	1 lea.	Vehlein	San Jacinto
Medrano, Jose Maria, Nov. 8, 1835	1 lea. 1 lab.	Taylor	Lea. Jasper Lab. Liber
Melton, William K., July 18, 1835	1 lea.	Burnet	3/5 Firesto 2/5 Ander
Menard, Michael B., June 3, 1835	1 lea.	Vehlein	San Jacinto
Menard, Peter J., July 18, 1835	1 lea.	Vehlein	Polk
Menchaca, Antonio, Nov. 2, 1833	11 lea.	Lessassier	6 Robertson 5 Bell
Menchaca, Joaquin, Oct. 5, 1835	1 lea. 1 lab.	Berry	(?)
Menchaca, Jose Nasario, Aug. 4, 1835	1/4 lea.	Burnet	Rusk
Menchaca, Luis, ? ? ?	11 lea. 2 lab.		3/5 Wilson 2/5 Karne
Menchaca, Miguel, See Santiago Serna			
Menchaca, Maria Dolores, Nov. 21, 1835	1 lea.	Taylor	(?)
Mendenhall, Peter, Jan. 18, 1836	1 lea.	Taylor	(?)
Meneffee, Francis, June 23, 1831	1 lea.	Austin 3	Jackson
Meneffee, Thomas, Dec. 4, 1830	1 lea.	Austin 3	Jackson
Meneffee, William, Nov. 24, 1830	1 lea.	Austin 3	Jackson
Meness, Shadrack, Sept. 9, 1835	1 lea.	Robertson	McLennan
Mercer, Eli, Dec. 13, 1830	1 lea.	Austin 3	Jackson
Mercer, George R., Oct. 14, 1835	1 lea.	Vehlein	Walker
Meredith, Thomas, Nov. 25, 1835	1 lea.	Taylor	(?)

Name and Date of Title	Amount	Colony or Commis-sioner	Present Location
Merry, John, Aug. 17, 1835	1 lea.	Vehlein	Harris
Metcalff, H. T., Nov. 23, 1835	1 lea. 1 lab.	Taylor	(?)
Mexia, Matilde A., See Pedro Varela			
Micheli, Vicente, June 12, 1810	2 lea.	Mora	Angelina
Micheli, Vicente, June 9, 1810	3/4 lea.	Procela	Nacogdoches ?
Micheli, Vicente, June 20, 1797	8 lea.	Zepeda	(?)
Mici, Pias, Mch. 27, 1835	1 lea.	Berry	Polk
Middleton, Henry, Nov. 23, 1835	1 lea.	Taylor	Jasper (?)
Middleton, J. F., Sept. 10, 1835	1 lea.	Zavala	San Augustine
Middleton, Samuel P., Sept. 12, 1831	1/4 lea.	DeWitt	Dewitt
Midkiff, Candis, Apr. 22, 1835	1 lea.	Burnet	Leon
Midkiff, Isaac J., Apr. 21, 1835	1 lea.	Burnet	Leon
Milburn, David H., May 27, 1828	1/4 lea.	Austin 2	Ft. Bend
Milburn, David H., (Thomas & Davis), July 29, 1824	1 lea.	Austin 1	Austin
Miles, James, Mch. 23, 1831	1 lea.	Austin 2	Fayette
Millard, Robert F., Nov. 20, 1835	1 lea.	Burnet	(?)
Miller, Andrew, Mch. 7, 1831	1 lea.	Austin 2	Washington
Miller, Edmond R., Mch. 10, 1831	1 lea.	Austin 2	Washington
Miller, Edward, Sept. 24, 1835	1 lea.	Zavala	Angelina
Miller, James B., Apr. 23, 1831	1 lea.	Austin 2	Washington
Miller, Joseph, Apr. 16, 1831	1 lea.	Austin 2	2/3 Harris 1/3 Mont-gomery
Miller, Leroy, Mch. 3, 1835	1/4 lea.	Zavala	San Augustine
Miller, Mathew S., June 25, 1835	5 lab. & 881,988 sq. vs.	Zavala	Liberty
Miller, Phillip, June 13, 1835	1 lea.	Vehlein	Liberty
Miller, Ruth, Aug. 17, 1835	1 lea.	Vehlein	San Jacinto
Miller, Samuel, Aug. 19, 1824	1 lea.	Austin 1	Washington
Miller, Samuel R., Aug. 19, 1824	1 lea.	Austin 1	Washington
Miller, Simon, Aug. 7, 1824	1/2 lea.	Austin 1	Ft. Bend
Miller, Simon, Mch. 20, 1831	1/4 lea.	Austin 2	Washington
Miller, Solomon, Nov. 27, 1834	1/4 lea.	Zavala	San Augustine
Miller, Thomas R., Sept. 20, 1831	1/4 lea.	DeWitt	Dewitt
Millett, Samuel, Nov. 20, 1832	1 lea.	Austin 2	3/4 Fayette 1/4 Bastrop
Millican, Andrew, Dec. 13, 1832	1 lea.	Austin 2	Brazos
Millican, Elliot M., Mch. 26, 1831	1 lea.	Austin 2	Brazos
Millican, James D., July 16, 1824	1 lea.	Austin 1	Brazos
Millican, Robert, July 16, 1824	2 1/2 lea.	Austin 1	Brazos
Millican, William, July 18, 1824	1 lea.	Austin 1	Brazos
Millon, Francis, Sept. 17, 1835	1 lea.	Zavala	18 3/4 lab. Liberty 6 1/4 Polk
Mills, David G., June 15, 1832	1/4 lea.	DeWitt	Dewitt
Mills, Robert, Sept. 13, 1831	1/4 lea.	DeWitt	Dewitt
Millspough, Nathaniel, May 2, 1831		Madero	Liberty
Mims, Benjamin F., May 22, 1835	1/4 lea.	Milam	Hays
Mims, Joseph, Aug. 19, 1824	1 lea.	Austin 1	Brazoria

Name and Date of Title	Amount	Colony or Commissioner	Present Location
Minckey, David, May 10, 1831	1 lea.	Madero	Liberty
Minckey, David, May 2, 1831		Madero	Liberty
Miranda, Pedro, Sept. 6, 1835	1/3 lea.	Taylor	Houston
Miranda, Pedro, Apr. 8, 1835	1 lea.	De Leon	Calhoun
Missenham, Jacob, Nov. 17, 1835	1 lea. 1 lab.	Smyth	(?)
Missenham, John, Nov. 27, 1835	1 lea. 1 lab.	Smyth	(?)
Mitchell, Asa, July 7, 1824	1 1/2 lea.	Austin 1	Brazoria
Mitchell, Asa, Aug. 24, 1824	1 lab.	Austin 1	Brazoria
Mitchell, Eli, Mch. 2, 1832	1/4 lea.	Austin 3	Brazoria
Mitchell, James, Apr. 2, 1835	1/4 lea.	Burnet	Tyler
Mitchell, James, Apr. 20, 1835	1 lea.	Vehlein	Madison
Mitchell, John W., Apr. 12, 1831	1/4 lea.	Austin 2	Burleson
Mixon, Noel, July 23, 1835	1 lea.	Milam	Blanco
Moffitt, N. C., Feb. 5, 1836	1 lea.	Austin 5	Fayette (?)
Moffitt, Robert, July 29, 1835	1 lea.	Robertson	2/3 Roberts 1/3 Falls
Mohan, Timothy, Nov. 21, 1835	1 lea.	Smyth	Henderson (
Molina, Carmen, Aug. 3, 1835	1 lea. 1 lab.	McMullen & McGloin	Bee
Molina, Juan, Aug. 3, 1835	1/3 lea.	McMullen & McGloin	Bee
Molina, Juan de Dios, Aug. 3, 1835	1 lea. 1 lab.	McMullen & McGloin	Bee
Molina, Teodoro, Aug. 3, 1835	1 lea. 1 lab.	McMullen & McGloin	Bee
Molina, Toribio, Aug. 3, 1835	1 lea. 1 lab.	McMullen & McGloin	San Patricio
Molloy, John Thomas, July 15, 1835	1 lea. 1 lab.	McMullen & McGloin	Bee
Monday, Samuel, Oct. 12, 1835	1 lea.	Smyth	Harrison
Money, John H., Mch. 31, 1831	1/4 lea.	Austin 3	Washington
Monks, John, Aug. 16, 1824	1 lea.	Austin 1	Brazoria (?
Monroe, Aug. C., Sept. 18, 1835	1 lea.	Burnet	3/5 Freesto 2/5 Anders
Monroe, Daniel, Mch. 20, 1835	24 lab.	Robertson	Milam
Monroe, Daniel, Feb. 15, 1835	1 lab.	Robertson	Falls
Montalba, Manuela, May 16, 1835	1 lea.	Vehlein	Trinity
Montano, Cesario, Nov. 16, 1835	11 lea.	Berry	(?)
Montgomery, Andrew, July 30, 1835	3/4 lea.	Robertson	Falls
Montgomery, Andrew, Feb. 2, 1835	1/4 lea.	Robertson	Falls
Montgomery, D. C., Aug. 29, 1835	1 lea.	Zavala	Hardin
Montgomery, Edley, Feb. 1, 1835	1/4 lea.	Robertson	Falls
Montgomery, John, Feb. 2, 1835	1/4 lea.	Robertson	Falls
Montgomery, William, Mch. 4, 1831	1 lea.	Austin 2	Grimes
Montone, Soto, Jan. 12, 1836	1 lea.	Taylor	Jefferson (?
Moore, Azariah G., June 21, 1835	1/4 lea.	Milam	Bastrop
Moore, Daniel S. D., Sept. 12, 1835	1 lea.	Zavala	Newton
Moore, Elisha, Apr. 19, 1831	1 lea.	Austin 2	Wharton
Moore, Francis, Mch. 3, 1830	1 lea.	Austin 3	Brazoria
Moore, James, Oct. 27, 1830	1 lea.	Austin 3	Matagorda
Moore, James W., Oct. 20, 1835	1 lea.	Austin 5	Grimes

Name and Date of Title	Amount	Colony or Commissioner	Present Location
Moore, John, Oct. 22, 1835	1 lea.	Vehlein	Houston
Moore, John, Mch. 7, 1835	1 lea.	Zavala	Sabine
Moore, John, Sept. 30, 1835	1 lea.	Zavala	Sabine
Moore, John, Apr. 15, 1831	1 lea.	Austin 2	Grimes
Moore, John H., See Thomas Gray			
Moore, John H., May 17, 1831	1/2 lea.	Austin 2	Fayette
Moore, John W., Apr. 28, 1831	1 lea.	Austin 2	3/4 Wharton 1/4 Ft. Bend
Moore, Lewis, Aug. 20, 1835	1/4 lea.	Robertson	McLennan
Moore, Luke, Aug. 3, 1824	1 lea.	Austin 1	Harris
Moore, Morris, Aug. 17, 1835	1/4 lea.	Robertson	McLennan
Moore, Rebecca, Nov. 2, 1835	1 lea.	Robertson	Milam
Moore, Robert D., June 22, 1831	1 lea.	Austin 3	Jackson
Moore, Samuel, Mch. 18, 1835	1/4 lea.	Robertson	Milam
Moore, Uriah, Jan. 3, 1835	1 lea.	Burnet	Cherokee
Moore, Vinson, Oct. 15, 1835	1 lea.	Burnet	Smith
Moore, William, Dec. 24, 1835	10 lea.	Williams, Johnson & Peebles	(?)
Mora, Esteban, Sept. 29, 1835	1 lea. 1 lab.	Smyth	Upshur
Mora, Jacinto, Dec. 10, 1795	6 lea.	Zepeda	(?)
Mora, Jose Maria, Oct. 1, 1799	(?)	Flores	Nacogdoches
Mora, Jose Maria, May 29, 1810	4 lea. 1 lab. & 640,000 sq. vs.	Flores	Nacogdoches
Mora, Jose Maria, Oct. 30, 1833	9 lea.	Aldrete	4 (?) 1 Jasper 1 Jefferson 1 Cherokee 2 Anderson
Mora, Juan, Dec. 3, 1833	11 lea.	Aldrete	(?)
Mora, Mariano, Dec. 6, 1833	11 lea.	Aldrete	(?)
Mora, Nicolas, May 11, 1792	273,529 sq. vs.	Zepeda	Nacogdoches (?)
Morales, Andres, Aug. 30, 1835	1 lea.	Vehlein	Polk
Morales, Benito, Apr. 11, 1835	1 lea.	De Leon	Calhoun
Morales, Crecencio, Dec. 4, 1835	1 lea. 1 lab.	Taylor	Liberty (?)
Morehead, John, Dec. 16, 1835	1 lea.	Taylor	Trinity (?)
Moreland, Isaac N., June 19, 1835	1/4 lea.	Vehlein	Polk
Moreland, John W., Oct. 27, 1835	1 lea.	Vehlein	Polk
Moreno, Joaquin, Apr. 20, 1835	11 lea.	Valmaceda	McLennan
Moreno, Maximo, Oct. 8, 1833	11 lea.	Lessassier	Bell
Morgan, Charles, June 3, 1835	1 lea.	Zavala	Orange
Morgan, George, Sept. 9, 1835	1 lea.	Robertson	Falls
Morgan, George W., Sept. 9, 1835	1 lea.	Robertson	Falls
Morgan, Hugh, Aug. 30, 1835	1 lea.	Vehlein	7/8 Liberty 1/8 Chambers
Morgan, James, Oct. 8, 1835	1 lea.	Vehlein	Polk
Morgan, James, Nov. 19, 1831	1 lea.	Austin 3	Jackson
Morgan, Joseph, Aug. 27, 1835	1 lea.	Vehlein	Polk
Morin, Jose, July 2, 1835	1 lea.	Vehlein	Angelina
Morris, Bethel, July 1, 1832	1/4 lea.	DeWitt	Gonzales

Name and Date of Title	Amount	Colony or Commissioner	Present Location
Morris, Domingo, Oct. 30, 1834	1 1/4 lea.	Power & Hewetson	Goliad
Morris, Elisha, Oct. 29, 1835	1 lea.	Zavala	Jasper
Morris, George, Oct. 27, 1834	1 lea.	Power & Hewetson	San Patrici
Morris, John, Sept. 16, 1832	1/4 lea.	DeWitt	3/5 Gonzal‹ 1/5 Fayet 1/5 Lavac
Morris, Johathan D., Apr. 6, 1831	1/4 lea.	Austin 2	Bastrop
Morris, Ritson, Nov. 14, 1832	1 lea.	Austin 3	Harris
Morris, Shadrack, June 17, 1835	16 lab. & 458,500 sq. vs.	Zavala	Sabine
Morris, Shadrack, July 11, 1835	8 lab. & 541,500 sq. vs.	Zavala	Jefferson
Morris, Silas M., June 22, 1832	1 lea.	DeWitt	Lavaca
Morris, Spencer, June 25, 1831	1 lea.	DeWitt	Caldwell
Morris, William, Oct. 14, 1835	1 lea.	Vehlein	San Jacinto
Morrison, Moses & Wm. Cooper, July 24, 1824	1 lea.	Austin 1	Matagorda
Morrison, Stephen B., June 22, 1831	1 lea.	DeWitt	Caldwell
Morton, Louisiana, Nov. 27, 1831	1 lea.	Austin 3	Brazoria
Morton, William, July 15, 1824	1 1/2 lea. & 1 lab.	Austin 1	Ft. Bend
Moss, Elihu, Nov. 25, 1831	1 lea.	DeWitt	Dewitt
Moss, Henry W., Mch. 18, 1835	1/4 lea.	Robertson	Robertson
Moss, James, Nov. 22, 1834	1/4 lea.	Zavala	San Augusti‹
Moss, Nathaniel, May 2, 1831		Madero	Liberty
Moss, William L., Feb. 15, 1835	1 lea.	Robertson	Robertson
Mott, Joseph, June 20, 1835	16 lab. 260,000 sq. vs.	Zavala	Sabine
Mott, William, Nov. 27, 1835	1 lea.	Taylor	(?)
Mouser, David, Aug. 19, 1824	1 lea.	Austin 1	Waller
Moya, Agustin & Juan, Dec. 3, 1834	1 1/4 lea.	Power & Hewetson	Bee
Mudd, Balthazar A., June 25, 1835	1 lea.	Zavala	Angelina
Muldoon, Miguel, Dec. 15, 1831	2 lea.	Austin 3	Galveston
Muldoon, Miguel, May 14, 1831	2 lea.	Arciniega	Wharton
Muldoon, Miguel, May 31, 1831	2 lea.	Arciniega	Fayette
Muldoon, Miguel, Feb. 28, 1832	5 lea.	Arciniega	2 lea. Faye‹ 3 Lavaca
Mullen, Patrick, Oct. 2, 1834	1 lea.	Zavala	Angelina
Mullen, Thomas, Sept. 18, 1834	1 lea.	Power & Hewetson	Refugio
Mullin, James Henry, Nov. 24, 1834	1/4 lea.	Power & Hewetson	Bee
Munford, David, Mch. 20, 1835	1 lea.	Robertson	Milam
Munford, Jesse, Feb. 25, 1835	1 lea.	Robertson	Bell
Munson, Elizabeth, May 3, 1831	1 lea.	Madero	Liberty

Name and Date of Title	Amount	Colony or Commissioner	Present Location
Munson, Henry W., Nov. 2, 1830	1 lea.	Austin 3	Jackson
Munson, William, Mch. 28, 1831	1 lea.	Austin 2	Washington
Murchison, Martin, Dec. 30, 1834	1 lea.	Burnet	Houston
Murrell, William, Jan. 15, 1836	1 lea.	Taylor	(?)
Murphrey, William, Jan. 17, 1831	1/4 lea.	Austin 3	Jackson
Murphy, Edmond, William & James, Oct. 29, 1834	1 1/4 lea.	Power & Hewetson	Goliad
Murphy, Edward, Oct. 18, 1791	1 lea.	Ybarbo	(?)
Murphy, Edward, Aug. ?, 1798	4 lea.	Zepeda	(?)
Murphy, James, Nov. 29, 1832	1/4 lea.	Austin 2	Wharton
Murphy, Samuel, Oct. 10, 1835	1 lea.	Smyth	Harrison
Murphy, Silvester, Oct. 25, 1832	1 lea.	Austin 3	Harris
Murphy, Willis, Nov. 26, 1834	1 lea.	Zavala	Sabine
Musquiz, Jose Maria, Nov. 8, 1833	5 lea.	Aldrete	3/5 Cherokee 2/5 Nacogdoches
Musquiz, Jose Miguel, Mch. 7, 1831	11 lea.	Madero	4 Leon 4 Houston 3 Madison
Musquiz, Miguel, Oct. 23, 1834	1 lea.	Power & Hewetson	San Patricio
Musquiz, Ramon, June 26, 1833	4 lea.	Aldrete	Karnes
Musquiz, Ramon, Aug. 20, 1835	1 1/2 lea.	Aldrete	2/3 Goliad 1/3 Karnes
Musquiz, Ramon, Jan. 2, 1833	5 1/2 lea.	De Leon	Jackson
Myers, Elias G., July 19, 1835	1 lea.	Burnet	Anderson
Myers, Henry, July 22, 1835	1/4 lea.	Burnet	Cherokee
Myrick, Eliakim P., Oct. 27, 1830	1 lea.	Austin 3	Brazoria
McAnulty, Sarah, July 7, 1835	1 lea.	Burnet	Limestone
McAuley, Francis Harrison, See Wm. Bartels			
McAuley, Malcolm, Oct. 30, 1834	1 lea.	Power & Hewetson	San Patricio
McCain, James, Mch. 23, 1831	1 lea.	Austin 2	Washington
McAllister, Joseph, Oct. 20, 1835	1/4 lea.	Austin 5	Fayette
McCamley, Samuel W., Nov. 30, 1834	1 lea.	Power & Hewetson	Goliad
McCarley, Samuel, May 14, 1831	1 lea.	Austin 2	3/5 Harris 2/5 Waller
McCarver, Morton M., Feb. 21, 1835	1 lea.	Milam	Hays
McClain, James, Oct. 12, 1835	1 lea.	Smyth	Rusk
McClain, William, Feb. 9, 1835	1/4 lea.	Robertson	Milam
McClure, Abraham O., July 6, 1831	1/4 lea.	DeWitt	Caldwell
McClure, Bartholomew D., Sept. 6, 1831	24 lab.	DeWitt	Gonzales
McClure, Bartholomew D., Sept. 12, 1831	1 lab.	DeWitt	Gonzales
McCormick, Arthur, Aug. 10, 1824	1 lea.	Austin 1	Harris
McCormick, David, July 21, 1824	1 lea.	Austin 1	Brazoria
McCormick, John, July 24, 1824	1/3 lea.	Austin 1	Austin (?)
McCormick, Joseph M., June 22, 1832	1 lea.	Austin 2	Ft. Bend
McCombs, Samuel, Nov. 4, 1835	1 lea.	Taylor	San Jacinto
McCoy, Alexander, Mch. 18, 1831	1/4 lea.	Austin 2	Washington

Name and Date of Title	Amount	Colony or Commissioner	Present Location
McCoy, Daniel, June 18, 1832	1 lea.	DeWitt	Gonzales
McCoy, David, Jan. 30, 1835	1 lea.	Vehlein	Angelina
McCoy, Jesse, Apr. 24, 1831	1/4 lea.	DeWitt	Gonzales
McCoy, John, Apr. 24, 1831	1 lea.	DeWitt	Gonzales
McCoy, John, Jr., May 5, 1831	1 lea.	DeWitt	Dewitt
McCoy, John S., June 22, 1835	1/4 lea.	Robertson	McLennan
McCoy, Joseph, May 1, 1831	1 lea.	DeWitt	Gonzales
McCoy, Joseph, Jr., July 11, 1832	1/4 lea.	DeWitt	Fayette
McCoy, Samuel, July 9, 1831	1/4 lea.	DeWitt	Dewitt
McCoy, Thomas & Daniel Deckro, July 24, 1824	1 lea.	Austin 1	Matagorda
McCrabb, John, July 13, 1831	1/4 lea.	DeWitt	Dewitt
McCrackin, Amanda, Feb. 19, 1836	1 lea.	Austin 5	Washington
McCrocklin, Jesse L., June 18, 1835	1 lea.	Milam	Blanco
McCrosky, John, Aug. 16, 1824	1 lea. 1 lab.	Austin 1	Lea. Brazo: Lab. Aust:
McCrosky, John, Oct. 29, 1831	1 lea.	Arciniega	Colorado
McCune, James, Nov. 30, 1834	1 lea.	Power & Hewetson	Goliad
McCune, James, July 18, 1835	1 lea.	Burnet	Rusk
McDaniel, James, Oct. 6, 1835	1/4 lea.	Vehlein	Houston
McDaniel, Robert C., July 6, 1835	1 lea.	Burnet	3/4 Hender-son 1/4 Ander
McDavid, Patrick, Nov. 21, 1835	1/3 lea.	Taylor	Jefferson (
McDonald, Donald, May 19, 1835	1 lea.	Zavala	Sabine
McDonald, Thomas, Oct. 22, 1835	1 lea.	Zavala	Jasper
McDonald, Thomas, Oct. 5, 1835	1 lea.	Austin 5	Grimes
McDonald, Thomas, June 20, 1835	1 lea.	Burnet	Rusk
McDonald, William, Nov. 12, 1834	1 lea.	Vehlein	Walker
McDonald, William S., June 20, 1835	1 lea.	Burnet	Anderson
McDonough, Edward, Oct. 15, 1834	1 lea.	Power & Hewetson	Victoria
McDowel, M., Oct. 17, 1835	1 lea.	Austin 5	Grimes
McElroy, Howard, Oct. 16, 1832	1 lea.	Austin 2	11/12 Color 1/12 Aust
McElroy, Phillip, Oct. 30, 1832	1 lea.ˑ	Austin 4	Travis
McFaddin, James, Apr. 26, 1831	1 lea.	Madero	3/4 Liberty 1/4 Cham
McFaddin, Nathan A., Oct. 20, 1832	1 lea.	Austin 2	Burleson
McFadin, William, Aug. 5, 1835	1 lea.	Vehlein	Polk
McFarlan, John, Aug. 10, 1824	1 1/4 lea. & 1 1/2 lab.	Austin 1	Waller
McFarlan, William, Apr. 6, 1831	1 lea.	Austin 2	Wharton
McFarland, Achilles, July 10, 1824	1 lea. 1 lab. & 510,000 sq. vs.	Austin 1	Lea. Brazo: Lab. Wall
McFarland, Nancy Artemisa, Dec. 17, 1830	1 lea.	Austin 3	Jackson
McFarland, Samuel P., Oct. 16, 1835	1/4 lea.	Vehlein	Angelina
McFarland, Thomas S., Mch. 18, 1835	1/4 lea.	Zavala	Jefferson
McFarland, William, Mch. 17, 1835	1 lea.	Zavala	Jefferson

Name and Date of Title	Amount	Colony or Commissioner	Present Location
McFarlane, Dugald, Oct. 29, 1830	1 lea.	Austin 3	Matagorda
McFarlin, William, Aug. 17, 1835	24 lab.	Robertson	Hill
McGahey, James S., Aug. 17, 1835	1 lea.	Vehlein	Chambers
McGalin, Thomas, July 24, 1835	1 lea.	Zavala	Jasper
McGarry, Bridget, Sept. 12, 1835	1 lea.	Robertson	McLennan
McGary, Edward, Feb. 25, 1835	1/4 lea.	Robertson	Falls
McGary, Isaac, Mch. 29, 1831	1 lea.	Austin 2	Ft. Bend
McGee, Anthony, Oct. 15, 1835	1 lea.	Zavala	(?)
McBee, Drury, Oct. 30, 1835	1 lea.	Taylor	San Jacinto
McGee, Jesse, Oct. 23, 1835	1 lea.	Zavala	1/2 Newton 1/2 Sabine
McGee, John, Nov. 2, 1834	1 lea.	Zavala	Newton
McGee, Ralph, Mch. 12, 1835	1 lea.	Vehlein	San Jacinto
McGeehans, James, Sept. 25, 1834	1 lea.	Power & Hewetson	3/5 Bee 2/5 Refugio
McGeehee, John G., Apr. 5, 1835	1 lea.	Milam	4/5 Hays 1/5 Travis
McGeehee, Thomas G., Feb. 19, 1835	1 lea.	Milam	Hays
McGill, Henry, Aug. 25, 1835	1 lea.	Zavala	Hardin
McGill, William, See Wm. Redmond			
McGloin, Edward J., Dec. 5, 1831	1 lea.	McMullen & McGloin	3/4 Live Oak 1/4 San Patricio
McGloin, James, Dec. 2, 1831	1 lea.	McMullen & McGloin	Live Oak
McGloin, James, Dec. 22, 1831	2 lab. & 295,000 sq. vs.	McMullen & McGloin	San Patricio
McGloin, James, Dec. 18, 1831	1 lea.	McMullen & McGloin	Live Oak
McGloin, John, July 5, 1835	1/3 lea.	McMullen & McGloin	Live Oak
McGloin, Patrick, Dec. 3, 1831	1 lea.	McMullen & McGloin	Lea. Live Oak 1/10 lab. San Patricio
McGowan, Denis, Dec. 3, 1831	1 lea.	McMullen & McGloin	Live Oak
McGregor, John, July 22, 1835	1/4 lea.	Burnet	Cherokee
McGrew, John Flood, Sept. 22, 1835	1/4 lea.	Robertson	Robertson
McGrew, William A., Sept. 22, 1835	1/4 lea.	Robertson	Robertson
McGuffin, Hugh, Nov. 22, 1831	1 lea.	Austin 3	Jackson
McGuffin, John, Oct. 22, 1830	1/4 lea.	Austin 3	Jackson
McGuffin, William, Nov. 12, 1832	1 lea.	Austin 2	Grimes
McHanks, Horatio, June 4, 1835	1/4 lea.	Zavala	Jefferson
McHenry, John, Oct. 26, 1832	1 lea.	De Leon	Jackson
McIlrain, William, Oct. 10, 1835	1/3 lea.	Smyth	Harrison
McIntire, Margaret, Apr. 5, 1831	1 lea.	Austin 2	Grimes
McIntire, William, Apr. 6, 1831	1/4 lea.	Austin 2	Grimes
McJohnson, Solomon, Nov. 10, 1835	1 lea.	Zavala	(?)
McKenzie, Daniel, July 9, 1835	1 lea.	Burnet	Freestone (?)
McKenzie, Elizabeth S., ? ? 1832	1 lea.	Austin 4	Wharton

Name and Date of Title	Amount	Colony or Commissioner	Present Location
McKey, Naomi, June 4, 1835	17 lab. & 301,291 sq. vs.	Zavala	Sabine
McKey, Thomas, Sept. 5, 1835	1 lea.	Robertson	Hill
McKim, James, Feb. 26, 1835	1 lea.	Zavala	Sabine
McKinney, James, Dec. 16, 1835	1 lea. 1 lab.	Smyth	Fannin (?)
McKinney, Thomas F., Aug. 16, 1824	1 lea.	Austin 1	Brazos
McKinney, Thomas F., Nov. 20, 1832	1 lab.	Austin 3	Brazoria
McKinney, Thomas F., Aug. 12, 1835	10 lea.	Williams, Johnson & Peebles	Fannin (?)
McKinney, Thomas F., Apr. 26, 1831	1 lea. .	Madero	Jefferson
McKinney, William C., Dec. 16, 1835	1 lea. 1 lab.	Smyth	Fannin (?)
McKinney, Hugh, See John Smith			
McKinstry, George B., Nov. 24, 1830	1 lea.	Austin 3	Harris
McKinza, Carter J., Nov. 20, 1835	1 lea.	Zavala	Jefferson (°
McKnight, George, Oct. 27, 1834	1/4 lea.	Power & Hewetson	Goliad
McLain, A. W. & J. McNair, July 24, 1824	1 lea.	Austin 1	Colorado
McLaughlin, James, Sept. 4, 1835	1 lea.	Robertson	Milam
McLaughlin, Laughlin, Sept. 28, 1835	1 lea.	Austin 5	Brazos
McLean, Daniel, Jan. 21, 1835	1 lea.	Burnet	Houston
McLean, Daniel, Feb. 20, 1835	1 lea.	Berry	Houston
McLennan, Neil, July 28, 1835	1 lea.	Robertson	Falls
McLinnan, Laughlin, Aug. 29, 1835	1 lea.	Robertson	Falls
McMahan, David B., Oct. 16, 1835	1 lea.	Austin 5	Grimes
McMahon, Samuel D., Oct. 11, 1835	1 lea.	Zavala	San August:
McMullen, John, Nov. 30, 1831	1 lea.	McMullen & McGloin	Live Oak
McMullen, John, Nov. 30, 1831	1 lea.	McMullen & McGloin	San Patrici
McNair, James, See A. W. McLain			
McNeal, John, Oct. 15, 1835	1 lea.	Burnet	Navarro
McNealy, Jesse B., Jan. 8, 1835	1 lea.	Burnet	Anderson
McNealy, Jesse B., Apr. 11, 1831	1 lea.	Austin 2	Grimes
McNeel, Daniel, Aug. 3, 1824	1 lea.	Austin 1	Brazoria
McNeel, John, July 7, 1831	1 lab.	Austin 3	Brazoria
McNeel, John G. & George W., Aug. 10, 1824	1 lea.	Austin 1	Brazoria
McNeel, Pleasant D., Aug. 7, 1824	1 lea.	Austin 1	Brazoria
McNeil, John, Aug. 3, 1824	1 lea.	Austin 1	Brazoria
McNeil, Sterling, Aug. 19, 1824	1 lea.	Austin 1	Brazoria
McNeill, Angus, Sept. 15, 1835	1 lea.	Vehlein	Liberty
McNeill, Henry C., Nov. 22, 1835	1/4 lea.	Vehlein	Polk (?)
McNutt, Elizabeth, July 21, 1824	1 lea.	Austin 1	Jackson
McQueen, David C., Sept. 20, 1828	1 lea.	Mora	Jasper (?)
McWilliams, William, July 19, 1824	1 lea.	Austin 1	Burleson
Nash, Hannah, Oct. 9, 1835	1 lea.	Vehlein	2/3 Chamb 1/3 Harri
Nash, Ira, May 1, 1831	1 lea.	DeWitt	5/6 Guadal 1/6 Gonza

Name and Date of Title	Amount	Colony or Commissioner-	Present Location
Nash, John D., July 25, 1835	20 lab. & 500,000 sq. vs.	Zavala	Polk
Nash, William, Sept. 12, 1835	1 lea.	Taylor	Polk
Nations, Joseph, Oct. 14, 1835	1/3 lea.	Smyth	Harrison
Nava (de), Nicolas, Sept. 18, 1835	4 lea.	Del Moral	(?)
Navarro, Angel, Dec. 4, 1833	1 lea.	Ximenes	Bexar
Navarro, Jose Antonio, Oct. 6, 1831	4 lea.	Salinas	Atascosa
Navarro, Jose Antonio, July 2, 1832	7 lea.	Arciniega	2/3 Travis 1/3 Bastrop
Navarro, Luciano, Apr. 7, 1835		De Leon	Victoria
Navarro, Luciano, Mch. 23, 1833	1 lea.	De Leon	6/7 Victoria 1/7 Dewitt
Navarro, Luciano, Oct. 5, 1835	3 lea.	Berry	1 Grayson 2 (?)
Navarro, Maria Concepcion, Nov. 4, 1835	1 lea. 1 lab.	Smyth	(?)
Needham, John, Dec. 30, 1834	1/4 lea.	Robertson	Bell
Neel, William, June 4, 1827	1/4 lea.	Austin 2	Ft. Bend
Neely, John M., Nov. 21, 1834	1 lea.	Zavala	San Augustine
Neill, James C., Nov. 26, 1832	1 lea.	Austin 4	2/3 Washington 1/3 Lee
Neill, James C., June 1, 1835	1 lea.	Milam	Travis
Neill, John A., June 20, 1831	1 lea.	DeWitt	Caldwell
Neill, William, Sept. 1, 1835	1 lea.	Robertson	McLennan
Neill, William, Dec. 27, 1834	1 lea.	Robertson	McLennan
Neilson, Joseph, Dec. 15, 1835	1 lea.	Taylor	Tyler (?)
Nelson, James, Aug. 7, 1824	1 lea.	Austin 1	Colorado
Nelson, Joshua, June 23, 1831	1/4 lea.	Austin 3	Matagorda
Nelson, O. C., Aug. 18, 1835	1 lea.	Zavala	Hardin
Nelson, Samuel, Feb. 25, 1835	1/4 lea.	Zavala	Sabine
Nelson, Samuel, Sept. 15, 1835	1 lea.	Robertson	Milam
Nevan, Patrick, Dec. 2, 1831	1 lea.	McMullen & McGloin	Live Oak
Nevill, Hardin, June 1, 1835	1 lea.	Robertson	McLennan
Neville, James, Oct. 22, 1835	1 lea.	Vehlein	Houston
New, William, Nov. 10, 1830	1/4 lea.	Austin 3	Jackson
Newell, John D., Oct. 23, 1832	1 lea.	Austin 3	Jackson
Newland, J. Alexander, June 15, 1835	9 lea.	Aldrete	(?)
Newman, Jonathan, Mch. 21, 1831	1 lea.	Austin 2	Washington
Newman, Joseph, Aug. 10, 1824	1 1/4 lea.	Austin 1	Lea. Wharton Lab. Austin
Newman, Thomas, June 20, 1835	1 lea.	Vehlein	Liberty
Newton, Joel, Sept. 15, 1835	1 lea.	Zavala	(?)
Nexon, Geo. M., June 23, 1831	1 lea.	Austin 3	Matagorda
Nicholls, Henry, July 7, 1835	1 lea.	Zavala	Sabine
Nicholls, John, Oct. 20, 1832	1 lea.	Austin 2	Austin
Nicholls, M. B., Aug. 3, 1824	1 lea. 1 lab.	Austin 1	22 lab. Matagorda 4 Brazoria

Name and Date of Title	Amount	Colony or Commissioner	Present Location
Nicholls, William, Nov. 20, 1835	1 lea.	Taylor	Trinity (?)
Nicholson, Stephen, July 25, 1835	1 lea.	Vehlein	Liberty
Niebling, Frederick, July 27, 1835	1 lea.	Robertson	Burleson
Nira, Desiderio, See Leonardo Rodriguez			
Nixon, Geo. Antonio, Feb. 9, 1835	11 lea.	Robertson	Robertson
Nixon, Geo. Antonio, Sept. 10, 1835	11 lea.	Bowie	(?)
Noblitt, John, Jan. 26, 1836	10 lea.	Grant, Durst & Williams	(?)
Norbeck, Nicholas, Dec. 1, 1835	1 lea. 1 lab.	Smyth	Wood (?)
Norris, Jesse, Nov. 26, 1835	1 lea.	Taylor	Jefferson (
Norris, Nathaniel, Sept. 1, 1835	10 lea.	Grant, Durst & Williams	(?)
Norris, Reymondo, July 29, 1824	4 lea.	Sepulveda	Nacogdoche
Northcross, James, Apr. 22, 1835	1 lea.	Milam	Travis
Northington, Andrew, May 28, 1831	1 lea.	Austin 2	Ft. Bend
Norvell, Lipscomb, July 13, 1835	1 lea.	Burnet	Limestone
Nowlan, Daniel, May 11, 1835	1/4 lea.	Vehlein	Angelina
Obar, Thomas, Oct. 13, 1835	1 lea.	Smyth	Rusk
O'Boyle, Daniel, July 20, 1835	1/3 lea.	McMullen & McGloin	Live Oak
O'Boyle, Daniel & John, Nov. 25, 1834	1 1/4 lea.	Power & Hewetson	Lea. San P tricio 1/4 Bee
O'Boyle, Edward, July 30, 1835	1 lea. 1 lab.	McMullen & McGloin	Atascosa
O'Boyle, Michael, July 14, 1835	1/3 lea.	McMullen & McGloin	McMullen
O'Boyle, Patrick, June 25, 1835	1 lea. 1 lab.	McMullen & McGloin	Bee
O'Boyle, Roderick, July 13, 1835	1/3 lea.	McMullen & McGloin	McMullen
O'Brien, Hugh, Nov. 22, 1834	1 lea.	Power & Hewetson	Bee
Oca (de), Manuel, May 26, 1810	6 lea.	Ceballos	Mexico (?)
Ocadiz (de), Miguel, Nov. 12, 1835	11 lea.	Berry	(?)
Ocampo, Carlos, Oct. 19, 1833	5 lea.	Lessassier	McLennan
Ocampo, Carlos, Dec. 16, 1835	6 lea.	Berry	(?)
O'Connor, James, Nov. 15, 1834	1/4 lea.	Power & Hewetson	1/2 Bee 1/2 San P tricio
O'Connor, Jeremiah Scanlan, Apr. 9, 1831	1 lea.	Austin 2	Ft. Bend
Odlum, Benjamin, July 12, 1835	1/3 lea.	McMullen & McGloin	McMullen
O'Docharty, George, June 25, 1835	1 lea. 1 lab.	McMullen & McGloin	Bee
O'Docharty, William, Dec. 3, 1831	2 lea.	McMullen & McGloin	Live Oak
Odum, Britain, Nov. 15, 1835	1 lea.	Zavala	(?)

Name and Date of Title	Amount	Colony or Commissioner	Present Location
Odom, Kinching, Sept. 17, 1835	1 lea.	Burnet	Cherokee
O'Donnell, Michael, Oct. 15, 1834	1 lea.	Power & Hewetson	3/4 Goliad 1/4 Refugio
O'Donnell, Michael, Sept. 26, 1834	1 lea.	Power & Hewetson	Bee
O'Farrell, James G., May 20, 1831	1 lea.	Austin 2	1/2 Colorado 1/2 Fayette
Oliver, Alfred, May 30, 1835	22 lab. 838,300 sq. vs.	Burnet	Nacogdoches
Oliver, John, May 1, 1831	24 lab.	DeWitt	Gonzales
Oliver, John, July 27, 1831	1 lab.	DeWitt	Gonzales
O'Reilly, James, Sept. 11, 1834	1 lea.	Power & Hewetson	Bee
Orr, George, Apr. 23, 1831	1 lea.	Madero	Liberty
Orr, George, May 2, 1832		Madero	Liberty
Orr, Priscilla Clark, May 2, 1832		Madero	Liberty
Orr, Thomas, May 2, 1832		Madero	Liberty
Orrick, James, Aug. 10, 1824	1 lab.	Austin 1	Austin
Orsett, Balthazar, Mch. 10, 1835	1 lea.	Vehlein	Walker
Ortega, Jose, Apr. 13, 1835, Apr. 14, 1835, Apr. 17, 1835	11 lea.	Mora	4 Walker & Trinity; 7 (?)
Ortiz, Miguel, Apr. 13, 1835	1 lea.	De Leon	Dewitt
Ortiz, Vicente, Sept. 19, 1835	11 lea.	Del Moral	(?)
Osborne, Heirs of Benjamin, Nov. 8, 1832	1 lea.	Austin 4	3/4 Bastrop 1/4 Travis
Osborne, Nathan, See Nathaniel Whiting			
Osborne, Spencer, Oct. 5, 1835	1 lea.	Zavala	Hardin
Overton, Greenberry, Feb. 3, 1836	1 lea.	Austin 5	Bastrop (?)
Owen, David F., Dec. 28, 1835	1 lea.	Robertson	Burnet
Pace, Wesley, Dec. 5, 1835	10 lea.	Williams, Johnson & Peebles	(?)
Pace, William, May 3, 1835	1 lea.	Vehlein	Polk
Padilla, Juan Antonio, Apr. 6, 1830	2 lea.	Arciniega	Waller
Padilla, Juan Antonio, ? ? ?			Galveston (?)
Padilla, Maria Josefa, Oct. 22, 1835	1 lea. 1 lab.	Taylor	(?)
Padilla, Pedro Silverio, ? ? ?	2 lea. 3 lab. & 730,000 sq. vs.	(?)	Nacogdoches
Padilla, Vicente, Jan. 3, 1835	1 lea.	Vehlein	Angelina
Padilla, Vicente, Mch. 28, 1830	7 lea.	Padilla	Chambers (?)
Padilla, Maria, ? ? ?	630,000 sq. vs.	(?)	Nacogdoches (?)
Padon, John, June 22, 1835	1/4 lea.	Burnet	Anderson
Page, David, Feb. 5, 1835	1 lea.	Burnet	Smith
Page, William, Aug. 23, 1831	1/4 lea.	DeWitt	Gonzales
Palacios, Maria Juana, See Antonio Arriola			
Palacios, Mariano Riva, Nov. 21, 1833	11 lea.	Aldrete	5 Limestone 3 Freestone 3 Anderson

Name and Date of Title	Amount	Colony or Commissioner	Present Location
Palbador, Juan Bautista, June 2, 1835	1 lea.	Vehlein	Angelina
Palmer, Martin, Feb. 28, 1835	1 lea.	Zavala	Orange
Pamplin, William, June 19, 1835	1 lea.	Zavala	20 1/2 lab. Tyler 4 1 Jasper
Pankey, James W., Oct. 19, 1835	1 lea.	Austin	Grimes
Pantaleon, Bernardo, July 7, 1835	1 lea.	Burnet	3/5 Freest 2/5 Ande
Pantaleon, Eusebio Isidero, Apr. 25, 1835	4 1/4 lea.	Vehlein	Trinity
Park, William, See Joshua Parker and William Park			
Parker, Argalus G., June 3, 1835	1 lea.	Zavala	Tyler
Parker, Christopher A., Nov. 20, 1835	1/4 lea.	Vehlein	Liberty (?
Parker, Daniel, Apr. 29, 1833	1 lea.	Austin 4	Madison
Parker, Daniel, Jr., Oct. 14, 1835	1/4 lea.	Burnet	Anderson
Parker, Dickerson, June 9, 1835	1/4 lea.	Burnet	Anderson
Parker, Henry, Feb. 5, 1833	1 lea.	Austin 3	Matagorda
Parker, Isaac, May 6, 1835	1 lea.	Vehlein	Polk
Parker, Isaac C., May 2, 1835	1/4 lea.	Burnet	Nacogdoch
Parker, James W., Apr. 1, 1835	1 lea.	Robertson	Limestone
Parker, Jesse, Feb. 11, 1835	1 lea.	Vehlein	Walker
Parker, John, May 21, 1835	1/4 lea.	Burnet	Anderson
Parker, John, Nov. 23, 1835	1 lea. 1 lab.	Taylor	Jefferson
Parker, Joshua, May 30, 1828	1/2 lea.	Austin 2	Wharton
Parker, Joshua & William Park, July 24, 1824	1 lea.	Austin 1	Wharton
Parker, Silas M., Apr. 1, 1835	1 lea.	Robertson	Limestone
Parker, William, July 8, 1824	1 lea. 1 lab.	Austin 1	Lea. Braz Lab. Wal
Parker, William S., Nov. 1, 1835	1/4 lea.	Robertson	Williamso
Parker, Wiley, Feb. 11, 1835	1 lea.	Vehlein	Walker
Parks, William, Jan. 17, 1833	1/4 lea.	Austin 3	Matagorda
Parmer, Isham, June 8, 1835	1 lea.	Zavala	San Augus
Parmer, Johnston, Sept. 16, 1835	1 lea.	Zavala	Angelina
Parmer, Johnston, Jr., Sept. 3, 1835	1 lea.	Zavala	(?)
Partin, John, Feb. 8, 1832	1 lea.	Austin 3	Matagorda
Patrick, George M., See Nicholas Clopper & Co.			
Patrick, George M., Nov. 13, 1830	1/4 lea.	Austin 3	Brazoria
Patrick, James B., Sept. 3, 1831	1 lea.	DeWitt	Gonzales
Patterson, G. H., Sept. 14, 1835	24 lab.	Smyth	Shelby
Patterson, John, Oct. 28, 1835	1/3 lea.	Smyth	Harrison
Patillo, Geo. A., June 7, 1835	1 lea.	Zavala	Orange
Patton, Moses L., Dec. 2, 1835	1/4 lea.	Vehlein	Polk
Patton, Moses L., Sept. 2, 1835	10 lea.	Grant, Durst & Williams	(?)
Patton, Robert S., Dec. 2, 1835	1 lea.	Vehlein	Polk (?)
Patton, William, Oct. 10, 1835	1/3 lea.	Smyth	Harrison
Payne, George T., Sept. 1, 1835	1 lea.	Zavala	Hardin
Payne, John, Oct. 16, 1835	1 lea.	Austin 5	3/5 Madis 2/5 Grim

Name and Date of Title	Amount	Colony or Commissioner	Present Location
Payne, Thomas, Feb. 18, 1835	1 lea.	Zavala	San Augustine
Peak, Eliza, Oct. 16, 1835	1 lea.	Austin 5	2/3 Burleson 1/3 Washington
Pease, Elisha M., Feb. 3, 1836	1/4 lea.	Austin 5	Bastrop (?)
Peebles, Robert, Mch. 22, 1831	1 lea.	Austin 2	Fayette
Peebles, Robert, June 27, 1831	1 lea.	Arciniega	Ft. Bend
Peirie, Maria D., Oct. 30, 1830	1/4 lea.	Austin 3	Matagorda
Pena, Francisco, See James Power			
Pena, Jose Antonio, Oct. 8, 1833	11 lea.	Lessassier	Milam
Pena, Jose Antonio, Jan. 31, 1836	11 lea.	Aldrete	(?)
Pena, Jose F., Nov. 21, 1835	1 lea.	Zavala	Hardin (?)
Pena, Manuel, Mch. 4, 1834	4 lea.	Vasquez	Goliad
Pena, Maria Velarde, Aug. 27, 1835	1 lea.	Smyth	Rusk
Pena, Matias, Nov. 30, 1796	1 lab. & 119,809 sq. vs.	Zepeda	Nacogdoches
Pena, Matias, See Mariano Santa Cruz			
Pena, Rafael, Oct. 22, 1834	11 lea.	Lewis	Ellis
Pena, Rosalio, Aug. 3, 1835	1 lea. 1 lab.	McMullen & McGloin	Bee
Pennington, Isaac, See David Randon			
Penticost, Geo. S., Aug. 19, 1824	1 lea.	Austin 1	Matagorda
Peoples, John, Oct. 11, 1835	1 lea.	Burnet	Navarro
Pepi, Justo, See Ignacio Sendeja			
Pepi, Justo & J. J. Grande (not titled)			
Pereda, Jose Manuel, Aug. 10, 1810	4 lea.		Zapata
Pereire, Pedro & J.J. & Mariano Grande, Dec. 17, 1833	11 lea.	Aldrete	2/3 Robertson 1/3 Leon
Perez, Alejo, Mch. 23, 1833	1/4 lea.	De Leon	Victoria
Perez, Candelario, Dec. 4, 1835	1 lea. 1 lab.	Taylor	(?)
Perez, Francisco, June 2, 1835	1 lea.	Vehlein	Houston
Perez, Francisco, Mch. 23, 1833	1 lea.	De Leon	Victoria
Perez, Ignacio, Mch. 24, 1808	4 lea.	Barrera	Bexar (?)
Perez, Ma. Francisca, Oct. 3, 1835	1/4 lea.	Taylor	Houston
Pereyra, Francisco, Apr. 18, 1834	11 lea.	Soto	2/3 Zavala 1/3 Dimmit
Perkins, James, Apr. 25, 1835	1 lea.	Zavala	Tyler
Perry, A. G., Mch. 18, 1835	1 lea.	Robertson	Milam
Perry, Burril, May 16, 1831	1 lea.	Austin 2	Fayette
Perry, Edward, Sept. 22, 1834	1 lea.	Power & Hewetson	Refugio
Perry, Harriet E., Mch. 12, 1835	1 lab.	Robertson	Falls
Perry, James, Dec. 6, 1832	1 lea.	Austin 2	Burleson
Perry, James F. and Emily M. Austin, May 26, 1830	8 lea.	Austin 3	5 Brazoria 2 Galveston 1/3 Brazoria 1/3 Harris 1/3 Galveston

Name and Date of Title	Amount	Colony or Commissioner	Present Location
Perry, James F., & Emily M. Austin, Oct. 29, 1831	1 lea.		2/3 Matagor 1/3 Brazo
Perry, James F., & Emily M. Austin, Nov. 3, 1831	2 lea.		Washington
Perry, Lawrence W., Feb. 12, 1836	1 lea.	Austin 5	Waller (?)
Perry, Orville, Oct. 12, 1835	1 lea.	Austin 5	Burleson
Perry, Orville, Aug. 10, 1835	1 lea.	Robertson	Williamson
Perry, Polly, Widow Day, Feb. 9, 1836	1 lea.	Austin 5	Fayette (?)
Perry, Richardson, Oct. 10, 1835	1 lea.	Austin 5	Brazos
Peske, John, Apr. 15, 1833	1/4 lea.	Austin 3	Brazoria
Peters, L. K., Sept. 15, 1835	1 lea.	Zavala	Polk
Peterson, John, Apr. 2, 1831	1 lea.	Austin 2	Grimes
Peterson, Niels, Feb. 20, 1835	1 lea.	Robertson	Lee
Peterson, Oliver, Sept. 19, 1835	1 lea.	Taylor	Polk
Peterson, William, July 30, 1835	1 lea.	Robertson	Falls
Pettit, Robert, Nov. 23, 1835	1 lea. 1 lab.	Taylor	(?)
Pettit, Walker, July 22, 1835	1 lea.	Zavala	Hardin
Pettus, Edward, May 15, 1831	1 lea.	Navarro	Guadalupe
Pettus, Edward, Aug. 12, 1835	10 lea.	Williams, Johnson & Peebles	(?)
Pettus, Freeman, Aug. 3, 1824	2 lea. 1 lab.	Austin 1	9/10 Colora 1/10 Faye 2/3 Mata- gorda 1/: Brazoria Lab. Colo do
Pettus, John, Dec. 12, 1835	10 lea.	Williams, Johnson & Peebles	(?)
Pettus, John F., May 11, 1831	1 lea.	Austin 2	Austin
Pettus, Samuel, Dec. 15, 1835	10 lea.	Williams, Johnson & Peebles	(?)
Pettus, Samuel, O., Jan. 21, 1832	1 lea. -	Austin 2	Austin
Pettus, William, July 10, 1824	2 lea. 1 lab.	Austin 1	1 Ft. Bend 1 Wharton lab. Walle
Pettus, William, May 15, 1831	2 lea.	Navarro	Caldwell
Pettus, William, Dec. 12, 1835	10 lea.	Williams, Johnson & Peebles	(?)
Petty, John, Aug. 10, 1824	1 lea.	Austin 1	Fayette
Pevehouse, James, Apr. 7, 1831	1 lea.	Austin 2	Montgomer
Pew, Thomas, June 30, 1835	1 lea. 1 lab.	McMullen & McGloin	Live Oak
Peyton, Jonothan C., May 25, 1827	1 lea.	Austin 1	Matagorda
Pharess, William, May 12, 1835	1 lea.	Zavala	Jasper
Pharis, Daniel, Sept. 2, 1834	1 lea.	Zavala	(?)
Pharr, Samuel, Apr. 27, 1821	1/4 lea.	Austin 2	Ft. Bend

Name and Date of Title	Amount	Colony or Commissioner	Present Location
Phelps, James E., Aug. 16, 1824	1 lea. 2 lab.	Austin 1	Brazoria
Phelps, Mary, Mch. 28, 1831	1 lea.	Austin 2	Fayette
Phillips, Isham B., May 9, 1827	1 lea.	Austin 1	Wharton
Phillips, James R., Apr. 23, 1831	1 lea.	Austin 2	Fayette
Phillips, Reuben, Aug. 30, 1835	1 lea.	Burnet	(?)
Phillips, Zeno, Feb. 24, 1832	1 lea.	Austin 1	Brazos
Phillips, Zeno, July 19, 1824	1 lea.	Austin 1	Brazoria
Piburn, John, Aug. 7, 1835	1 lea.	Burnet	Rusk
Picket, Pamelia, July 21, 1824	1 lea. 1 lab.	Austin 1	Lea. Matagorda Lab. Austin
Pieper, Peter, Feb. 11, 1836	1 lea.	Austin 5	Colorado (?)
Pierson, John G. W., ? ? 1832	1 lea.	Austin 4	Fayette
Pierson, John G. W., Dec. 10, 1834	1 lea.	Robertson	Falls
Pierson, John H., Feb. 25, 1835	1/4 lea.	Robertson	Falls
Pierson, John S., May 2, 1831		Madero	Liberty
Pifermo, Juan Ignacio, Sept. 13, 1794	4 lea.	Zepeda	Sabine
Pillow, Sarah, Mch. 20, 1835	1 lea.	Robertson	Falls
Pineda, Jose, Apr. 4, 1834	11 lea.	Aldrete	8 Cherokee 3 Anderson
Pinkney, John T., Apr. 30, 1835	1 lea.	Vehlein	Polk
Pitts, Jonathan C., Sept. 13, 1835	1 lea.	Vehlein	Montgomery
Pitts, Heirs of Obadiah, Oct. 29, 1835	1 lea.	Austin 5	4/5 Waller 1/5 Grimes
Pittuck, George, July 30, 1835	1 lea. 1 lab.	McMullen & McGloin	McMullen
Pittuck, James, July 14, 1835	1/3 lea.	McMullen & McGloin	McMullen
Pivetot, Michael, Oct. 15, 1835	1 lea.	Zavala	Jefferson
Plummer, Luther, T.M., Apr. 1, 1835	1 lea.	Robertson	Limestone
Pobedano, Juan, Sept. 22, 1834	1 lea.	Power & Hewetson	Refugio
Poe, Aaron, Oct. 10, 1835	1 lea.	Smyth	Harrison
Poland, John, Oct. 30, 1834	1 lea.	Power & Hewetson	San Patricio
Polland, Frederick H., Mch. 5, 1835	1 lea.	Zavala	(?)
Polley, Joseph H., Aug. 16, 1824	1 lea.	Austin 1	Ft. Bend
Pollitt, George, Apr. 10, 1835	12 lab. & 498,300 sq. vs.	Vehlein	Nacogdoches
Pollitt, George, Sept. 10, 1835	11 lea.	Bowie	Upshur (?)
Polly, Joseph & H. & S. Chance, July 27, 1824	1 lea.	Austin 1	5/6 Brazoria 1/6 Matagorda
Polvador, Maria H., Sept. 19, 1832	1 lea. 1 lab.	Smyth	Upshur
Ponton, Andrew, June 18, 1832	1/4 lea.	DeWitt	Lavaca
Ponton, William, Nov. 27, 1832	1 lea.	Austin 2	Lavaca
Pool, Beverly, July 19, 1835	1 lea.	Burnet	Cherokee
Pool, Walter F., Nov. 7, 1835	1 lea.	Burnet	Anderson
Poorhouse, James, Apr. 7, 1831	1 lea.	Austin 2	Montgomery

Name and Date of Title	Amount	Colony or Commissioner	Present Location
Porter, Alexander, June 22, 1831	1 lea.	DeWitt	Lavaca
Porter, Beverly, A., Apr. 30, 1831	1 lea.	Austin 2	Burleson
Porter, John James, May 5, 1835	1 lea.	Vehlein	Walker
Portilla, Jose Maria & Felipe, Oct. 23, 1834	1/2 lea.	Power & Hewetson	San Patrici
Portilla, Juan, Calisto, Franco., & Encarnacion, Oct. 23, 1834	4 lea.	Power & Hewetson	San Patrici
Portilla, Felipe Roque, Oct. 23, 1834	1 lea.	Power & Hewetson	San Patrici
Powell, Archibald, Aug. 21, 1835	24 lab.	Robertson	3/4 Limest 1/4 Falls
Powell, Elizabeth, Mch. 21, 1835	1 lea.	Austin 2	Ft. Bend
Powell, Isaac, July 22, 1835	1 lea.	Zavala	Sabine
Powell, James, Dec. 10, 1834	1 lea.	Robertson	Falls
Powell, James, Feb. 22, 1836	1/4 lea.	Austin 5	Grimes (?)
Powell, John, Feb. 17, 1836	1 lea.	Austin 5	Lavaca (?)
Powell, Joseph, May 2, 1831	1/4 lea.	Austin 2	Ft. Bend
Powell, Peter, See William Kingston			
Power, James, Sept. 10, 1834	1 lea.	Power & Hewetson	Refugio
Power, James, Nov. 28, 1834	11 lea.	Power & Hewetson	San Patrici
Power, James Son, Oct. 20, 1834	1 1/2 lea.	Power & Hewetson	Refugio
Power, Martin, Sept. 29, 1834	1 lea.	Power & Hewetson	Refugio
Power & Hewetson, Sept. 15, 1834	7 1/4 lea.	Power & Hewetson	Refugio (?)
Power & Hewetson, Oct. 12, 1834	4 1/2 lea.	Power & Hewetson	Refugio
Power & Hewetson, Oct. 30, 1834	9 1/2 lea.	Power & Hewetson	3 1/3 Aran 1 2/3 Cal houn 4 1/ Refugio ('
Power & Hewetson, Nov. 22, 1834	4 3/4 lea.	Power & Hewetson	2 1/2 Refug 1 1/4 San tricio 1 houn and Aransas
Power & Hewetson, Dec. 30, 1834	5 lea.	Power & Hewetson	Aransas Calhoun
Power & Hewetson, Nov. 20, 1834	11 lea.		San Patric
Prado, Francisco, See above title			
Prado, Jose Antonio, Oct. 17, 1834	1 lea.	Vehlein	Angelina
Prado, Jose Martin, May 18, 1835	1 lea.	Vehlein	3/4 Trinity 1/4 Houst
Prado, Juan, Dec. 4, 1835	1/3 lea.	Taylor	Hardin
Prather, Stephen, Nov. 23, 1835	10 lea.	Williams, Johnson & Peebles	(?)

Name and Date of Title	Amount	Colony or Commis- sioner	Present Location
Prater, William, July 19, 1824	1 lea. 1 lab.	Austin 1	Lea. Brazoria Lab. Austin
Prentiss, Henry S., Apr. 20, 1833	1 lea.	Austin 2	Harris
Prewitt, Beasley, May 2, 1831		Madero	Liberty
Prewitt, Beasley, Apr. 23, 1831	1 lea.	Madero	Liberty
Prewitt, Cinda Riley, May 2, 1831		Madero	Liberty
Prewitt, Jacob, Feb. 16, 1835	1 lea.	Burnet	2/3 Houston 1/3 Trinity
Price, G. W., July 10, 1835	1/4 lea.	Burnet	Freestone
Price, James, Feb. 22, 1832	1 lea.	Austin 2	Lee
Prickett, Jacob, Jan. 21, 1835	1/4 lea.	Robertson	Robertson
Priestley, Philander, Dec. 10, 1831	1/4 lea.	DeWitt	2/3 Gonzales 1/3 Lavaca
Price, R., Sept. 30, 1835	1 lea.	Zavala	Tyler (?)
Prior, Mary, Dec. 20, 1834	1 lea.	Robertson	Falls
Prissick, William, June 15, 1835	1 lea.	Vehlein	Houston
Pritchard, Joseph, June 21, 1835	1/4 lea.	Vehlein	Houston
Procela, Jose de Jesus, July 22, 1835	1 lea.	Burnet	Houston
Procela, Jose Maria, July 17, 1835	1 lea.	Burnet	2/3 Smith 1/3 Cherokee
Procela, Jose, Maria, Feb. 7, 1833	1 lea.	Sterne	Houston
Procela, Jose P., Oct. 12, 1835	1 lea.	Vehlein	Houston
Procela, Manuel, Nov. 13, 1835	1 lea.	Taylor	Polk
Procela, Pedro, ? ? ?	3 lea. 3 lab.& 708,000 sq. vs.	(?)	Nacogdoches
Pru, Maria Josefa, Aug. 26, 1835	1 lea.	Smyth	Rusk
Pruit, Pleasant M., July 24, 1824	1 lea.	Austin 1	Matagorda
Pruitt, John, July 9, 1831	1 lea.	Zavala	Tyler (?)
Pry, Peter B., Nov. 7, 1834	1 lea.	Zavala	Jasper
Pryor, William, Aug. 24, 1824	1 lab.	Austin 1	Waller
Pryor, William, May 21, 1828	1 lea.	Austin 2	Washington
Pugh, Spencer A., May 6, 1831	1 lea.	Austin 2	Fayette
Punchard, Joseph (Heirs of), July 6, 1835	24 lab.	Robertson	Hill
Punchard, William, Sept. 11, 1835	1 lea.	Robertson	Milam
Purdom, Henry, Sept. 17, 1835	24 lab.	Robertson	1/2 Bell 1/2 Milam
Purdom, Henry, Mch. 18, 1835	1 lab.	Robertson	Falls
Purdy, Litson, Dec. 30, 1834	1 lab.	Robertson	Robertson
Quevedo, Tomas, Sept. 23, 1835	11 lea.	Berry	7 Smith 1 Angelina 3 Cherokee
Quinalty, John L., Nov. 10, 1835	1/4 lea.	Zavala	Sabine
Quinalty, John Lewis, Apr. 27, 1835	1 lea.	Zavala	Angelina
Quin, Bridget, Oct. 12, 1834	1 lea.	Power & Hewetson	2/3 San Pa- tricio 1/3 Bee
Quin, James, Apr. 23, 1835		DeLeon	Victoria
Quin, William, Dec. 12, 1834	1 lea.	Power & Hewetson	San Patricio

Name and Date of Title	Amount	Colony or Commissioner	Present Location
Quin, William, Nov. 22, 1834	1/4 lea.	Power & Hewetson	Bee
Quin, Wm. & Patrick, Nov. 20, 1834	1/2 lea.	Power & Hewetson	3/5 San Patricio 2/5 Bee
Quirk, Edmund, Feb. 19, 1800	4 lea.	Zepeda	San Augusti
Quirk, Edward & Son, Oct. 30, 1834	1 1/4 lea.	Power & Hewetson	Bee
Quirk, Thomas, Dec. 25, 1834	1/4 lea.	Power & Hewetson	Bee
Rabago, Miguel, Jan 13, 1834	11 lea.	Aldrete	6/7 McLenr 1/7 Bosqu
Rabb, Andrew, Aug. 10, 1824	1 1/2 lea.	Austin 1	Wharton
Rabb, John, July 8, 1824	1 lea.	Austin 1	Lea. Ft. Be Lab. Aust
Rabb, Thomas, July 24, 1824	1 lea.	Austin 1	Wharton
Rabb, William, July 19, 1824	5 lea.	Austin 1	3 Fayette 2 Matagor
Rabb, William, Aug. 24, 1824	2 lab.	Austin 1	Fayette
Rafferty, James, Aug. 18, 1835	1 lea.	Zavala	Hardin
Ragsdale, John D., Feb. 16, 1836	1 lea.	Austin 5	Lavaca (?)
Raguet, Henry, May 21, 1835	1 lea.	Vehlein	Houston
Rains, Emery, Feb. 19, 1835	1 lea.	Zavala	Jefferson
Raleigh, William, Aug. 16, 1824	1 lea.	Austin 1	Burleson
Ramey, Lawrence, May 23, 1827	1 lea.	Austin 1	Matagorda
Ramirez, Antonio, Dec. 2, 1835	5 lea.	Falcon	Nueces
Ramirez, Francisco, Nov. 30, 1833	5 lea.	Aldrete	4 (?) 1 Leo
Ramirez, Jose de Jesus, Nov. 4, 1835	1/3 lea.	Smyth	Wood
Ramon, Francisco, Oct. 20, 1834	1 lea.	Power & Hewetson	Victoria
Randon, David, Dec. 5, 1832	1/2 lea.	Austin 2	Ft. Bend
Randon, David & Isaac Pennington, Aug. 3, 1824	1 lea.	Austin 1	Ft. Bend
Randon, John, Aug. 19, 1824	1 lea.	Austin 1	Ft. Bend
Raney, Clement, Mch. 18, 1835	1/4 lea.	Robertson	Milam
Raney, John, Dec. 16, 1831	1 lea.	Austin 2	Matagorda
Rankin, Frederick H., July 7, 1824	1 lea. 1 lab.	Austin 1	Harris & Liberty
Rankin, James, Sr., Oct. 22, 1835	1 lea.	Vehlein	San Jacinto
Rankin, James, Jr., Oct. 30, 1835	1 lea.	Vehlein	San Jacinto
Rankin, Robert, Apr. 24, 1835	1 lea.	Vehlein	San Jacinto
Rankin, William, Aug. 10, 1831	1 lea.	Austin 3	Montgomer
Rankin, William, Jr., Nov. 3, 1835	1 lea.	Taylor	San Jacinto
Ratliff, Elijah, Jan. 3, 1835	1 lea.	Vehlein	Polk
Rawls, Amos, July 24, 1824	1 lea.	Austin 1	Matagorda
Rawls, Benjamin & Owen Stout, Aug. 3, 1824	1 lea.	Austin 1	Matagorda
Rawls, Daniel, July 24, 1824	1 1/4 lea.	Austin 1	Matagorda
Ray, Jonathan D., Oct. 18, 1835	1 lea.	Zavala	Newton
Ray, Robert, Apr. 9, 1831	1/4 lea.	Austin 2	Grimes
Raymond, Alfred, Oct. 14, 1835	1 lea. 1 lab.	Smyth	(?)

Name and Date of Title	Amount	Colony or Commis-sioner	Present Location
Raymond, John, Nov. 26, 1835	1 lea. 1 lab.	Smyth	(?)
Rea, Andrew, June 18, 1831	1/4 lea.	Austin 2	Grimes
Reagan, William, May 4, 1835	1 lea.	Burnet	Rusk
Rector, Joseph, Dec. 6, 1830	1 lea.	Austin 3	Jackson
Rector, Morgan, Oct. 19, 1832	1 lea.	Austin 2	Brazos
Redlich, August C., Nov. 4, 1835	1 lea.	Zavala	Hardin
Redmond, William & William McGill, Sept. 16, 1834	1/2 lea.	Power & Hewetson	1/2 Wharton 1/2 Goliad
Redmond, Zachariah, Nov. 20, 1834	1 lea.	Zavala	San Augustine
Reed, Henry, Jan. 1, 1835	1 lea.	Robertson	Robertson
Reed, Isaac, June 22, 1835	1 lea.	Burnet	Cherokee
Reed, Isaac H., July 15, 1835	1 lea.	Burnet	Freestone
Reed, Jacob, May 9, 1831	1 lea.	Austin 2	Burleson
Reed, James, Sept. 12, 1835	1 lea.	Robertson	Milam
Reed, Jefferson, Nov. 3, 1834	1/4 lea.	Robertson	Bell
Reed, Michael, Dec. 29, 1834	1 lea.	Robertson	Bell
Reed, Thomas J., Dec. 10, 1830	1 lea.	Austin 3	Jackson
Reed, William, Dec. 25, 1834	1/4 lea.	Robertson	Bell
Reed, William B., July 9, 1835	1 lea.	Burnet	Freestone
Reed, William B., Nov. 3, 1835	1 lea.	Zavala	Liberty
Reed, Wilson, Dec. 15, 1834	1/4 lea.	Robertson	3/4 Robert-son 1/4 Brazos
Reel, Daniel, May 16, 1835	1 lea.	Burnet	Rusk
Reel, Henry, May 15, 1835	1/4 lea.	Burnet	Rusk
Reel, James, May 15, 1835	1/4 lea.	Burnet	Rusk
Reel, Patrick & John Troubough, May 1, 1827	1 lea.	Austin 1	Harris
Reel, R. J. W., Oct. 21, 1835	1 lea.	Austin 5	1/2 Washing-ton 1/2 Burleson
Rees, Joseph, Apr. 14, 1830	1 lea.	Austin 3	Matagorda
Reese, Charles K., See A. Bowman			
Reeves, Absolom, Oct. 8, 1835	1/3 lea.	Taylor	Harris
Reiley, Michael, Oct. 5, 1834	1 lea.	Power & Hewetson	Refugio
Rejon, Manuel Crecencio, Nov. 18, 1833	11 lea.	Aldrete	7 Limestone 2 Leon 2 Robertson
Rener, Juan & Son, Oct. 28, 1834	1 1/4 lea.	Power & Hewetson	3/4 Goliad 1/4 Victoria
Rener, Inez, Nov. 20, 1834	1 lea.	Power & Hewetson	Goliad
Rendon, Enrique, Apr. 8, 1835	1 lea.	De Leon	Calhoun
Reojas, Anastacio, Sept. 1, 1834	1 lea.	Power & Hewetson	Refugio
Resendis, Luciano, Aug. 3, 1835	1 lea. 1 lab.	McMullen & McGloin	2/3 Bee 1/3 Goliad
Retherford, Joseph, June 21, 1835	1 lea.	Robertson	McLennan

Name and Date of Title	Amount	Colony or Commissioner	Present Location
Reyes, Blas, Apr. 18, 1834	11 lea.	Soto	Dimmit
Reyes, Buenaventura, Sept. 22, 1835	11 lea.	Del Moral	Jefferson (?
Reyes, Juan Jose, Oct. 12, 1835	1 lea.	Vehlein	2/3 Houston 1/3 Trinit
Reynolds, Albert G., June 19, 1831	1 lea.	Austin 3	5/6 Brazor 1/6 Galve ton
Reynolds, Allen C., Apr. 23, 1831	1 lea.	Austin 2	Harris
Reynolds, James, Nov. 30, 1834	1/4 lea.	Power & Hewetson	3/4 Victoria 1/4 Goliad
Reynolds, Joseph, Oct. 22, 1835	1/3 lea.	Taylor	(?)
Rhea, John R., Aug. 17, 1835	1 lea.	Vehlein	Harris
Ricardo, Guadalupe, Oct. 14, 1835	1 lea.	Vehlein	Trinity
Richards, Jesse, Oct. 10, 1835	1 lea.	Austin 5	7/8 Fayette 1/8 Lavac
Richards, William, Oct. 11, 1835	1/4 lea.	Vehlein	Trinity
Richardson, Daniel L., Sept. 20, 1835	1 lea.	Milam	Kendall
Richardson, George F., Dec. 17, 1832	1/4 lea.	Austin 4	Lavaca
Richardson, Stephen, July 10, 1824	1 lea.	Austin 1	Brazoria
Richardson, Stephen, Apr. 23, 1831	1/3 lea.	Austin 2	Austin
Richardson, Stephen, Nov. 28, 1835	1 lea. 1 lab.	Taylor	(?)
Richardson, William, Nov. 20, 1835	1/4 lea.	Vehlein	Polk (?)
Richey, Joseph, May 12, 1835	1/4 lea.	Zavala	Orange
Richey, Uel, July 24, 1835	1/4 lea.	Zavala	Orange
Richeson, Edwin, Sept. 15, 1831	1 lea.	DeWitt	Lavaca
Rigby, Benjamin, Apr. 14, 1831	1 lea.	Austin 2	Montgomery
Riley, James, Mch. 19, 1835	1 lea.	Burnet	Leon
Rio (del), Jose, Nov. 30, 1835	1 lea.	Taylor	Liberty (?)
Rio (del), Melchora, ? ? ?	16 lab. & 250,000 sq. vs.	(?)	Nacogdoche
Rio (del), Pedro, Aug. 11, 1835	1 lea.	Smyth	Smith
Rio (del), Simon, Oct. 17, 1835	1/4 lea.	Burnet	Rusk
Rionda, Manuel, Nov. 26, 1833	11 lea.	Aldrete	1/2 Anders 1/2 Free-stone
Rios, Antonio, Oct. 16, 1835	1 lea.	Austin 5	Madison
Rios, Florentino, Aug. 28, 1834	1 lea.	Power & Hewetson	Refugio
Rios, Jose Maria, Apr. 10, 1835		De Leon	Victoria
Rios, Jose Maria, Apr. 10, 1835	1 lea.	De Leon	Calhoun
Rios, Maria Josefa, Oct. 12, 1834	1 lea.	Power & Hewetson	Goliad
Rivas, Antonio, Oct. 2, 1835	1 lea.	Berry	Cooke
Rivas, Francisco, Dec. 4, 1833	1 lea. 1 lab.	Ximenes	Bexar
Roache, Garret, Sept. 15, 1834	1 lea.	Power & Hewetson	Bee
Roache, John, Sept. 16, 1834	1/4 lea.	Power Hewetson	Bee
Roache, Mary & Ann, Sept. 18, 1834	1 lea.	Power & Hewetson	Refugio

Name and Date of Title	Amount	Colony or Commissioner	Present Location
Roarck, Elijah, July 10, 1824	1 lea. 1 lab.	Austin 1	Lea. Ft. Bend Lab. Waller
Roarck, John, July 23, 1835	1 lea.	Vehlein	1/2 San Jacinto 1/2 Walker
Roarck, Russell, Oct. 14, 1835	1/4 lea.	Vehlein	3/4 San Jacinto 1/4 Walker
Roarck, William, June 22, 1835	1 lea.	Vehlein	Walker
Robbins, Early, July 19, 1824	1 lab.	Austin 1	Austin
Robbins, Early, Apr. 27, 1828	1/4 lea. 1/4 lab.	Austin 2	Austin
Robbins, George, Oct. 16, 1834	1 lea.	Vehlein	Houston
Robbins, Nathaniel, Oct. 16, 1834	1 lea.	Vehlein	Madison
Robbins, William, July 19, 1824	1 lea. 1 lab.	Austin 1	Lea. Brazoria Lab. Austin
Roberts, Abraham, Mch. 24, 1831	1 lea.	Austin 2	2/3 Harris 1/3 Montgomery
Roberts, Andrew, May 11, 1827	1 lea.	Austin 1	Ft. Bend
Roberts, Charles S., Apr. 10, 1835	1/4 lea.	Vehlein	Trinity
Roberts, Edward, Apr. 11, 1835	1/4 lea.	Vehlein	Trinity
Roberts, Elisha, Sept. 7, 1835	1 lea.	Smyth	San Augustine
Roberts, Elisha, Apr. 26, 1831	1 lea.	Madero	Trinity
Roberts, John S., Dec. 5, 1835	10 lea.	Williams, Johnson & Peebles	Red River (?)
Roberts, John S., Jan. 12, 1835	1 lea.	Zavala	Chambers
Roberts, Noel F., July 15, 1824	1 1/4 lea.	Austin 1	Ft. Bend
Roberts, Noel G., Sept. 8, 1835	1 lea. 1 lab.	Smyth	San Augustine
Roberts, William, July 8, 1824	1 lea.	Austin 1	Brazoria
Roberts, William, Feb. 10, 1836	1 lea.	Austin 1	Wharton (?)
Roberts, William, Nov. 12, 1835	1 lea.	Zavala	3/4 Sabine 1/4 San Augustine
Robertson, Baldwin, Dec. 23, 1834	24 lab.	Robertson	Bell
Robertson, Heirs of Daniel, Oct. 1, 1835	1 lea.	Robertson	Milam
Robertson, E., Sept. 23, 1835	1 lea.	Zavala	Angelina
Robertson, Edward, Mch. 31, 1828	1 lea.	Austin 1	Ft. Bend
Robertson, Elijah S. C., July 29, 1835	1/4 lea.	Robertson	Milam
Robertson, Euphemia L., Dec. 1, 1834	1 lea.	Robertson	McLennan
Robertson, George, Dec. 11, 1834	1 lea.	Robertson	Robertson
Robertson, Isaac E., Nov. 19, 1832	1 lea.	Austin 3	Matagorda
Robertson, James, Oct. 12, 1835	1 lea. 1 lab.	Smyth	Grayson
Robertson, Joel W., Feb. 20, 1835	1/4 lab.	Robertson	Falls
Robertson, Larkin, Nov. 5, 1835	1 lea.	Burnet	Limestone
Robertson, Sterling C., Jan. 5, 1835	1 lea.	Robertson	Burleson (?)
Robertson, Sterling C., Mch. 18, 1835	1 lea.	Robertson	Burleson
Robertson, Sterling C., July 31, 1835	5 lea.	Robertson	Bell (?)
Robertson, Sterling C., Mch 18, 1835	1 lea.	Robertson	Burleson
Robertson, Sterling C., June 22, 1835	1 lea.	Robertson	Robertson
Robertson, Sterling C., Feb. 27, 1835	5 lea.	Robertson	4 Falls 1 Robertson

Name and Date of Title	Amount	Colony or Commis- sioner	Present Location
Robertson, Sterling C., July 31, 1835	1 lea.	Robertson	Bell (?)
Robertson, Sterling C., July 30, 1835	1 lea.	Robertson	Bell (?)
Robertson, Sterling C., Apr. 1, 1835	4 lea.	Robertson	Milam
Robertson, Sterling C., Jan. 12, 1835	1 lab.	Robertson	Falls
Robertson, Sterling C., Feb. 10, 1835	1 lab.	Robertson	Falls (?)
Robertson, Sterling C., Feb. 25, 1835	1 lea.	Robertson	McLennan (
Robertson, Sterling C., Mch. 18, 1835	1 lea.	Robertson	Burleson
Robertson, Sterling C., Mch. 18, 1835	1 lea.	Robertson	Burleson
Robertson, Sterling C., July 2, 1835	1 lea.	Robertson	Hill
Robertson, Sterling C., Dec. 24, 1834	1 lea.	Robertson	Burleson
Robertson, Sterling C., Apr. 25, 1835	2 lea.	Robertson	Milam
Robertson, Sterling C., July 1, 1835	1 lea.	Robertson	Hill
Robertson, Sterling C., July 1, 1835	1 lea.	Robertson	Bosque (?)
Robertson, Sterling C., July 2, 1835	1 lea.	Robertson	Hill (?)
Robertson, Sterling C., July 2, 1835	1 lea.	Robertson	Bosque (?)
Robertson, Sterling C., July 2, 1835	1 lea.	Robertson	Bosque (?)
Robertson, Sterling C., July 2, 1835	1 lea.	Robertson	Bosque (?)
Robertson, Sterling C., July 2, 1835	1 lea.	Robertson	Hill (?)
Robertson, William, Oct. 6, 1834	1 lea.	Power & Hewetson	Refugio
Robeson, James, May 9, 1831	1 lea.	Madero	Liberty
Robeson, James, May 2, 1831		Madero	Liberty
Robinet, Calvin C., Dec. 8, 1835	1 lea.	Zavala	Hardin (?)
Robinson, Andrew, July 10, 1824	2 lea. 1 lab.	Austin 1	1 1/2 Brazo 1/2 Wash- ington Lab. Wall
Robinson, Benjamin W., Aug. 18, 1835	1 lea.	Vehlein	Walker
Robinson, George, July 8, 1824	1 lea.	Austin 1	Brazoria
Robinson, Isaac, Nov. 20, 1834	1 lea.	Power & Hewetson	Bee
Robinson, James W., Oct. 6, 1835	1 lea.	Vehlein	San Jacinto
Robinson, Jesse, May 5, 1831	1/4 lea.	DeWitt	Gonzales
Robinson, Joel, May 6, 1835	1/4 lea.	Zavala	Jasper
Robinson, John G., Feb. 12, 1836	1 lea.	Austin 5	Fayette (?)
Robinson, Neill K., June 2, 1835	1 lea.	Robertson	Falls
Robinson, William, Mch. 7, 1835	1 lea.	Vehlein	Walker
Robinson, William, Apr. 6, 1831	1 lea.	Austin 2	Wharton
Robinson, Zoraster, Oct. 16, 1835	1 lea.	Austin 5	Madison
Robitson, Lavina, Feb. 8, 1835	1 lea.	Robertson	Robertson
Robleau, Honore, Mch. 18, 1835	1 lea.	Zavala	Polk (?)
Roblo, Pierre, Dec. 16, 1835	1 lea. 1 lab.	Taylor	Angelina (?
Rodgers, R. C. Oct. 20, 1835	1 lea.	Vehlein	Hardin
Rodriguez, Bonifacio, Apr. 14, 1835	1 lea.	De Leon	Calhoun
Rodriguez, Bonifacio, Apr. 24, 1835		De Leon	Victoria
Rodriguez, Fernando, Sept. 27, 1834	1 lea.	De Leon	Jackson
Rodriguez, Fernando, Oct. 29, 1833	3 lea.	Lessassier	Milam
Rodriguez, Franco. & Jose Maria, Dec. 9, 1834	1/2 lea.	Power & Hewetson	Victoria
Rodriguez, Jose Anto., Dec. 7, 1835	1 lea. 1 lab.	Taylor	Orange (?)
Rodriguez, Jose Maria, Oct. 22, 1835	1 lea. 1 lab.	Taylor	(?)

Name and Date of Title	Amount	Colony or Commissioner	Present Location
Rodriguez, Leonardo and D. Nira, Oct. 15, 1834	2 lea.	Power & Hewetson	Victoria
Rodriguez, Maria F., Feb. 24, 1834	1 lea. 1 lab.	Bustillo	Bexar
Rodriguez, Maria J., Feb. 20, 1834	2 lea. 1 lab.	Bustillo	Bexar
Rodriguez, Mariano, Mch. 17, 1808	2 lea.	Barrera	Bexar (?)
Rodriguez, Narciso, Mch. 25, 1833	1 lea.	De Leon	Jackson
Rodriguez, Narciso, Apr. 8, 1835		De Leon	Victoria
Roe, John, July 10, 1832	1/4 lea.	DeWitt	Caldwell
Rogers, Bethany, Oct. 15, 1835	1 lea.	Smyth	Harrison
Rogers, John R., Nov. 27, 1835	1 lea. 1 lab.	Taylor	Jefferson (?)
Rogers, Joseph, Oct. 30, 1832	1 lea.	Austin 4	Bastrop
Rogers, Raleigh, May 6, 1831	1 lea.	Austin 2	Montgomery
Rogers, Robert, May 23, 1835	1 lea.	Burnet	Leon
Rogers, Samuel, Nov. 15, 1830	1 lea.	Austin 3	Jackson
Rogers, Samuel, Sept. 4, 1835	1 lea.	Taylor	Walker
Rogers, Stephen, May 23, 1835	1 lea.	Burnet	Houston
Rojos (de), Andres, Nov. 22, 1835	1/3 lea.	Taylor	Walker (?)
Rojo (de), Francisco, Nov. 21, 1835	1 lea.	Smyth	Anderson (?)
Rojo (de), Francisco, Oct. 3, 1835	4 lea.	Berry	(?)
Romero, Manuel A., Sept. 16, 1835	1 lea. 1 lab.	Smyth	Lea. Panola Lab. Rusk
Roney, James, June 11, 1832	1/4 lea.	DeWitt	Gonzales
Rosa (de la), Nicolas, Dec. 7, 1835	1 lea.	Taylor	Liberty (?)
Rosales, Antonio, May 16, 1792	1 lab. & 794,000 sq. vs.	Zepeda	Nacogdoches (?)
Rosales, Encarnacion, See Francisco Farias			
Rosales, Jose A., July 16, 1800	20,300 sq. vs.	De la Bega	Nacogdoches (?)
Rosales, Julian, May 31, 1808	(?)	Guadiana	Nacogdoches (?)
Rose, John E., Nov. 27, 1835	1 lea. 1 lab.	Smyth	(?)
Ross, James, July 19, 1824	1 lea.	Austin 1	Colorado
Roth, Jacob, June 18, 1835	1 lea.	Burnet	Rusk
Rousseau, Mozea, Apr. 4, 1831	1 lea.	Austin 2	Bastrop
Routh, James, Nov. 19, 1832	1/4 lea.	Austin 3	Harris
Rowe, James, July 24, 1835	6 lab. & 127,500 sq. vs.	Zavala	Jefferson
Rowe, Robert, Sept. 10, 1835	1 lea.	Zavala	Tyler (?)
Royall, Richard R., Dec. 10, 1830	1 lea.	Austin 2	Jackson
Rozell, Ashley B., Oct. 20, 1833	1 lea.	Vehlein	2/3 San Jacinto 1/3 Liberty
Rubble, Fielden, Dec. 27, 1834	1 lea.	Robertson	Falls
Ruddell, George, May 4, 1835	1 lea.	Burnet	Cherokee
Ruiz, Francisco, Aug. 31, 1833	9 lea.	Lessassier	4 Robertson 2 Brazos 2 Milam 1 Burleson
Ruiz, Francisco, Mch. 16, 1834	2 lea.	Seguin	Karnes
Rumayor, Joaquin F., Mch. 15, 1834	2 lea.	Aldrete	Red River (?)

Name and Date of Title	Amount	Colony or Commissioner	Present Location
Rumayor, Joaquin F., Apr. 25, 1831	6 lea.	Madero	7/12 Libert 1/12 Polk 4/12 San cinto
Rumayor, Joaquin F., Feb. 27, 1834	2 lea.	Aldrete	1 Jefferson 1 Orange
Rumayor, Joaquin F., Mch. 5, 1834	1 lea.	Aldrete	(?)
Rumpfeldt, Soloman, Feb. 12, 1836	1 lea.	Austin 5	Waller (?)
Runnels, Mathilda, Oct. 23, 1835	1 lea.	Zavala	Newton
Runnels, Sina, June 22, 1835	1 lea.	Vehlein	Polk
Rusk, David, Jan. 30, 1836	1 lea.	Grant, Durst & Williams	(?)
Rusk, Joseph, Sept. 30, 1835	1 lea.	Zavala	(?)
Rusk, Thomas J., Nov. 5, 1835	1 lea.	Burnet	Cherokee
Russell, Aurelia, Aug. 27, 1835	1 lea.	Zavala	Sabine
Russell, Edward, Aug. 21, 1835	1 lea.	Vehlein	San Jacinto
Russell, Eli, Oct. 16, 1835	1 lea.	Burnet	Freestone
Russell, Reuben R., Dec. 23, 1834	1 lea.	Vehlein	Houston
Russell, Robert, Oct. 13, 1835	1/4 lea.	Zavala	Sabine
Russell, Robert W., Oct. 14, 1835	1 lea.	Vehlein	Polk
Russell, William J., Apr. 23, 1831	1 lea.	Austin 2	Fayette
Russell, William J., Nov. 16, 1832	1 lab.	Austin 3	Brazoria
Ryan, Edward, Aug. 3, 1835	1/3 lea.	McMullen & McGloin	Bee
Ryan, James, Nov. 20, 1832	1 lea.	Austin 2	Lavaca
Ryan, James, May 2, 1835	1/4 lea.	De Leon	Lavaca
Ryan, John, June 25, 1835	1 lea. 1 lab.	McMullen & McGloin	Bee
Ryan, Patrick, Mch. 26, 1835	1 lea.	De Leon	Lavaca
Ryan, Simon, July 5, 1835	1 lea. 1 lab.	McMullen & McGloin	Live Oak
Sacco, Michael, Sept. 23, 1835	24,325,795 sq. vs.	Smyth	Nacogdoche
Saddler, John, Apr. 29, 1835	1 lea.	Vehlein	3/4 Walker 1/4 Montgomery
Sais, Rafael G., July 25, 1836	2 lea. 9 lab. & 350,000 sq. vs.		Starr
Salas, Marcelino, Nov. 11, 1832	2 lea.	Mora	Shelby & Sa Augustine
Salas, Marcelino, Feb. 5, 1833	1 lea.	Sterne	Houston
Salas, Marcelino, Dec. 2, 1833	2 lea.	Aldrete	1 Red Rive
Salinas, Jose Maria, Aug. 31, 1831	4 lea.	Navarro	Gonzales
Salinas, Jose Maria, Mch. 20, 1834	1 lea.	McMullen & McGloin	Atascosa
Salinas, Pedro, Mch. 18, 1835	1 lea.	Robertson	Falls
Salinas, Rafael G., Mch. 21, 1835	5 lea.	De la Fuente	Starr
Sambrano, Caciana, Feb. 11, 1833	1 lea.	De Leon	Victoria
Samuel, Santiago, May 18, 1810	227,000 sq. vs.	Mora	Nacogdoche

Name and Date of Title	Amount	Colony or Commissioner	Present Location
Sanchez, Antonio, Sept. 3, 1835	10 lea.	Grant, Durst & Williams	(?)
Sanchez, Candido, July 30, 1835	1 lea.	Vehlein	Trinity
Sanchez, Felix, July 29, 1835	1/4 lea.	De Leon	Calhoun
Sanchez, Guadalupe, Dec. 15, 1835	5 lea.	Falcon	Hidalgo
Sanchez, Jose, Nov. 26, 1835	1/3 lea.	Smyth	Harrison (?)
Sanchez, Jose David, Oct. 3, 1833	10 lea.	Lessassier	4 McLennan 3 Milam 3 Bell
Sanchez, Jose Maria, Oct. 19, 1833	5 lea.	Lessassier	2 1/2 Falls 2 1/2 Burleson
Sanchez, Jose Maria, July 16, 1835	1 lea.	Burnet	3/5 Freestone 2/5 Leon
Sanchez, Juan Jose, June 18, 1835	1 lea.	Vehlein	Walker
Sanchez, Luis, Nov. 27, 1834	1 lea.	Burnet	Nacogdoches
Sanchez, Marcos, Sept. 24, 1835	6 lea.	Berry	3 Harrison 2 Cooke 1 Grayson (?)
Sanchez, Marcos, Dec. 10, 1834	5 lea.	Flores	2 Fannin 2 Lamar (?)
Sanchez, Maria G., Apr. 9, 1835		De Leon	Victoria
Sanchez, Maria J., Aug. 15, 1835	1 lea. 1 lab.	Taylor	Houston
Sanchez, Maria T., Oct. 15, 1835	1 lea.	Burnet	Limestone
Sanchez, Mariano, Nov. 26, 1834	1 lea.	Burnet	Nacogdoches
Sanchez, Maximo, Feb. 5, 1835		De Leon	Victoria
Sanchez, Maximo, Mch. 26, 1835	1 lea.	De Leon	Calhoun
Sanchez, Simon, July 12, 1833	1 lea.	Ybarvo	Freestone
Sanchez, Simon, July 13, 1833	1 lea.	Ybarvo	Freestone
Sanchez, Simon, July 14, 1833	1 lea.	Ybarvo	Freestone
Sanchez, Simon, July 15, 1833	1 lea.	Ybarvo	Freestone
Sanchez, Simon, July 17, 1833	1 lea.	Ybarvo	Freestone
Sanchez, Simon, July 18, 1833	1 lea.	Ybarvo	Freestone
Sanchez, Simon, July 20, 1833	1 lea.	Ybarvo	Leon
Sanchez, Simon, July 22, 1833	1 lea.	Ybarvo	Leon
Sanchez, Simon, July 24, 1833	1 lea.	Ybarvo	Leon
Sanchez, Simon, July 28, 1833	1 lea.	Ybarvo	Anderson
Sanchez, Simon, July 30, 1833	1 lea.	Ybarvo	Anderson
Sandefur, Marmaduke, Apr. 18, 1831	1 lea.	Austin 2	
Sandejas, Ignacio & J.J. Pepi, Vol. 29, P. 196			
Sandenus, Indalecio, Apr. 24, 1834	2 lea.	Vasquez	Goliad
Sanders, George, Nov. 15, 1835	1 lea. 1 lab.	Smyth	(?)
Sanders, Stephen F., Nov. 22, 1831	1/4 lea.	DeWitt	Caldwell
Sanders, Thomas, Nov. 4, 1835	1 lea.	Taylor	Jefferson (?)
Sanders, Uriah, Nov. 9, 1835	1/4 lea.	Robertson	McLennan
Sanders, William, Nov. 4, 1835	1 lea. 1 lab.	Smyth	(?)
Sanford, Joseph, Nov. 26, 1835	1 lea.	Taylor	Jefferson (?)
Sandoval, Jose, Nov. 20, 1824	1/2 lea.	Flores	Bexar
San Felipe (Town of), July 1, 1834	4 lea.	Austin 1	Austin

Name and Date of Title	Amount	Colony or Commissioner	Present Location
San Miguel, Agustine, ? ? ?	14 lab. & 175,000 sq. vs.		Nacogdoches
San Miguel, Vicente, See Antonio Rosales			
San Patricio (Town of), Oct. 24, 1831	4 lea.	McMullen & McGloin	San Patricio
San Patricio (Town of), June 26, 1835		McMullen & McGloin	San Patricio
San Pierre, Joseph, June 15, 1831	1 lea.	Austin 2	Jackson
San Pierre, Joseph, Aug. 24, 1824	1 lab.	Austin 1	Ft. Bend
Santa Cruz, Francisco & Bros., May 16, 1792	1 lea.	Zepeda	Nacogdoches
Santa Cruz, Mariano, Aug. 31, 1794	6 lea.	Zepeda	Nacogdoches
Santos (de los), Francisco, Sept. 16, 1835	1 lea.	Robertson	Williamson
Santos (de los), Jose S., Dec. 2, 1835	1 lea.	Taylor	Liberty (?)
Santos (de los), Miguel, Dec. 24, 1835	1 lea.	Power & Hewetson	Bee
Sartuche, Ignacio, Oct. 27, 1826	1 lea.	Norris	Leon & Walker (?)
Saul, John, Dec. 23, 1834	1 lea.	Zavala	Jasper
Saul, Thomas S., Mch. 29, 1831	24 lab.	Austin 2	Washington
Savage, Emilius, Apr. 30, 1831	1 lea.	Austin	Fayette
Savery, Asahel, Apr. 13, 1835	1 lea.	Zavala	Jefferson
Savery, Henry P., July 14, 1835	1/4 lea.	Zavala	Jefferson
Sawyer, Samuel, Apr. 4, 1831	1/4 lea.	Austin 2	Bastrop
Sayre, Charles D., May 4, 1831	1 lea.	Austin 2	Ft. Bend
Sayre, Daniel, Oct. 29, 1835	1/4 lea.	Austin 5	Austin
Scanlan, Christopher, July 13, 1835	1/3 lea.	McMullen & McGloin	Live Oak
Scanlan, Jerry, July 5, 1835	1 lea. 1 lab.	McMullen & McGloin	McMullen
Scanlan, Michael, Dec. 20, 1832	1/4 lea.	Austin 4	Wharton
Scates, Joseph W., June 25, 1835	1 lea.	Vehlein	Polk
Schrier, James, Mch. 22, 1831	1 lea.	Austin 2	Washington
Schrier, John, Nov. 5, 1834	1 lea.	Zavala	Jasper
Scobey, Robert, Aug. 3, 1824	1 lea.	Austin 1	Wharton
Scott, George, Aug. 25, 1835	10 lea.	Williams, Johnson & Peebles	(?)
Scott, Geo. W. & Wm. H., Apr. 30, 1831	1 lea.	Austin 2	Lavaca
Scott, Henry, Apr. 8, 1831	1 lea.	Austin 2	Ft. Bend
Scott, James, Apr. 7, 1824	1 lea.	Austin 1	Ft. Bend
Scott, James, Sept. 30, 1835	1 lea.	Zavala	Jasper (?)
Scott, James W., Nov. 23, 1832	1 lea.	Austin 2	Brazos
Scott, John, Sept. 2, 1834	1 lea.	Power & Hewetson	Refugio
Scott, John, Sept. 17, 1834	1/4 lea.	Power & Hewetson	Refugio
Scott, John, July 11, 1835	1 lea.	Vehlein	Walker

Name and Date of Title	Amount	Colony or Commissioner	Present Location
Scott, John H., Dec. 20, 1830	1/4 lea.	Austin 3	Matagorda
Scott, Jonathan, July 9, 1831	1/4 lea.	DeWitt	Lavaca
Scott, Jonathan, Heirs of, Apr. 29, 1831	1 lea.	Austin 2	Wharton
Scott, Joseph E., Nov. 22, 1832	1 lea.	Austin 2	Brazos
Scott, Patrick, Oct. 21, 1830	1 lea.	Austin 3	Jackson
Scott, Peter, Oct. 7, 1834	1/4 lea.	Power & Hewetson	4/5 Refugio 1/5 Goliad
Scott, Thomas, Sept. 2, 1834	1/4 lea.	Power & Hewetson	Refugio
Scott, William, Aug. 19, 1824	2 lea. 1 lab.	Austin 1	Harris
Scott, William, See Heirs of Jonathan Scott			
Scott, William, Jr., Aug. 20, 1835	10 lea.	Williams, Johnson & Peebles	Fannin (?)
Scott, William, Sr., Oct.3, 1835	10 lea.	Williams, Johnson & Peebles	(?)
Scott, William H., See Geo. W. Scott			
Scott, W.J.L., July 6, 1835	1 lea.	Burnet	Henderson
Scritchfield, John, July 24, 1835	24 lab.& 620,000 sq. vs.	Burnet	Leon
Scritchfield, Polly, July 18, 1835	1 lea.	Burnet	Anderson
Scrungham, Edward W.B., June 25, 1835	1 lea. 1 lab.	McMullen & McGloin	Live Oak
Seal, Christopher C., Feb. 22, 1835	1/4 lea.	Robertson	Robertson
Seal, Eli, Mch. 18, 1835	1 lea.	Robertson	Limestone
Seal, Solomon, July 1, 1831	1 lea.	DeWitt	Caldwell
Seely, Sarah (wife of DeWitt), Apr. 15, 1831	1 lea.	Navarro	Gonzales
Seguin Erasmo, Mch. 16, 1834	5 lea.	Seguin	Karnes
Seguin, Erasmo, Oct. 5, 1835	1 lea. 1 lab.	Berry	(?)
Seguin, Juan Angel, See Jose I. Arocha			
Seguin, Juan Angel, Dec. 30, 1834	1 lea.	Flores	Red River
Seguin, Juan Nepomuceno, July 30, 1834	1 lea.	Wood	Galveston
Segura, Marcelino, July 30, 1835	1 lea. 1 lab.	McMullen & McGloin	Atascosa
Self, Jacob, E., Apr. 26, 1831	1 lea.	Madero	Liberty
Selkirk, William, Aug. 10, 1824	1 lea.	Austin 1	Matagorda
Selser, Nimrod R., Apr. 12, 1835	1 lea.	Zavala	Tyler
Sepulveda, Jose Anto., Mch. 3, 1834	7 lea.	Aldrete	Bowie & Red River (?)
Sepulveda, Jose Anto, Apr. 3, 1834	4 lea.	Aldrete	Red River (?)
Supulveda, Jose Anto., Dec. 17, 1825	1 lea.	Procela	Nacogdoches (?)
Sepulveda, Jose Anto., Mch. 16, 1826	4 lea.	Procela	3/4 Trinity 1/4 Houston
Sepulveda, Jose Anto., May 16, 1826	3 1/2 lea.	Norris	Houstin (?)
Sepulveda, Jose Anto., Aug. 27, 1835	1 lea.	Vehlein	Trinity
Serda (de la), Anastacio, ? ?, 1833	11 lea.	Lessassier	Falls
Serda (de la), Ramon, Apr. 2, 1834	5 lea.	Aldrete	1 Bowie (?) 4 (?)

Name and Date of Title	Amount	Colony or Commissioner	Present Location
Sergeant, Jasper A., May 20, 1831	1 lea.	Austin 2	Fayette
Serna, Santiago, Oct. 18, 1834	2 lea.	Power & Hewetson	Victoria
Serna, Santiago, Oct. 16, 1834	3 lea.	Power & Hewetson	Refugio
Serna, Santiago & Lazaro, Oct. 8, 1834	2 lea.	Power & Hewetson	Victoria
Servantes, Jose M., Nov. 4, 1835	1/3 lea.	Smyth	Wood
Servantes, Pedro, Nov. 4, 1835	1/3 lea.	Smyth	(?)
Sessam, Michael, Aug. 3, 1835	1 lea.	Robertson	Falls
Shackelford, Joseph S., Nov. 27, 1835	1/4 lea.	Taylor	Walker (?
Shackelford, M.B., Aug. 25, 1835	1/4 lea.	Robertson	Hill
Shannon, Jacob, Apr. 30, 1831	1 lea.	Austin 2	Montgome
Shannon, John, Apr. 8, 1831	1 lea.	Austin 2	Walker
Shannon, Owen, Apr. 8, 1831	1 lea.	Austin 2	Montgome
Shannon, William T., Oct. 12, 1835	21 lab.	Zavala	19 lab. Sar Augustin 2 Jasper
Sharnac, Margil, Oct. 22, 1835	1 lea. 1 lab.	Taylor	(?)
Shavano, Faustino, Oct. 22, 1835	1/3 lea.	Taylor	Hardin
Shaw, James, June 16, 1832	1/4 lea.	DeWitt	Gonzales acres in Fayette
Shaw, John, Mch. 31, 1831	1 lea.	Austin 2	Fayette
Shearn, Charles & James, Oct. 31, 1834	1 lea & 1/4 lab.	Power & Hewetson	Goliad
Shelby, David, Mch. 28, 1831	3/4 lea.	Austin 2	Austin
Shelby, David, Frazier & McCormick, July 24, 1824	1 lea.	Austin 1	2/3 Austin 1/3 Ft. I
Shelly, John, Sept. 15, 1834	1 lea.	Power & Hewetson	4/5 Goliad 1/5 Refu
Shelly, Patrick, Sept. 15, 1834	1 lea.	Power & Hewetson	Goliad
Shelton, Jacob, Sept. 15, 1835	1 lea.	Zavala	Angelina
Shepherd, Hugh, July 9, 1835	1 lea.	Burnet	Freestone
Shepherd, William W., Apr. 16, 1831	1 lea.	Austin 2	11/12 Faye 1/12 Aus
Sheridan, John, June 11, 1835	1 lea.	Burnet	Houston
Sherry, John, Oct. 28, 1834	1/4 lea.	Power & Hewetson	Goliad
Shields, Gilbert, Oct. 7, 1835	1 lea.	Zavala	(?)
Ship, Joseph, June 26, 1835	1 lea.	Zavala	San Augus
Shipler, Isaac E., Feb. 18, 1836	1/4 lea.	Austin 5	Bastrop (?
Shipman, Daniel & I. N. Charles, May 21, 1827	1 lea.	Austin 1	Brazoria
Shipman, Edward, Dec. 14, 1830	1/4 lea.	Austin 3	Harris
Shipman, Moses, July 19, 1824	1 lea. 1 lab.	Austin 1	Lea. Ft. B Lab. Aus
Shire, Michael, Oct. 12, 1835	1 lea.	Burnet	Navarro

Name and Date of Title	Amount	Colony or Commis- sioner	Present Location
Shoemaker, Evans, Oct. 17, 1835	1 lea.	Zavala	Newton
Shuff, Washington, Feb. 22, 1836	1 lea.	Austin 5	Washington
Shupe, Samuel, May 5, 1831	1/4 lea.	DeWitt	Caldwell
Sideck, Anthony, Oct. 27, 1834	1 lea.	Power & Hewetson	1/2 Goliad 1/2 Victoria
Sideck, John B., Oct. 28, 1834	1 lea.	Power & Hewetson	Goliad
Sierra, Juana M., See Joaquin Cordova			
Sigler, William N., Jan. 3, 1835	1 lea.	Zavala	Jefferson
Silsbe, Albert, Aug. 16, 1831	1/4 lea.	Austin 3	Matagorda
Simmons, James, June 20, 1835	1 lea.	Vehlein	Polk & Tyler
Simpson, Dinsmore, Sept. 5, 1835	1 lea.	Smyth	Rusk
Simpson, Isaac, July 8, 1835	1 lea.	Burnet	Anderson
Simpson, John S., Sept. 20, 1835	11 lea.	Bowie	(?)
Simpson, John J., Feb. 5, 1835	1 lea.	Vehlein	San Jacinto
Simpson, William, Feb. 25, 1833	1 lea.	Austin 3	Matagorda
Sims, Bartlett, Aug. 7, 1824	1 lea.	Austin 1	Wharton
Sims, Charles H., Sept. 10, 1835	11 lea.	Bowie	(?)
Sims, Ignatius, Oct. 26, 1835	1 lea.	Austin 5	3/5 Grimes 2/5 Madison
Sims, Richard, June 30, 1835	1 lea.	Zavala	Newton
Singleton, George W., Oct. 15, 1832	1 lea.	Austin 2	Brazos
Singleton, George W., May 14, 1827	1 lea.	Austin 1	Wharton
Singleton, Phillip, Aug. 19, 1824	1 lea.	Austin 1	3/5 Burleson 2/5 Washing- ton
Sinnott, John, Aug. 6, 1835	1 lea.	Power & Hewetson	Refugio
Sisneros, Agaton, Apr. 3, 1835	1 lea.	De Leon	Calhoun
Sisneros, Estevan, Apr. 8, 1835		De Leon	Victoria
Sisneros, Jose E., Apr. 16, 1835	1 lea.	De Leon	Jackson
Skelton, John, Oct. 15, 1834	1 lea.	Burnet	Nacogdoches
Skillern, Isaac C., Oct. 28, 1835	1 lea. 1 lab.	Smyth	Gregg
Skinner, Manuel, July 13, 1835	1 lea.	Burnet	Leon
Skinner, William, July 12, 1835	1 lea.	Burnet	Freestone
Slatter, Narcisa, Dec. 10, 1834	1 lea.	Robertson	Falls
Slattern, John, Oct. 13, 1835	1 lea.	Taylor	Liberty (?)
Slaughter, Richard, Sept. 3, 1835	1 lea.	Smyth	Sabine
Slaughter, Stephen F., Feb. 23, 1835	1 lea.	Milam	Travis
Slaughter, Thomas, May 21, 1827	1 lea.	Austin 2	Wharton
Slaughter, William F., Aug. 16, 1835	1 lea.	Zavala	Tyler
Small, James, Nov. 29, 1830	1/4 lea.	Austin 3	Jackson
Smalley, Heirs of Andrew, Apr. 12, 1830	1 lea.	Austin 3	Matagorda
Smeathers, John, May 8, 1832	1 lea.	DeWitt	Lavaca
Smeathers, William, July 16, 1824	1 lea.	Austin 1	Austin
Smiley, John, See Charles Smith			
Smith, Abner, Dec. 9, 1835	1 lab.	Robertson	Bell (?)
Smith, Alexander, Aug. 17, 1835	1/4 lea.	Vehlein	Polk (?)
Smith, Anthony G., Dec. 2, 1835	10 lea.	Williams, Johnson & Peebles	(?)

Name and Date of Title	Amount	Colony or Commissioner	Present Location
Smith, A. W., Aug. 18, 1835	1 lea.	Zavala	Hardin
Smith, Chas. & Abs., Oct. 30, 1834	1 lea.	Power & Hewetson	Goliad
Smith, Charles S., Oct. 14, 1835	1 lea.	Austin 5	Bastrop
Smith, Christian, July 19, 1824	1 lea.	Austin 1	3/5 Chambe 2/5 Harri
Smith, Christian, July 28, 1835	1 lea.	Vehlein	San Jacinto
Smith, Cornelius, Aug. 10, 1824	1 lea.	Austin 1	Brazoria
Smith, Elizabeth, May 13, 1831	1 lea.	Austin 2	Harris
Smith, Erastus, Oct. 5, 1835	1/4 lea.	Robertson	Robertson
Smith, Erastus, Dec. 25, 1833	1 lea.	Ximenes	Guadalupe
Smith, Francis, May 7, 1831	1 lea.	Austin 2	Burleson
Smith, Francis, Mch. 23, 1835	1 lea.	De Leon	Lavaca
Smith, Henry, Oct. 22, 1830	1 lea.	Austin 3	Jackson
Smith, James, May 13, 1831	1/4 lea.	Austin 2	Montgomer
Smith, James or Jonas, ? ? 1832	1 lea.	Austin 4	Williamson
Smith, John, Feb. 26, 1835	23 lab. & 381,339 sq. vs.	Zavala	Sabine
Smith, John & H. McKinsey, Aug. 3, 1824	1 lea.	Austin 1	2/3 Wharto 1/3 Mata- gorda
Smith, John D., Mch. 18, 1835	1/4 lea.	Robertson	Milam
Smith, John D., Feb. 25, 1835	1 lab.	Robertson	Falls
Smith, John W., Jan. 20, 1835	1 lea.	Robertson	Milam
Smith, Joseph, Mch. 31, 1831	1/4 lea.	Austin 2	Washington
Smith, Joseph, Mch. 26, 1835	1/4 lea.	De Leon	Lavaca
Smith, Joshua G., Mch. 18, 1835	1/4 lea.	Robertson	McLennan
Smith, Leander, Feb. 11, 1836	10 lea.	Grant, Durst & Williams	(?)
Smith, Luther, Sept. 4, 1835	8 lea.	Grant, Durst & Williams	Grayson (?
Smith, Major, Dec. 13, 1834	1 lea.	Zavala	San Augusti
Smith, Maurice, Sept. 5, 1835	1 lea.	Vehlein	Liberty
Smith, Nelson, Mch. 30, 1831	1 lea.	Austin 2	Washington
Smith, Niles F., Dec. 30, 1834	1 lea.	Robertson	Milam
Smith, Richard, Oct. 12, 1835	1 lea.	Austin 5	Fayette
Smith, Robert, May 5, 1831	1 lea.	DeWitt	Guadalupe
Smith, Robert W., May 13, 1835	1/4 lea.	Burnet	Rusk
Smith, Samuel, June 10, 1835	1/4 lea.	Robertson	Williamson
Smith, Samuel C., June 10, 1835	1/4 lea.	Robertson	Robertson
Smith, Sion, Feb. 28, 1835	1 lea.	Robertson	Milam
Smith, Sion, Feb. 24, 1835	1 lea.	Zavala	Sabine
Smith, Stephen, Apr. 15, 1831	1 lea.	DeWitt	1/2 Gonzale 1/2 Guada lupe
Smith, Thomas, Aug. 12, 1835	1 lea.	Vehlein	Angelina
Smith, Wiley B.D., Apr. 5, 1831	1/4 lea.	Austin 2	Montgomer

Name and Date of Title	Amount	Colony or Commis- sioner	Present Location
Smith, William, Jan. 27, 1835	1 lea.	Zavala	Jefferson
Smith, William, Oct. 12, 1835	1 lea.	Smyth	Harrison
Smith, William D., Apr. 30, 1835	1 lea.	Vehlein	Liberty
Smith, William D., Apr. 30, 1835	1 lea.	Vehlein	1/4 Liberty 3/4 Chambers
Smith, William H., Dec. 12, 1835	10 lea.	Williams, Johnson & Peebles	(?)
Smith, William T., July 2, 1835	1 lea.	Burnet	Cherokee
Smither, Lancelot, Apr. 4, 1831	1/4 lea. & 382,000 sq. vs.	Austin 2	Ft. Bend
Smithson, John P., June 27, 1835	1/4 lea.	Robertson	Milam
Smithwick, Nicholas, Nov. 4, 1835	1 lea.	Robertson	Falls (?)
Smothers, Archibald, Mch. 27, 1835	1/4 lea.	De Leon	Lavaca
Smyth, Geo. W., May 6, 1835	1 lea.	Zavala	Jasper
Snider, Gabriel Straw, Aug. 7, 1824	1 lea.	Austin 1	Colorado
Snively, Jacob, July 25, 1835	1/4 lea.	Burnet	Anderson
Sojourner, Albert Lloyd, See Pumphrey Burnet			
Solis, Antonio, Feb. 7, 1835	1 lea.	Vehlein	Angelina
Solis, Rafael, Feb. 18, 1833	1 lea.	De Leon	Jackson
Sommerville, Alexander, Apr. 29, 1833	1/4 lea.	Austin 2	Wharton
Sosa, Guadalupe, Apr. 11, 1835	1 lea.	Vehlein	Trinity
Soto, Jose Maria, Feb. 9, 1835	1 lea.	Vehlein	Angelina
Soto (de Beales), Maria Dolores, Apr. 15, 1835	11 lea.	Soto	Kinney
Sowell, John, May 5, 1831	24 lab.	DeWitt	Guadalupe
Sowell, John, July 1, 1831	1 lea.	DeWitt	Guadalupe
Sowell, Lewis D., June 25, 1831	1/4 lea.	DeWitt	Gonzales
Sowell, William A., June 22, 1831	1/4 lea.	DeWitt	Gonzales
Spain, Elihu D., Oct. 10, 1835	1 lea.	Smyth	Harrison
Sparks, James, July 8, 1835	1 lea.	Burnet	Freestone
Sparks, Matthew, Oct. 3, 1835	1 lea.	Austin 5	Lee
Sparks, Richard, Aug. 15, 1835	1 lea.	Taylor	Walker
Sparks, Richard, Nov. 13, 1835	1 lea.	Bowie	Panola (?)
Sparks, Richard, Sept. 22, 1835	11 lea.	Bowie	Upshur (?)
Sparks, Wilkinson, July 21, 1835	1/4 lea.	Milam	Travis
Sparks, William C., Nov. 21, 1832	1 lea.	Austin 4	Brazos
Sparks, William C., Oct. 20, 1834	1 lea.	Robertson	Bell
Spear, Abner B., Dec. 28, 1835	1 lea.	Robertson	Burnet
Spears, John, July 10, 1835	1/4 lea.	Zavala	Newton
Spears, William, Oct. 17, 1835	1 lea.	Taylor	Liberty (?)
Speer, Andrew, May 23, 1835	1 lea.	Zavala	San Augustine
Speer, Thomas, Sept. 19, 1835	1 lea.	Zavala	2/3 Jefferson 1/3 Hardin
Spencer, Nancy, Aug. 19, 1824	1 lea.	Austin 1	Ft. Bend
Spinks, Baker M., Apr. 25, 1831	1 lea.	Madero	Liberty
Splane, Peyton R., Apr. 30, 1831	1 lea.	Austin 2	Colorado
Splane, Thomas M., June 20, 1832	1 lea.	Austin 2	Brazos

Name and Date of Title	Amount	Colony or Commissioner	Present Location
Spring, Amos, Jan. 5, 1836	6 lab.	Taylor	(?)
Spurgin, William, Dec. 28, 1834	1 lea.	Robertson	Falls
St. John, Edmond, Sept. 3, 1834	1 lea.	Power & Hewetson	Refugio
St. John, James & Wm., Sept. 30, 1834	1/2 lea.	Power & Hewetson	3/4 Refugio 1/4 Bee
St. John, William, June 12, 1832	1/4 lea.	DeWitt	Gonzales
Stack, Florence, Oct. 29, 1830	1/4 lea.	Austin 3	Jackson
Stafford, Adam, Aug. 24, 1824	1 lab.	Austin 1	Waller
Stafford, William, Aug. 16, 1824	1 1/2 lea. & 1 lab.	Austin 1	Lea. Ft. Be Lab. Wall
Stagner, Henry, Oct. 20, 1835	1 lea.	Taylor	Angelina
Stalings, Jacob, Dec. 18, 1835	1 lea. 1 lab.	Smyth	Lamar (?)
Standefur, Marmaduke, Apr. 18, 1831	1 lea.	Austin 2	Lavaca
Standiferd, Elizabeth, Nov. 8, 1832	1 lea.	Austin 4	Bastrop
Standiferd, James, Nov. 8, 1832	1 lea.	Austin 4	Bastrop
Stanley, Stephen, Aug. 10, 1835	1 lea.	Zavala	Angelina
Stanley, Stephen J., June 27, 1835	1 lea.	Zavala	Angelina
Stanley, Willafred, June 15, 1835	1 lea.	Vehlein	Angelina
Stanley, Willis, Apr. 23, 1831	1 lea.	Austin 2	Austin
Stapp, Darwin M., July 19, 1831	1/4 lea.	DeWitt	Gonzales
Stapp, Elijah, July 16, 1831	1 lea.	DeWitt	Victoria
Stapp, William P., July 9, 1831	1/4 lea.	DeWitt	Gonzales
Steele, James S., Aug. 17, 1835	1 lea.	Robertson	Bosque
Steele, William H., Aug. 10, 1835	1/4 lea.	Burnet	1/2 Cherok 1/2 Smith
Steinson, John, Nov. 25, 1835	1 lea.	Zavala	Liberty (?)
Stephens, Amos, Dec. 11, 1835	1 lea.	Smyth	(?)
Stephens, James, Mch. 8, 1831	1 lea.	Austin 2	Washington
Stephens, Joel, Nov. 4, 1835	1 lea.	Taylor	Jefferson ('
Stephenson, Andrew, Sept. 30, 1835	1 lea.	Zavala	(?)
Stephenson, Henry, June 13, 1835	1 lea.	Zavala	Hardin
Stephenson, James, Mch. 7, 1831	1 lea.	Austin 2	7/8 Austin 1/8 Washington
Stephenson, James P., Apr. 9, 1831	1 lea.	Austin 2	Austin
Stephenson, William, Jan. 29, 1835	1 lea.	Zavala	Orange
Sterne, Adolfo, Oct. 21, 1835	1 lea.	Taylor	Tyler
Stevens, Ashley R., Nov. 22, 1832	1 lea.	Austin 2	3/5 Washington 2/5 Lee
Stevens, Corbet, July 15, 1835	1/4 lea.	Zavala	3 1/2 Newt 3 Orange
Stevens, Jacob, May 4, 1831	1 lea.	Austin 2	Austin
Stevens, Madison M., Feb. 9, 1835	1 lea.	Robertson	McLennan
Stevens, Miles G., Oct. 26, 1835	1 lea.	Vehlein	San Jacinto
Stevens, Thomas, Mch. 2, 1835	1 lea.	Vehlein	Walker
Stevens, Thomas, Aug. 7, 1824	1 lea.	Austin 1	Waller
Stevenson, John F., ? ? 1832	1 lea.	Austin 4	Wharton
Stevenson, Robert, Nov. 19, 1832	1 lea.	Austin 2	Brazos
Stewart, Charles B., May 17, 1831	1/4 lea.	Austin 2	Ft. Bend
Stewart, John, Sept. 18, 1835	1 lea.	Vehlein	San Jacinto

Name and Date of Title	Amount	Colony or Commissioner	Present Location
Stewart, John & James C., Apr. 9, 1831	1 lea.	Austin 2	Bastrop
Stiffler, Meinrad, Feb. 5, 1836	1/4 lea.	Austin 5	2/3 Gonzales (?) 1/3 Caldwell
Stinnett, Clayborne, Apr. 15, 1831	1/4 lea.	DeWitt	Gonzales
Stivers, Samuel, Feb. 21, 1835	1 lea.	Zavala	Jefferson
Stockman, Henry, Aug. 7, 1833	1 lea.	Ybarbo	Rusk
Stockman, Jose Anto., Apr. 23, 1834	2 lea.	Aldrete	(?)
Stockman, Jose Anto., Apr. 22, 1834	2 lea.	Aldrete	(?)
Stockton, Stephen, Sept. 28, 1835	1 lea.	Zavala	Angelina
Stoddart, J. W., Feb. 6, 1836	1 lea.	Austin 5	Madison (?)
Stone, R., Sept. 2, 1835	1 lea.	Zavala	Jasper
Stone, Reuben P. T., Oct. 22, 1832	1/4 lea.	Austin 3	Matagorda
Stout, Isaac L., Sept. 4, 1835	1 lea.	Zavala	(?)
Stout, Owen H., See Benjamin Rawls			
Strange, James, Aug. 24, 1824	1 lab.	Austin 1	Harris
Strange, John, Nov. 26, 1835	1 lea. 1 lab.	Smyth	(?)
Striker, Peter, Jan. 21, 1836	1 lea.	Taylor	(?)
Strode, Jeremiah, May 18, 1835	1 lea.	Vehlein	Houston
Strode, William, June 15, 1832	1 lea.	DeWitt	1/2 Gonzales 1/2 Lavaca
Strong, Samuel, May 9, 1831	1 lea.	Madero	Liberty
Strong, Theron, Mch. 19, 1835	23 lab.	Zavala	Orange
Stuart, James, July 17, 1835	1 lea.	Milam	Bastrop
Stuart, John, Sept. 20, 1835	1 lea.	Milam	Hays
Stubbins, Christopher B., Aug. 28, 1835	1 lea.	Robertson	Falls
Stubbins, Christopher B., Sept. 17, 1835	1 lab.	Robertson	Falls
Sublett, Philip A., Oct. 9, 1835	1 lea.	Vehlein	1/2 Liberty 1/2 Polk
Sublett, Philip A., Sept. 8, 1835	7 lab. & 659,972 sq. vs.	Smyth	San Augustine
Summers, Henry C. G., May 1, 1835	1 lea.	De Leon	Lavaca
Summers, William E., May 1, 1835	1/4 lea.	De Leon	Lavaca
Sutherland, George, Nov. 24, 1830	1 lea.	Austin 3	Jackson
Sutherland, Thomas S., Apr. 17, 1833	1/4 lea.	Austin 3	Calhoun
Sutherland, Walter, Aug. 10, 1824	1 lea.	Austin 1	Brazos
Sutherland, William, Mch. 22, 1831	1 lea.	Austin 2	Austin
Sutherland, William D., Apr. 17, 1833	1/4 lea.	Austin 3	Jackson
Swaggert, Mary, Mch. 24, 1835	1/4 lea.	Milam	Bastrop (?)
Swail, William, May 12, 1831	1 lea.	Madero	Liberty
Swain, William L., Mch. 14, 1835	1/4 lea.	Robertson	McLennan
Sward, Samuel, Dec. 20, 1834	1 lea.	Robertson	Falls
Swearingen, Ebimeleck, May 7, 1831	1 lea.	Austin 2	Burleson
Swearingen, Samuel, Oct. 3, 1835	1 lea.	Austin 5	Burleson
Sweeney, William, Feb. 16, 1836	1 lea.	Austin 5	Lavaca (?)
Sweet, Sidney A., July 9, 1835	1 lea.	Burnet	Freestone
Talley, Ephram, Oct. 16, 1835	1/4 lea.	Zavala	2/3 Sabine 1/3 Newton
Talley, David, Aug. 16, 1824	1 lea. 1 lab.	Austin 1	Lea. Brazoria Lab. Austin

Name and Date of Title	Amount	Colony or Commissioner	Present Location
Tannehill, Jesse C., Oct. 29, 1832	1 lea.	Austin 4	Travis
Tanner, George, Nov. 26, 1835	1 lea. 1 lab.	Smyth	(?)
Tannile, Benjamin, June 1, 1835	1 lea.	Milam	Bastrop
Tapp, Charles, Feb. 16, 1836	1/4 lea.	Austin 5	Bastrop (?
Tares, Victoriano & Pedro Villareal, Nov. 26, 1834	2 lea.	Power & Hewetson	San Patrici
Tascan, Manuel, Sept. 17, 1835	1 lea.	Vehlein	1/2 Housto 1/2 Polk
Tate, Elijah, May 5, 1831	1/4 lea.	DeWitt	Gonzales
Tatum, Edward, Aug. 24, 1835	1/4 lea.	Robertson	Burleson
Tatum, Henry, Oct. 16, 1835	1 lea.	Taylor	(?)
Taylor, Charles S., Oct. 30, 1835	1 lea.	Smyth	(?)
Taylor, Felix, May 1, 1831	1 lea.	DeWitt	Gonzales
Taylor, Hepzibeth, July 26, 1831	1 lea.	DeWitt	Dewitt
Taylor, Jane, Mch. 21, 1835	1 lea.	Vehlein	Tyler
Taylor, John, Oct. 12, 1835	1 lea.	Smyth	Lamar
Taylor, John, Oct. 12, 1835	1 lea.	Burnet	Navarro
Taylor, John D., Aug. 10, 1824	1 lea.	Austin 1	Harris
Taylor, John R., Sept. 13, 1835	10 lea.	Grant, Durst & Williams	(?)
Taylor, Levi, Aug. 18, 1835	1 lea.	Robertson	Milam
Taylor, Robert, Jr., Apr. 20, 1831	1/4 lea.	Austin 2	Washington
Taylor, Thomas, Apr. 27, 1831	1 lea.	Austin 2	Fayette
Taylor, William, Aug. 6, 1831	1 lea.	DeWitt	Lavaca
Taylor, William H., Apr. 4, 1831	1 lea.	Austin 2	Fayette
Teague, Joseph C., Mch. 10, 1835	1 lea.	Vehlein	Houston
Teal, Peter, June 4, 1835	1 lea.	Vehlein	Walker (?)
Teal, Peter, May 29, 1831	1/4 lea.	DeWitt	Dewitt
Teal, Peter, Oct. 13, 1834	1 lea.	Power & Hewetson	Victoria
Teel, George, Aug. 5, 1824	1 lea.	Austin 1	Ft. Bend (?
Teel, Richard, Feb. 21, 1835	1/4 lea.	De Leon	Victoria
Teel, Rosa Anna, Feb. 20, 1835	1 lea.	De Leon	Victoria (?
Tejada, Ventura, Oct. 17, 1835	1 lea.	Burnet	Smith
Tennill, Benjamin, May 2, 1831		Madero	Liberty
Tennille, George, Apr. 5, 1830	1 lea.	Austin 3	Brazoria
Tevis, Noah, Jan. 16, 1835	1/2 lea.	Zavala	Jefferson
Thames, Amos, Dec. 27, 1834	1/4 lea.	Zavala	(?)
Thomas, Ezekiel, Aug. 19, 1824	1 lea.	Austin 1	Harris
Thomas, Geraldus S., Mch. 2, 1835	1 lea.	Vehlein	Polk
Thomas, Jacob, Aug. 24, 1824	1 lab.	Austin 1	Waller
Thomas, Jacob, May 19, 1831	1/4 lea.	Austin 2	Harris
Thomas, James, Nov. 25, 1835	1 lea.	Zavala	Liberty (?)
Thomas, James J., June 7, 1835	1 lea.	Vehlein	Houston
Thomas, Josiah, Nov. 26, 1835	1 lea. 1 lab.	Smyth	(?)
Thomas. J. D., Sept. 12, 1835	1 lea.	Taylor	Polk
Taylor, Mary, Sept. 23, 1835	1 lea.	Taylor	Polk
Thomas, Montgomery B., July 10, 1835	1/4 lea.	Burnet	Leon
Thomas, Wiley S., Nov. 25, 1835	1/3 lea.	Taylor	Polk (?)
Thompson, Alexander, June 20, 1832	1 lea.	Austin 2	Fayette

Name and Date of Title	Amount	Colony or Commissioner	Present Location
Thompson, Alexander, Oct. 28, 1834	1 lea.	Robertson	Burleson
Thompson, C. F., Dec. 5, 1835	1 lea. 1 lab.	Smyth	Upshur (?)
Thompson, Ephraim, Oct. 31, 1834	1 lea.	Zavala	10 1/4 lab. Jasper 14 3/4 Tyler
Thompson, James, Apr. 24, 1831	1 lea.	DeWitt	Gonzales
Thompson, Jesse, Aug. 7, 1824	1 lea.	Austin 1	Brazoria
Thompson, John A., Apr. 5, 1831	1/4 lea.	Austin 2	Fayette
Thompson, Joseph, Nov. 16, 1832	1 lea.	Austin 2	Colorado
Thompson, Joseph, Feb. 23, 1836	1 lea.	Austin 5	Washington (?)
Thompson, Seth Orville, June 10, 1835	1/4 lea.	Vehlein	Liberty
Thompson, Thomas, Apr. 5, 1831	1/4 lea.	Austin 2	Bastrop
Thompson, Thomas, Nov. 19, 1832	3/4 lea.	Austin 2	2/3 Fayette 1/3 Bastrop
Thompson, William W.W., Apr. 20, 1831	1 lea.	Austin 2	Colorado
Thompson, Zacharia S., July 25, 1835	1/4 lea.	Burnet	Houston
Thorn, Frost, Aug. 25, 1835	1 lea.	Smyth	Gregg
Thorn, Frost, Sept. 10, 1835	11 lea.	Bowie	Upshur (?)
Thorn, John S., June 11, 1835	1/4 lea.	Vehlein	Houston
Thouvenin, Arnold, Apr. 24, 1835	1/4 lea.	Vehlein	Polk
Thurwachter, Henry, Oct. 19, 1832	1/4 lea.	Austin 2	Harris
Tilly, Josiah, Jan. 23, 1832	1 lea.	Austin 3	Matagorda
Timmins, Thomas, Dec. 24, 1834	1 lea.	Burnet	Cherokee
Timmins, Thomas G., Sept. 22, 1835	1/4 lea.	Smyth	Cherokee
Timmons, James F., Oct. 22, 1835	1/4 lea.	Burnet	Anderson
Tinnan, Jeremiah, Mch. 20, 1835	1 lea.	Robertson	Robertson
Tinney, Ambrose, June 22, 1832	1 lea.	DeWitt	Caldwell
Tinsley, Isaac F., Apr. 6, 1831	1/4 lea.	Austin 3	Fayette
Tobar, Juan, June 13, 1834	1 lea.	Aldrete	Nacogdoches
Tobar, Juan, Francisco & Fermin, Dec. 7, 1835	1 lea. 1 lab.	Taylor	Jefferson (?)
Todd, Conrad, Oct. 3, 1835	1 lea.	Zavala	Tyler (?)
Todd, John, Nov. 22, 1835	1 lea.	Taylor	Orange (?)
Tolbert, John, May 28, 1835	1 lea.	Vehlein	Madison
Tone, Thomas & Thomas Jamison, July 24, 1824	1 lea.	Austin 1	24 lab. Matagorda 1 Brazoria
Tong, James F., Aug. 19, 1824	1 lea.	Austin 1	Brazoria (?)
Tong, John B., July 24, 1835	1/4 lea.	Vehlein	Montgomery
Tool, Jeremiah, Sept. 11, 1834	1 lea.	Power & Hewetson	Bee
Tool, John, Nov. 24, 1834	1/4 lea.	Power & Hewetson	San Patricio
Tool, Domenique, ? ? 1834	1/4 lea.		
Tool, Martin, Michael & John, Sept. 12, 1834	3/4 lea.	Power & Hewetson	Bee
Toro (del), Pedro, Sept. 17, 1835	1 lea.	Robertson	Williamson
Torralva, Jose Maria, See Manuel de Oca			

Name and Date of Title	Amount	Colony or Commis- sioner	Present Location
Torres, Anacleto, Oct. 27, 1835	1 lea.	Berry	(?)
Torres, Jose Andres, Dec. 15, 1835	1 lea. 1 lab.	Taylor	(?)
Torres, Maria del Pilar, Sept. 22, 1835	1 lea. 1 lab.	Smyth	Upshur
Torres, Maria Josefa, Oct. 7, 1835	1 lea.	Vehlein	Madison (?
Torres, Miguel, Mch. 26, 1835	1 lea.	Vehlein	Trinity
Torres (de), Patricio, Oct. 19, 1835	1 lea.	Berry	(?)
Torres (de), Patricio, Jan. 30, 1835	1 lea.	Zavala	Nacogdoch
Totin, Remigio, Dec. 23, 1834	1 lea.	Zavala	Nacogdoch
Toulson, Thomas, June 23, 1832	1/4 lea.	Austin 4	Fayette
Townsend, Edward, See G. H. Hall			
Townsend, Isabella, Oct. 14, 1835	1 lea.	Vehlein	Madison
Townsend, Jacob, Apr. 30, 1835	1/4 lea.	Vehlein	Chambers
Townsend, John, Mch. 30, 1831	1/4 lea.	Austin 2	3/5 Fayett 2/5 Wash ton
Townsend, Nathaniel, Mch. 28, 1831	1 lea.	Austin 2	Fayette
Townsend, Thomas R., Feb. 7, 1835	1 lea.	Burnet	Houston
Townsend, William, Oct. 20, 1835	1 lea.	Austin 5	3/5 Madis 2/5 Grim
Townsend, William S., Mch. 30, 1831	1/4 lea.	Austin 2	Fayette
Toy, Samuel, May 7, 1827	1 lea.	Austin 1	Austin
Toy, William H., Oct. 12, 1835	1 lea.	Austin 5	Fayette
Toy, William H., Dec. 4, 1835	10 lea.	Williams, Johnson & Peebles	(?)
Travieso, Maria Josefa de Anda, Oct. 8, 1834	1 lea.	Power & Hewetson	Victoria
Travis, Wm. Barrett, Apr. 10, 1835	1 lea.	Milam	Hays
Tredwell, Timothy, June 25, 1835	5 lab. & 844,740 sq. vs.	Zavala	Liberty
Trevino, Alexandro, Dec. 19, 1833	4 lea.	Ximenes	Wilson
Trevino, Ignacio, May 22, 1829	5 lea. 2 lab.	Fernandez	Cameron
Trevino, Maria del Coronel, Oct. 22, 1835	1 lea. 1 lab.	Taylor	(?)
Trevino, Pedro, Feb. 26, 1834	11 lea.	Vasquez	8 Goliad 3 Karnes
Trobough, John, See Patrick Reels			
Troutman, Hiram B., May 3, 1835	1 lea.	Burnet	Cherokee
Tucker, John, Aug. 12, 1835	1 lab.	Robertson	Falls
Tucker, John, July 30, 1835	1 lea.	Robertson	McLennan
Tumlinson, Andrew (Heirs of), See H. Cottle			
Tumlinson, David C., Dec. 15, 1831	1/4 lea.	DeWitt	Gonzales
Tumlinson, Elizabeth, Aug. 16, 1824	1 lea. 1 lab.	Austin 1	Colorado
Tumlinson, James, Dec. 8, 1831	1/4 lea.	DeWitt	Gonzales
Tumlinson, James, Aug. 19, 1824	1 1/2 lea.& 1 lab.	Austin 1	1 lea. Colo 1/2 lea. Wharton Lab. Col rado

Name and Date of Title	Amount	Colony or Commissioner	Present Location
Tumlinson, John J., June 15, 1831	1 lea.	DeWitt	Dewitt
Tumlinson, Joseph, Aug. 8, 1831	1/4 lea.	DeWitt	Dewitt
Tumlinson, Littleton, Dec. 7, 1831	1/4 lea.	DeWitt	Gonzales
Turnbough, Elizabeth, Nov. 5, 1835	1 lea. 1 lab.	Taylor	Lea. Hardin Lab. Liberty
Turner, John, June 30, 1835	1 lea. 1 lab.	McMullen & McGloin	Live Oak
Turner, Jonathan, Sept. 15, 1835	1 lea.	Zavala	(?)
Turner, Ruffun, June 23, 1835	1 lea.	Zavala	Jasper
Turner, Winslow, Apr. 15, 1831	1 lea.	DeWitt	Gonzales
Turner, Winslow, Jr., May 1, 1831	1/4 lea.	DeWitt	Gonzales
Tyler, Daniel, Oct. 22, 1835	1/4 lea.	Austin 5	Grimes
Tyler, John K., Feb. 12, 1835	1 lea.	Robertson	Milam
Tyler, Orville T., Feb. 27, 1835	1 lea.	Robertson	Bell
Underwood, Ammon, Jan. 25, 1836	1/4 lea.	Austin 5	Burleson (?)
Underwood, Gaston, Oct. 16, 1835	1 lea.	Taylor	Chambers (?)
Uranga, Jose Maria, Mch. 17, 1834	11 lea.	Vasquez	10 1/2 Bee 1/2 Goliad
Urban, Joseph, Jan. 29, 1836	1 lea.	Austin 5	Wharton (?)
Vacocu, Baptiste Andre, June 13, 1835	1 1/4 lea.	Zavala	Jefferson
Vail, Daniel H., Dec. 12, 1835	1 lea.	Smyth	Henderson (?)
Vairin, T. and A. L. Fernet, See A. L. Fernet			
Vajardo, Pascual, Apr. 12, 1835	1 lea.	De Leon	Calhoun
Valdez, Jose Anto., June 10, 1824	4 lea.	Saucedo	Victoria
Valdez, Jose Maria & Indalecio, Oct. 8, 1834	1 1/4 lea.	Power & Hewetson	Victoria
Valdez, Manuel M., Feb. 27, 1835	1/4 lea.	Robertson	Milam
Valdez, Meliton, Apr. 18, 1834	11 lea.	Soto	Kinney
Valdez, Perfecto vol. 29, p. 199			
Valdez y Gonzales, Jose Antonio, Oct. 25, 1833	1 lea.	Patrick	DeWitt
Vallanova, Francisco Jacinto, Aug. 25, 1835	1 lea.	Smyth	Cherokee
Valle (del), Fernando, May 8, 1831	11 lea.	Madero	2/3 Leon 1/3 Houston
Valle (del), Santiago, June 12, 1832	10 lea.	Lessassier	Travis
Valmore, Francisco, Sept. 2, 1835	1 lea.	Taylor	3/4 Jefferson 1/4 Chambers
Vance, Jesse, June 4, 1827	1/4 lea.	Austin 2	Ft. Bend
Vandever, Cornelius H., Nov. 26, 1830	1 lea.	Austin 3	Matagorda
Vandorn, Isaac & Daniel E. Balis, Apr. 14, 1828	1 lea.	Austin 1	Matagorda
Vanmeter, S.K., Aug. 30, 1835	1 lea.	Zavala	Hardin
Varela, Andres, Nov. 22, 1833	11 lea.	Aldrete	Limestone
Varela, Pedro, Nov. 23, 1833	11 lea.	Aldrete	Limestone
Varga, Juan, May 13, 1835	1 lea.	Burnet	Smith
Varner, Martin, July 8, 1824	1 lea. 1 lab.	Austin 1	Lea. Brazoria Lab. Walker

Name and Date of Title	Amount	Colony or Commissioner	Present Location
Varrelmann, John D.G., Oct. 20, 1835	1 lea.	Austin 5	Lee
Vasquez, Juan, Mch. 29, 1835	1 lea.	Robertson	Limestone
Vaughn, George, Nov. 4, 1835	1 lea. 1 lab.	Smyth	(?)
Vaughn, John, Jan. 20, 1835	1 lea.	Burnet	Cherokee
Vaughn, Richard, June 17, 1835	1/4 lea.	Milam	Hays
Veatch (Veitch), John A., Oct. 26, 1835	1 lea.	Vehlein	Trinity
Veatch (Veitch), John A., Oct. 14, 1835	5 lab. & 538,670 sq. vs.	Zavala	Hardin
Veatch (Veitch), John A., Feb. 6, 1835	19 lab.& 481,003 sq. vs.	Zavala	Jefferson
Veatch (Veitch), John A., Feb. 12, 1836	10 lea.	Grant, Durst & Williams	(?)
Vega (de la), Tomas, Oct. 4, 1833	11 lea.	Lessassier	McLennan
Veider, Luis L., Oct. 29, 1830	1/4 lea.	Austin 3	Matagorda
Venabides, Eugenio, Mch. 17, 1835		De Leon	Victoria
Venabides, Nicolas, Feb. 18, 1833	1/4 lea.	De Leon	Victoria
Venabides, Placido, Mch. 23, 1835		De Leon	Victoria
Venabides, Placido, Jan. 25, 1833	1 lea.	De Leon	Victoria
Venabides, Isidro, Apr. 2, 1833	1 lea.	De Leon	Calhoun
Venabides, Isidro, Mar. 25, 1835		De Leon	Victoria
Venabides, See Benavides			
Venites, Manuela, Mch. 14, 1835	1 lea.	De Leon	Calhoun
Veramendi, Juan, Nov. 10, 1831	2 lea.	Navarro	Comal
Veramendi, Juan, Nov. 15, 1831	1 lea.	Navarro	Comal
Veramendi, Juan, Nov. 20, 1831	2 lea.	Navarro	Hays
Vess, Jonathan, May 21, 1831	1 lea.	Austin 2	Jackson
Vialpando, Francisco, ? ? ?	21 lab.		Nacogdoches
Vickers, John A., Aug. 27, 1835	1 lea.	Zavala	Hardin
Victoria, Town of, July 29, 1835	4 lea.	De Leon	Victoria
Vidaurri, Jose, See Santiago Serna			
Vidales, Manuel, Sept. 11, 1835	1/3 lea.	Smyth	Rusk
Viesca, Agustin, Nov. 11, 1833	11 lea.	Aldrete	Polk
Viesca, Jose Maria, June 3, 1835	11 lea.	Balmaceda	4/7 Roberts 3/7 Leon
Villa, Juan Jose, Aug. 4, 1835	1 lea.	Vehlein	Trinity
Villa, Pedro & Geo. Sarats, Oct. 14, 1834	1 1/2 lea.	Power & Hewetson	Goliad
Villareal, Enrique, Nov. 18, 1834	10 lea.	Fernandez	Nueces
Villareal, Ignacio, Mch. 26, 1833	4 1/2 lea.	Molano	Cameron
Villareal, Juan, Dec. 4, 1835	1 lea.	Taylor	Jefferson (?
Villareal, Pedro, See Victoriano Tares			
Villareal, Sacarias, Nov. 26, 1834	1/4 lea.	Power & Hewetson	San Patricio
Villegas, Ignacio, Nov. 6, 1835	1 lea. 1 lab.	Taylor	Lea. Hardin Lab. (?)
Vina (de la), Antonio, Sept. 10, 1834	1 lea.	Power & Hewetson	Refugio

Name and Date of Title	Amount	Colony or Commissioner	Present Location
Vina (de la), Juana C., Aug. 24, 1835	1 lea.	Smyth	Rusk
Vince, Allen, See Morris Callahan			
Vince, Allen, Apr. 30, 1831	1/2 lea.	Austin 2	3/4 Grimes 1/4 Montgomery
Vince, John T., May 4, 1831	1/4 lea.	Austin 2	Montgomery
Vince, Richard and Robert, Aug. 21, 1824	1 lea.	Austin 1	Harris
Vince, Robert, Nov. 16, 1832	1/2 lea.	Arciniega	Harris
Vince, Susan, May 2, 1831	1/4 lea.	Austin 2	Walker
Vince, William, July 21, 1824	1 lea.	Austin 1	Harris
Vince, William, Nov. 14, 1832	1 lab.	Austin 3	Harris
Vinton, Oliver M., June 10, 1835	1 lea.	Vehlein	Houston
Vonderwertes, John, Feb. 23, 1836	1 lea.	Austin 5	Fayette (?)
Votaw, Isaac, Oct. 12, 1835	1 lea.	Austin 5	Madison
Vueno, Fulgencio, Mch. 25, 1833	1 lea.	De Leon	Victoria
Vueno, See Bueno			
Wade, David, Dec. 8, 1835	10 lea.	Williams, Johnson & Peebles	(?)
Wade, David, Oct. 18, 1835	1 lea.	Austin 5	Wharton
Wade, John, Nov. 3, 1835	1 lea.	Zavala	Liberty (?)
Wade, John K., Jan. 17, 1833	1/4 lea.	Austin 3	Matagorda
Wadlington, James, Dec. 3, 1832	1/4 lea.	Austin 4	1/2 Bastrop 1/2 Lee
Wagner, John A., Nov. 20, 1835	1/4 lea.	Vehlein	Angelina (?)
Wakefield, Robert, Aug. 29, 1835	1 lea.	Zavala	(?)
Walker, Hiram, Oct. 5, 1835	19 lab. & 026,122 sq. vs.	Burnet	Madison
Walker, James, July 21, 1824	1 lea.	Austin 1	Washington
Walker, Joel, Feb. 14, 1835	1 lea.	Zavala	Nacogdoches
Walker, John, Jan. 8, 1835	1 lea.	Burnet	Cherokee
Walker, Joseph, Oct. 14, 1835	1 lea.	Zavala	Sabine
Walker, Sheigh, July 30, 1835	1/4 lea.	Robertson	Robertson
Walker, Tandy, Apr. 27, 1831	1 lea.	Austin 2	Grimes
Walker, Thomas, See Henry W. Johnson			
Walker, William H., Dec. 16, 1834	1 lea.	Robertson	Milam
Wallace, Caleb, May 14, 1828	1 lea.	Austin 1	Grimes
Wallace, James, Apr. 9, 1831	1 lea.	Austin 2	Grimes
Wallace, John Y., Oct. 8, 1835	1 lea.	Austin 5	Lee
Wallace, Joseph W.E., Dec. 18, 1830	1 lea.	Austin 3	Matagorda
Waller, Edwin, July 20, 1831	1 lea.	Austin 3	Brazoria
Walling, John, Aug. 15, 1835	1 lea.	Smyth	Rusk
Wallop, Joseph, Oct. 13, 1835	1 lea.	Taylor	Jefferson (?)
Walmsley, James, See Charles Smith			
Walters, Jacob, Feb. 3, 1836	1 lea.	Austin 5	Bastrop (?)
Walters, James, Dec. 30, 1834	1 lea.	Robertson	Milam
Walters, John B., Oct. 29, 1832	1/2 lea.	Austin 4	Bastrop
Walters, John B., Nov. 21, 1832	1/2 lea.	Austin 4	Travis
Walters, Lemuel S., Mch. 10, 1835	1 lea.	Zavala	2/3 Angelina 1/3 Jasper

Name and Date of Title	Amount	Colony or Commissioner	Present Location
Ward, Elliott, Oct. 14, 1334	1 lea.	Power & Hewetson	Goliad
Ward, James S., April 11, 1835	1 lea.	Vehlein	Trinity
Ward, Russel, July 20, 1831	1/4 lea.	DeWitt	Gonzales
Ward, Seth, Nov. 24, 1835	1 lea. 1 lab.	Taylor	(?)
Ware, Joseph, May 1, 1835	1/4 lea.	De Leon	Dewitt
Warin, Lewis, June 9, 1835	1/4 lea.	Zavala	Sabine
Warnoch, James P., Nov. 1, 1835	1/4 lea.	Robertson	Williamson
Watson, Harrison E., Oct. 23, 1835	1 lea.	Vehlein	(?)
Watson, H. E., Sept. 15, 1835	1 lea.	Taylor	Polk
Watson, Lemuel, Sept. 3, 1835	1 lea.	Zavala	Hardin
Watson, Willis B., Nov. 24, 1835	1 lea.	Vehlein	Walker (?)
Watts, John, Mch. 14, 1835	1 lea.	Vehlein	Polk
Watts, Thomas, Dec. 23, 1834	1 lea.	Zavala	Jasper
Waugh, John, Dec. 27, 1834	1/4 lea.	Robertson	Bell
Waugh, John, Nov. 12, 1835	1 lea.	Vehlein	San Jacinto
Webb, Andrew J., Dec. 30, 1834	1/4 lea.	Robertson	Robertson
Webb, Henry, Nov. 6, 1835	1 lea. 1 lab.	Taylor	Lea. Jasper Lab. Liber
Webb, James D., Feb. 28, 1835	1 lab.	Robertson	Falls
Webb, James D., Mch. 20, 1835	1 lea.	Robertson	McLennan
Webb, Jesse, Dec. 30, 1834	1 lea.	Robertson	Robertson
Webb, John B., Dec. 30, 1834	1/4 lea.	Robertson	Robertson
Webb, Joseph, Jan. 12, 1835	1 lea.	Robertson	Robertson
Webb, Thomas R., Nov. 1, 1835	1/4 lea.	Robertson	Falls
Webb, Thomas R., Oct. 26, 1835	1/4 lea.	Robertson	Milam
Webb, William, July 16, 1835	1 lea.	Zavala	Angelina
Webber, John F., June 22, 1832	1/2 lea.	Austin 4	Travis
Weekes, Joseph, Nov. 21, 1834	1 lea.	Burnet	Nacogdoche
Weir, William, Aug. 17, 1835	1 lea.	Vehlein	Montgomer
Welch, Charles C.P., Sept. 5, 1835	1 lea.	Vehlein	Liberty
Welch, William, July 28, 1835	1 lea.	Robertson	Robertson
Weldon, Isaac, June 30, 1831	1/4 lea.	DeWitt	Caldwell
Wells, Francis F., July 21, 1824	1 lea. 1 lab.	Austin 1	Lea. Jacksc Lab. Braz ia
Wells, Martin, Oct. 29, 1832	1 lea.	Austin 4	Bastrop
Wells, Samuel G., June 7, 1835	1 lea.	Burnet	Anderson
Welsh, John, June 20, 1835	1 lea.	Vehlein	Houston
Wentworth, Tobias, May 18, 1832	1/4 lea.	DeWitt	Dewitt
West, Claiborne, May 20, 1835	1 lea.	Zavala	Orange
West, Jordan, Sept. 5, 1835	1 lea.	Vehlein	Liberty
Westall, Andrew E., July 5, 1835	1 lea.	Vehlein	Trinity
Westall, James M., May 21, 1827	1/4 lea.	Austin 2	Washington
Westall, Thomas, July 19, 1824	2 lea. 2 lab.	Austin 1	1 lea. Whar 1 lea. Ft. 2 lab. Aus
Westover, Ira, Sept. 22, 1834	1 lea.	Power & Hewetson	Refugio
Whatley, Seaborn J., May 19, 1835	1 lea.	Milam	Hays
Wheaton, Joel, Dec. 24, 1831	1 lea.	Austin 2	Harris
Wheelock, Ann, Sept. 20, 1835	24 lab.	Robertson	Bosque

Name and Date of Title	Amount	Colony or Commissioner	Present Location
Wheelock, E.L.R., Jan. 19, 1835	1 lea.	Robertson	Robertson
Wheelock, George R., Jan. 21, 1835	1/4 lea.	Robertson	Robertson
Whitaker, Alexander, Mch. 25, 1835	1/4 lea.	Robertson	Falls
Whitaker, Benjamin, June 4, 1835	1 lea.	Burnet	Leon
Whitaker, William, May 18, 1831	1 lea.	Austin 2	Jackson
Whitcomb, Joseph, Sept. 26, 1835	1 lea.	Zavala	Chambers
White, Alexander, Dec. 18, 1835	1 lea. 1 lab.	Smyth	Grayson (?)
White, Amy, Aug. 16, 1824	1 lea.	Austin 1	Harris
White, Ann, May 12, 1831	1 lea.	Austin 2	Montgomery
White, Archibald S., May 5, 1831	1 lea.	Austin 2	2/3 Jackson 1/3 Lavaca
White, Benjamin J., Nov. 24, 1830	1 lea.	Austin 3	Jackson
White, David, June 18, 1835	1/4 lea.	Zavala	Sabine
White, Dudley J., May 31, 1831	1 lea.	Austin 2	2/3 Grimes 1/3 Waller
White, George, Oct. 7, 1835	1 lea.	Vehlein	Harris
White, Henry, July 6, 1835	1/4 lea.	Vehlein	San Jacinto
White, James T., Nov. 19, 1835	1 lea. 1 lab.	Smyth	Sabine (?)
White, Jesse, Nov. 15, 1830	1 lea.	Austin 3	Jackson
White, Jesse, Aug. 17, 1835	1/4 lea.	Vehlein	Harris
White, Joseph, Aug. 16, 1824	1 lea.	Austin 1	Brazoria
White, Martin, July 24, 1835	1 lea.	Zavala	9/10 Sabine 1/10 San Augustine
White, Mathew G., Apr. 23, 1831	1 lea.	Madero	Liberty
White, Peter, Oct. 22, 1830	1 lea.	Austin 3	Jackson
White, Reuben, Aug. 19, 1824	1 lea.	Austin 1	Harris
White, Samuel W., Mch. 10, 1835	1 lea.	Robertson	Falls
White, Walter C., See Knight &White			
White, William, Mch. 14, 1835	1 lea.	Burnet	Houston
White, William C., Aug. 19, 1824	1 lea.	Austin 1	Austin
Whitehead, Edward P., Oct. 7, 1835	1/4 lea.	Austin 5	Ft. Bend
Whitehead, Ephraim, Nov. 14, 1831	1 lea.	Austin 2	Lavaca
Whitehead, Nicholas, Nov. 18, 1832	1/4 lea.	Austin 2	Washington
Whiteley, William, Mch. 14, 1835	1/4 lea.	Vehlein	Houston
Whiteside, George W., Nov. 23, 1832	1 lea.	Austin 2	8/12 Bastrop 3/12 Fayette 1/12 Lee
Whiteside, John J., Oct. 14, 1831	1 lea.	Austin 2	Grimes
Whiteside, John T., Nov. 20, 1832	1 lea.	Austin 2	Fayette
Whitesides, Henry & Bowlin, Aug. 10, 1824	1 lea.	Austin 1	Brazos
Whitesides, James, July 16, 1824	1 lea. 1 lab.	Austin 1	4/5 lea. Grimes 1/5 Brazos Lab. Waller
Whitesides, John J., Aug. 12, 1835	1 lea.	Robertson	Milam
Whitesides, William, July 19, 1824	1 lea.	Austin 1	Walker
Whiting, Nathaniel and Nathan Osborn, July 24, 1824	1 lea.	Austin 1	Colorado
Whiting, Samuel, Aug. 18, 1835	1 lea.	Taylor	Chambers (?)
Whitlock, William, Aug. 16, 1824	1 lea.	Austin 1	Harris
Whitlock, William, May 11, 1831	1 lea.	Madero	Liberty

Name and Date of Title	Amount	Colony or Commissioner	Present Location
Whittington, Thomas M., Jan. 25, 1836	1 lea.	Austin 5	(?)
Wickson, Asa, Apr. 23, 1831	1/4 lea.	Austin 2	Ft. Bend
Wickson, Barnabas, Apr. 4, 1831	1 lea.	Austin 2	Ft. Bend
Wickson, Byrum, May 1, 1831	1/4 lea.	DeWitt	Gonzales (?)
Wickson, Byrum, Dec. 28, 1834	1 lea.	Robertson	Milam
Wier, Omy, Oct. 16, 1835	1 lea.	Vehlein	Houston
Wiggins, James F., Nov. 5, 1835	1 lea.	Taylor	Jefferson (?)
Wiggins, Roderick, Apr. 15, 1835	1 lea.	Zavala	Tyler
Wightman, Hiers of Benjamin, Oct. 28, 1830	1 lea.	Austin 3	Matagorda
Wightman, Elias R., May 25, 1827	1 lea.	Austin 1	Matagorda
Wightman, Margaret, Oct. 30, 1830	1 lea.	Austin 3	Matagorda
Wilbarger, Josiah, June 22, 1832	1 lea.	Austin 4	Bastrop
Wilburn, Daniel, June 2, 1835	1 lea.	Vehlein	Polk
Wilburn, William, Mch. 21, 1835	1 lea.	Vehlein	Tyler
Wilhelm, Sarah, Mch. 20, 1835	1 lea.	Robertson	Milam
Wilkins, Jane, May 26, 1827	1 lea.	Austin 1	Ft. Bend
Wilkinson, James G., Oct. 14, 1835	1 lea.	Austin 5	Fayette
Williams, Allam B., May 10, 1832	1 lea.	DeWitt	Gonzales
Williams, Augustus, Nov. 19, 1832	1 lea.	Austin 2	Brazos
Williams, Benjamin, July 27, 1835	1 lea.	Milam	Blanco
Williams, Brooks, July 24, 1835	1 lea.	Vehlein	Cherokee
Williams, Brooks, Aug. 15, 1835	1 lea.	Berry	Cherokee
Williams, Charles, Dec. 24, 1834	1 lea.	Zavala	Jefferson
Williams, Christopher, May 12, 1832	1/4 lea.	DeWitt	4/5 Fayette 1/5 Gonza
Williams, Ezechiel, May 1, 1831	1/4 lea.	DeWitt	Gonzales
Williams, George J., Aug. 19, 1824	1 lea.	Austin 1	Matagorda
Williams, Henry, See John J. Bowman			
Williams, Henry, Feb. 20, 1835	1 lea.	Zavala	San Augusti
Williams, Hezekiah, Dec. 24, 1834	1 lea.	Zavala	Jefferson
Williams, Hezekiah, Jr., Dec. 24, 1834	1/4 lea.	Zavala	Jefferson
Williams, Hezekiah, R., Dec. 24, 1834	1/4 lea.	Zavala	Jefferson
Williams, Job, Oct. 22, 1830	1 lea.	Austin 3	Jackson
Williams, John, Sr., See Mills M. Battle			
Williams, John, Aug. 24, 1834	1 lab.	Austin 1	Waller
Williams, John A., Apr. 23, 1831	1 lea.	Madero	Liberty
Williams, John A., Mar. 2, 1831		Madero	Liberty
Williams, John P., Oct. 15, 1835	1 lea.	Taylor	Liberty (?)
Williams, John R., July 29, 1824	1 lea. 1 lab.	Austin 1	Lea. 3/4 Ga veston 1/ Harris Lab. Harr
Williams, Leonard, Jan. 13, 1831	1 lea.	Vehlein	Houston
Williams, Leonard, Mch. 28, 1829	1 lea.	Ybarbo	Rusk
Williams, Malkijah, Nov. 20, 1831	1/4 lea.	DeWitt	1/2 Jackso 1/2 Lavac
Williams, Mary Ann, Sept. 16, 1832	1 lea.	DeWitt	Gonzales
Williams, Matthew R., Oct. 29, 1830	1 lea.	Austin 3	Matagorda
Williams, Matthew R., Dec. 10, 1835	10 lea.	Williams, Johnson & Peebles	(?)

Name and Date of Title	Amount	Colony or Commissioner	Present Location
Williams, Parker, Dec. 13, 1832	1/4 lea.	Austin 3	Brazoria
Williams, Richard, Oct. 22, 1835	1 lea. 1 lab.	Smyth	Lea. Newton Lab. Jasper
Williams, Robert H., Aug. 19, 1824	1 lea.	Austin 1	Matagorda
Williams, Samuel, June 15, 1832	1/4 lea.	DeWitt	Guadalupe
Williams, Samuel M., Aug. 10, 1824	2 lea.	Austin 1	Brazoria
Williams, Samuel M., Aug. 10, 1824	3 lab.	Austin 1	1 Austin 1 Brazoria 1 Waller
Williams, Samuel M., Apr. 11, 1828	1 lea.	Arciniega	Ft. Bend
Williams, Samuel M., Apr. 11, 1828	1 lea.	Arciniega	Harris
Williams, Samuel M., Apr. 11, 1828	2 lea.	Arciniega	2/3 Washington 1/3 Austin
Williams, Samuel M., Dec. 28, 1831	1 lea.	Arciniega	Waller
Williams, Samuel M., Dec. 28, 1831	1 lea.	Arciniega	Washington
Williams, Samuel M., Dec. 28, 1831	1 lea.	Arciniega	Burleson
Williams, Samuel M., Dec. 28, 1831	2 lea.	Arciniega	Fayette
Williams, Samuel M., Dec. 28, 1831	1 lea.	Arciniega	Bastrop
Williams, Samuel M., Dec. 28, 1831	1 lea.	Arciniega	3/5 Fayette 2/5 Bastrop
Williams, Solomon, Aug. 7, 1824	1 lea. 1 lab.	Austin 1	Lea. Matagorda Lab. Waller
Williams, Stephen, Nov. 7, 1834	1/4 lea.	Zavala	Jasper
Williams, Thomas, Aug. 16, 1824	1 lea.	Austin 1	Matagorda
Williams, Thomas, Mch. 24, 1829	1 lea.	Ybarbo	Rusk
Williams, William, Oct. 30, 1834	1 lea.	Burnet	Rusk
Williams, William, Nov. 7, 1834	1 lea.	Zavala	Newton
Williams, William, Oct. 22, 1835	1 lea.	Zavala	Jasper
Williams, Zacharia, Nov. 21, 1835	1 lea.	Taylor	(?)
Williamson, Russel, Oct. 13, 1835	1 lea.	Smyth	Rusk
Williamson, R. M., Apr. 23, 1831	1 lea.	Arciniega	Austin
Williamson, William, Mch 21, 1831	1 lea.	Austin 2	Fayette
Wilson, Amelia, Apr. 21, 1835	1 lea.	Milam	Hays
Wilson, David, Nov. 20, 1835	1 lea.	Vehlein	San Jacinto (?)
Wilson, George W., Oct. 15, 1835	1 lea.	Burnet	Houston
Wilson, Jefferson, Oct. 10, 1835	1 lea.	Vehlein	Nacogdoches
Wilson, Jesse, Mch. 14, 1835	1 lea.	De Leon	Jackson
Wilson, Robert, See Wm. P. Harris			
Wilson, Robert, Dec. 10, 1830	1 lea.	Austin 3	Harris
Wilson, Thomas, Oct. 15, 1835	1 lea.	Vehlein	Walker
Wilson, Walker, Mch. 12, 1835	1 lea.	Milam	Travis
Walker, William C., Feb. 10, 1835	1/4 lea.	Robertson	Falls
Walker, William R., July 12, 1835	1 lea.	Burnet	Anderson
Win, John B., Aug. 27, 1835	1 lea.	Vehlein	Polk
Winburn, McHenry, Oct. 3, 1835	1/4 lea.	Austin 5	Washington
Winchester, David R., Oct. 18, 1835	1 lea.	Burnet	(?)
Winchester, Henry, See Charles Smith			
Winfree, Benjamin, Oct. 7, 1835	1 lea.	Taylor	Chambers
Winn, James, March 31, 1831	1 lea.	Austin 2	Fayette

Name and Date of Title	Amount	Colony or Commissioner	Present Location
Winston, Thomas J., Nov. 20, 1830	1 lea.	Austin 3	3/4 Wharton 1/4 Jackson
Winters, James, Aug. 18, 1835	1 lea.	Vehlein	1/2 San Jaci 1/2 Walker
Winters, William, Oct. 30, 1835	1 lea.	Vehlein	San Jacinto
Wiseman, Robert, May 4, 1831	12 lab. & 317,500 sq. vs.	Madero	2/3 Liberty 1/3 Chamb
Witte, Bernhart, Feb. 6, 1836	1/4 lea.	Austin 5	Bastrop (?)
Wolfenberger, Samuel, Feb. 12, 1836	1 lea.	Austin 5	Bastrop (?)
Womack, Mark S., Aug. 27, 1835	1 lea.	Vehlein	Polk
Wood, James T., June 22, 1831	1 lea.	DeWitt	Lavaca
Wood, Mitchell, Oct. 28, 1835	1/4 lea.	Vehlein	San Jacinto
Wood, Reuben, June 25, 1835	1 lea.	Zavala	Hardin
Wood, Reuben D., Nov. 24, 1832	1 lea.	Austin 2	Ft. Bend
Woodford, William, Dec. 23, 1834	1 lea.	Robertson	Bell
Woodlief, Devereux J., Oct. 27, 1835	1/4 lea.	Zavala	San Augustin (?)
Woodruff, John, Oct. 20, 1832	1 lea.	Austin 2	Madison
Woods, James B., Apr. 9, 1835	1 lea.	Vehlein	4/5 Polk 1/5 Tyler
Woods, James B., Mch. 2, 1831		Madero	Liberty
Woods, Leander, Apr. 4, 1831	1/4 lea.	Austin 2	Bastrop
Woods, Montreville, Apr. 4, 1831	1 lea.	Austin 2	Fayette
Woods, Norman, Apr. 4, 1831	1/4 lea.	Austin 2	Fayette
Woods, Reuben, Nov. 3, 1835	1 lea.	Robertson	McLennan
Woods, Zadock, May 15, 1827	1 lea.	Austin 1	Matagorda
Woodward, Alvin B., Feb. 23, 1836	1/4 lea.	Austin 5	Matagorda
Woodward, Sanford, Mch. 11, 1831	1 lea.	Austin 2	Washington
Woody, Freelove, Mch. 30, 1835	1 lea.	Milam	Hays
Wooldridge, Ann, Feb. 20, 1836	1 lea.	Austin 5	Burleson (?
Woolsey, Abner W., Oct. 29, 1835	1/4 lea.	Austin 5	Fayette
Wooton, Thomas J., Feb. 14, 1832	1 lea.	Austin 2	Brazos
Wooton, Thomas J., Dec. 9, 1834	1 lea.	Robertson	Robertson
Work, Richard, Oct. 4, 1835	1 lea.	Zavala	(?)
Wright, Alexander, Feb. 20, 1835	1 lea.	Zavala	Jasper
Wright, David, June 1, 1835	1 lea.	Robertson	Williamson
Wright, Felix, Feb. 22, 1836	1/4 lea.	Austin 5	Austin (?)
Wright, James G., Apr. 16, 1831	1 lea.	Austin 2	Harris (?)
Wright, John D., Oct. 18, 1831	1 lea.	De Leon	Victoria
Wright, Ralph, June 4, 1827	1/4 lea.	Austin 2	Wharton (?)
Wright, Sharod, Feb. 19, 1835	1 lea.	Zavala	Jasper
Wroe, William, Jan. 18, 1832	1 lea.	Austin 3	Matagorda
Wroton, Isaiah, Nov. 25, 1835	1 lea.	Taylor	Liberty (?)
Wyllie, Anderson, Aug. 30, 1835	1/4 lea.	Vehlein	Polk
Ximenes, Juan, Aug. 31, 1835	1 lea.	Smyth	Rusk
Ximenes, Manuel, Mch. 13, 1834	1 lea. 1 lab.	Seguin	22 lab. Wils 4 lab. Gua lupe and Hardin
Ximenes, Maria, Nov. 2, 1835	1 lea.	Vehlein	Hardin

Name and Date of Title	Amount	Colony or Commissioner	Present Location
Yates, Andrew J., Nov. 23, 1835	1 lea.	Zavala	Liberty (?)
Ybarbo, Anastacio, Oct. 8, 1835	1 lea.	Vehlein	Chambers
Ybarbo, Domingo, Nov. 14, 1835	1 lea.	Vehlein	Liberty (?)
Ybarbo, Jose Damasio, May 4, 1835	1 lea.	Vehlein	Angelina
Ybarbo, Juan Jose, Aug. 23, 1830	10 lea. & 23 1/2 lab.	Flores	
Ybarbo, Jose Ignacio, ? ? ?	3 1/2 lea.	(?)	Nacogdoches
Ybarbo, Jose Ignacio, ? ? ?	2 lab. & 661,925 sq. vs.	(?)	Nacogdoches (?)
Ybarbo, Maria Antonia, ? ? ?	?	(?)	San Augustine (?)
Ybarbo, Maria de Jesus, July 16, 1833	4 lea.	Aldrete	7/8 Goliad 1/8 Karnes
Ybarbo, Maria de Jesus, Feb. 27, 1834	1 lea. 1 lab.	Vasquez	Goliad
Ybarbo, Maria T., Sept. 21, 1835	1 lea. 1 lab.	Smyth	Upshur
Ybarbo, Martin, Oct. 17, 1835	1 lea.	Vehlein	Angelina
Ybarbo, Miguel, Oct. 12, 1835	1 lea.	Smyth	Grayson
Ybarbo, See also Ibarbo			
Ydalgo, Eusebio, Apr. 8, 1835		De Leon	Victoria
Ydalgo, See also Hidalgo			
Yeamans, Asa, July 8, 1835	1 lea.	Austin 2	Grimes
Ynojosa (de), Ramon, Nov. 16, 1831	10 lea.	Fernandez	Nueces
Ynojosa, Diego, Dec. 15, 1835	5 lea.	S.P. 1-441	
York, John, Dec. 12, 1835	10 lea.	Williams, Johnson & Peebles	(?)
York, John, May 2, 1831		Madero	Liberty
Yocom, Thomas D., Mch. 2, 1835	15 lab. & 250,760 sq. vs.	Vehlein	Liberty
Yocom, Thomas D., Aug. 17, 1835	9 lab. & 749,240 sq. vs.	Vehlein	2/3 Jefferson 1/3 Hardin
Young, Jarrett, Feb. 25, 1835	1 lea.	Robertson	1/2 Lime- stone 1/2 Robert- son
Young, Jesse, Nov. 25, 1835	1 lea.	Vehlein	Montgomery (?)
Young, Joseph, June 20, 1835	1 lea.	Vehlein	Liberty
Young, Michael, May 5, 1831	1 lea.	Austin 2	Ft. Bend
Young, Samuel, Apr. 21, 1831	1/4 lea.	Austin 2	Lavaca
Young, William, Feb. 12, 1835	1 lea.	Robertson	Limestone
Young, William W., Sept. 2, 1835	1 lea.	Zavala	Hardin
Yancy, John, Aug. 11, 1835	1/3 lea.	Smyth	Nacogdoches
Ysleta, Town of, Jan. 31, 1854	2 lea.	Special Act	El Paso
Zaragoza, Miguel, Nov. 22, 1835	11 lea.	Aldrete	(?)
Zarza, Juan, Dec. 16, 1835	10 lea.	Berry	(?)
Zarza, Pedro, Oct. 17, 1833	11 lea.	Lesassier	6 Williamson 5 Falls

Name and Date of Title	Amount	Colony or Commissioner	Present Location
Zavala, Julian, Aug. 3, 1835	1 lea. 1 lab.	McMullen & McGloin	11/12 Bee 1/12 Golia
Zekainski, John, May 3, 1831	1/4 lea.	Austin 2	Ft. Bend (?)
Zepeda, Manuel, Apr. 4, 1833	7 lab.	De Leon	Victoria
Zepeda, Manuel, Sept. 29, 1834	18 lab.	De Leon	Victoria
Zepeda, Manuel, Oct. 1, 1835	2 lea.	Berry	(?)
Zepeda, Victoriano, July 6, 1833	2 lea.	Aldrete	Karnes
Zosa (de), Jose F., Oct. 10, 1835	1 lea. 1 lab.	Berry	(?)
Zubar, Abraham, Mch. 4, 1833	1 lea.	Austin 4	Grimes
Zumwalt, Abraham, Aug. 12, 1831	1 lea.	DeWitt	Gonzales
Zumwalt, Adam, Nov. 23, 1831	24 lab.	DeWitt	Gonzales
Zumwalt, Adam, Aug. 11, 1831	712,400 sq. vs.	DeWitt	Gonzales
Zumwalt, Adam, Jr., May 8, 1832	1 lea.	DeWitt	1/4 Gonzale 3/4 Fayett
Zumwalt, Andrew, Apr. 4, 1835	1/4 lea.	De Leon	Lavaca

MAP OF
TEXAS
IN
1836

COMPILED & PUBLISHED
BY

J.D. FREEMAN LICENSED LAND SURVEYOR

FORT WORTH, TEXAS

drawn by n.b. poff fort worth, texas

LEGEND

● Towns
▲ Indian Village
▲ Masonic Lodge meeting
⊠ Old Forts
† Roads
------- Roads
------- Outline of Grants
✶ Battlefield

SCALE
0 5 MILES

This map, compiled from old maps and records
by J.D. Freeman, while doing research work
in the State Archives and General Land office of
the State of Texas.

REMEMBER THE ALAMO

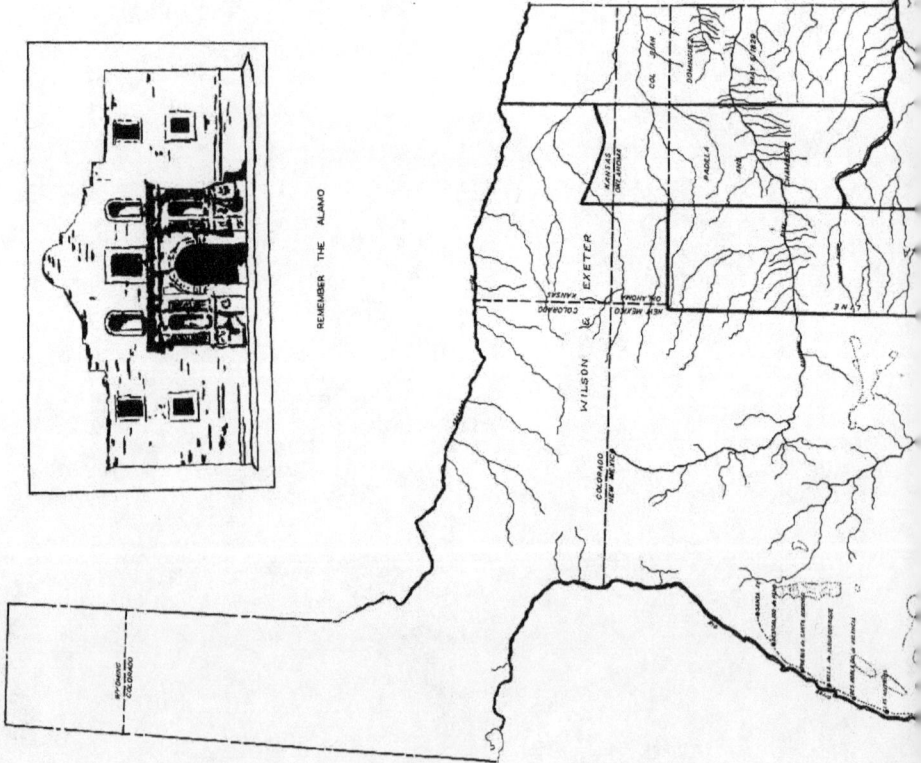

EMPRESARIO GRANTS
1828 ~ 1835

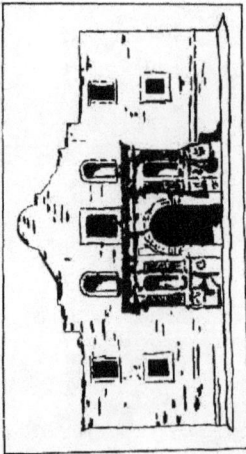

WILSON

COLORADO
NEW MEXICO

EXETER

KANSAS
OKLAHOMA

PADELLA

COLORADO

NEW MEXICO

OKLAHOMA

COL. 9AM

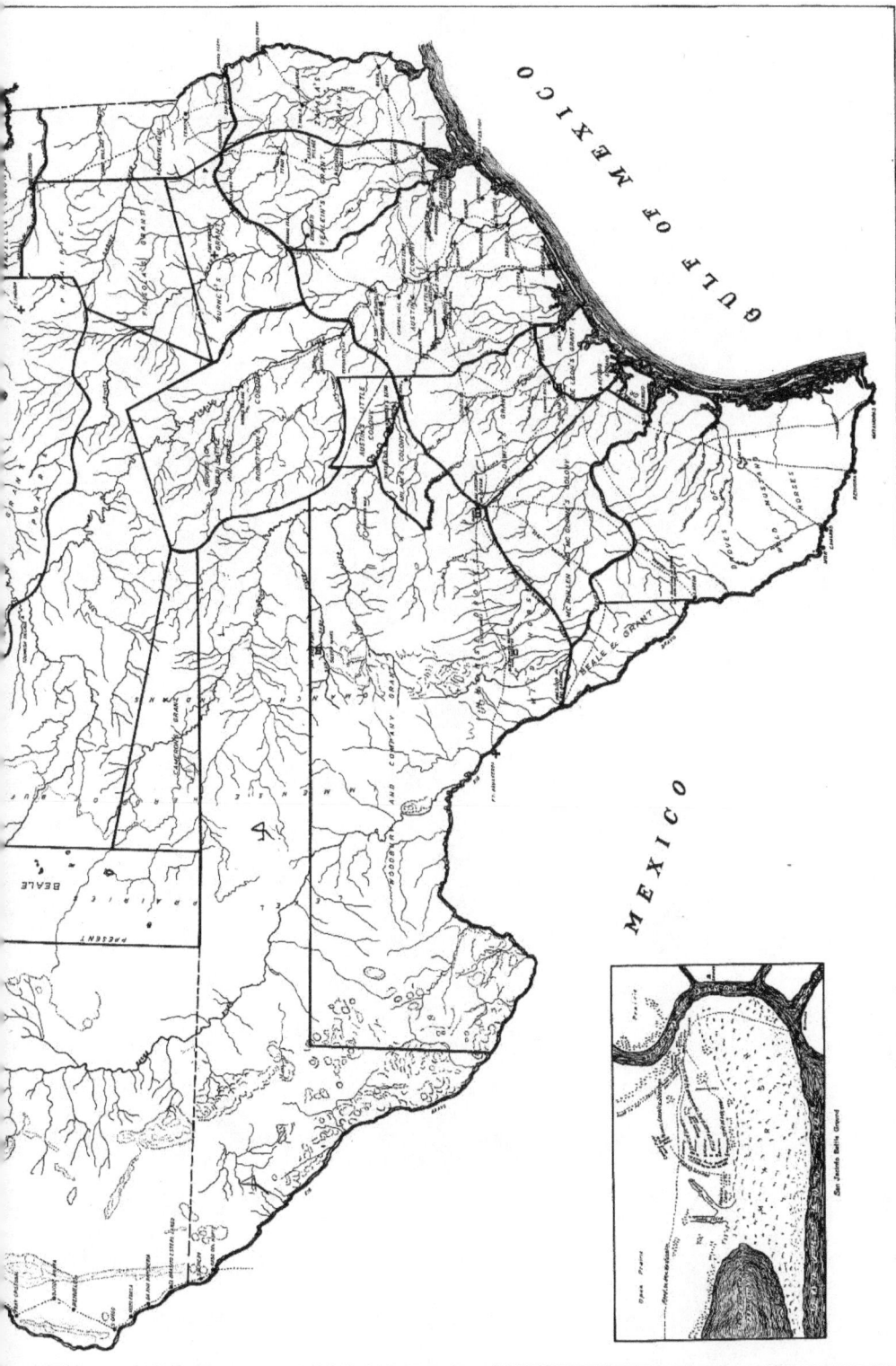

GULF OF MEXICO

MEXICO

San Jacinto Battle Ground

www.ingramcontent.com/pod-product-compliance
Lightning Source LLC
Chambersburg PA
CBHW021854020426
42334CB00013B/333